Lecture Notes in Computer Science 7855

Commenced Publication in 1973
Founding and Former Series Editors:
Gerhard Goos, Juris Hartmanis, and Jan van Leeuwen

Mark Chignell   James R. Cordy
Ryan Kealey   Joanna Ng   Yelena Yesha (Eds.)

The Personal Web

A Research Agenda

 Springer

Volume Editors

Mark Chignell
Universtiy of Toronto
Toronto, ON, Canada
E-mail: chignell@mie.utoronto.ca

James R. Cordy
Queen's University
Kingston, ON, Canada
E-mail: cordy@cs.queensu.ca

Ryan Kealey
University of Toronto
Toronto, ON, Canada
E-mail: ryan.kealey@utoronto.ca

Joanna Ng
IBM Canada Software Laboratory
Markham, ON, Canada
E-mail: jwng@ca.ibm.com

Yelena Yesha
University of Maryland at Baltimore
County, Baltimore, MD, USA
E-mail: yeyesha@umbc.edu

ISSN 0302-9743
e-ISSN 1611-3349
ISBN 978-3-642-39994-7
e-ISBN 978-3-642-39995-4
DOI 10.1007/978-3-642-39995-4
Springer Heidelberg Dordrecht London New York

Library of Congress Control Number: 2013944290

CR Subject Classification (1998): H.4, H.3, I.2, D.2, H.5, C.2

LNCS Sublibrary: SL 3 – Information Systems and Application, incl. Internet/Web and HCI

Typesetting: Camera-ready by author, data conversion by Scientific Publishing Services, Chennai, India

Printed on acid-free paper

Springer is part of Springer Science+Business Media (www.springer.com)

Preface

This book grew out of the First Symposium on the Personal Web, sponsored by the IBM Canada Centre for Advanced Studies Research and co-located with CASCON 2010 in Markham, Ontario, Canada. The purpose of the symposium was to bring together prominent researchers and practitioners from a diverse range of research areas relevant to the advancement of science and practice relating to the Personal Web. Research on the Personal Web is an outgrowth of the Smart Internet initiative, which seeks to extend and transform the Web to be centered on the user, with the Web as a calm platform ubiquitously providing cognitive support to its user and his or her tasks. As with the preceding SITCON workshop (held at CASCON 2009), this symposium involved a multidisciplinary effort that brought together researchers and practitioners in data integration; Web services modelling and architecture; human-computer interaction; predictive analytics; cloud infrastructure; semantics and ontology; and industrial application domains such as health care and finance.

During the symposium we discussed different aspects of the architecture and functionality needed to make the Personal Web a reality. After the symposium the authors reworked their presentations into draft chapters that were submitted for peer evaluation and review. Every chapter went through two rounds of reviewing by at least two independent expert reviewers, and accepted chapters were then revised and are presented in this book.

In the first paper presented here, Joanna Ng introduces her vision of the Personal Web. It is a user-centric (rather than server-) centric vision of the Web where general users can personalize tasks and services for their needs without having to get involved in programming activities. In addition to motivating the need for, and inevitability of, the Personal Web, Ng's chapter also discusses research challenges associated with development of the Personal Web. She suggests RDF linked data as an infrastructure for Web integration and she discusses the primacy of links between people and objects as a basis for Web integration and personalization. The paper by Chechik and her colleagues then introduces a Personal Web Workflow Methodology that aims to elicit the users goals for a particular task and create a customizable workflow to accomplish it. Chechik et al. build their workflow approach around artificial intelligence style planning, but they also incorporate a crowdsourcing approach to fill in the gaps. They demonstrate their workflow methodology with a detailed walkthrough of the example of ordering and arranging delivery of a crib.

The paper by Ye et al. then approaches the Web integration problem from a Web services perspective. They present a model of service subscription and consumption where Web data are collected and organized automatically according to the end-users' context and preferences. They show how their methods would work using an automated ticket-booking scenario. Their prototype uses the POLARIS event exposure framework that is built on top of the PADRES broker network.

The paper by Upadhyaya et al. presents a third, service discovery, approach to the problem of Web integration. The authors propose a framework for building a personalized Web space that assists a user in managing various Web resources and composing Web resources for automatic reuse. The personalized Web space described by Upadhyaya et al. builds on the Personal Web sphere concept introduced by Ng in the opening paper of this volume. Upadhyaya proposes a three-layer architecture for the personal Web space working down from a concept later at the top, through a model layer to an instance layer at the most detailed level. They use a travel-booking scenario to illustrate their approach and they describe a prototype that they built to show how the user can change simple Web resources into reusable services by annotating the data with them.

Clever integration of services using planning, publishing and subscription, and service discovery seem like good ways to integrate services for personal use, but how are new services, or new uses of services, constructed? The paper by Matheson et al. addresses this problem from the perspective of predictive analytics. They describe the PASIF framework for incorporating predictive analytics into intelligent services. To show how predictive analytics might function in the Personal Web, they give the example of analyzing data about products in a shopping cart, along with demographic information about the user, to come up with useful predictions. These predictions might generate a product recommendation for the user, or layout changes to the website to make browsing more personalized based on user activity.

The goals of the Personal Web require intelligence in Web integration and predictive analytics, and much of this intelligence will rely on an understanding of user context. In their paper, Villegas and Muller present a semantic ontology to assist in describing user content for Personal Web applications. The Smarter-Context ontology that they introduce is based on RDF and a subset of a Web Ontology Language. To validate their approach, they apply it to a number of case studies, including smarter commerce, where they developed a deal recommendation system that exploits users changing personal context information to deliver highly relevant offers. These new tools for modeling context promise to greatly enhance our understanding of personal preferences and situations online.

The paper by Stroulia examines the social aspect of context, focusing on collaboration in the Social Web. She introduces a suite of collaborative platforms that her team has developed to explore the space of collaborative Web-based tools. She also introduces SociQL, a language for querying and analyzing systems supporting the activities of teams. Stroulia's paper discusses some of the emergent properties of collaborative and social networking environments, including forming of communities, sharing of contributions, and propagation of influence. While the emphasis of her paper is on the Social Web, the automation and facilitation of social and collaborative tasks will also be highly relevant to the Personal Web, since so many of the tasks that people perform online now involve collaboration in varying degrees.

The drive toward personalization and automation of tasks in the Personal Web comes with potential threats to privacy. Thus the paper by Samavi et al. is particularly timely in proposing tools for evaluating the privacy implications of different online operations. While Samavi et al. focus on personal health applications, the techniques that they develop have broad applicability to online transactions and data management. They provide a comprehensive analysis of privacy management online that includes a model that helps privacy experts encode their knowledge. This model fills the gap between the end users' high-level privacy intentions and what personal health applications offer as privacy features. They also introduce a second smart privacy model in their framework, which is an ontological model that supports privacy enforcement. The model allows privacy settings that are selected, by a user, to be translated as enforceable constraints on the data and processes of a personal workflow. We see these privacy protection mechanisms as an essential component of the Personal Web.

The final paper in this volume (by Ghajar-Khosravi et al.) looks at the application of group gift giving. This is a complex application that is faced with many challenges but that has a great deal of revenue potential if it can be implemented effectively. It is an application that would also benefit greatly from the Personal Web technologies discussed in this volume, since dealing with groups of people is an onerous task, particular where complex product search and gift selection tasks have to be carried out. Ghajar-Khosravi et al. review the literature on group gift giving and identify some of the key research issues. They then report the results of two studies that establish some requirements for online group gift giving, one an interview study and the other an online survey with 250 respondents. They demonstrate that there are age and gender differences in attitudes toward group gift giving, and that the attractiveness of giving in a group depends on the type of gift-giving occasion. They show that gift-giving situations where the intended gift recipients are weak social ties (i.e., not friends or close family members) are more suitable for group gift giving than are situations involving gift recipients who are strong social ties.

We thank the authors of this volume for tackling the problem of defining the development of the Personal Web from each of their areas of expertise. This volume has laid out some of the groundwork for the Personal Web but much remains to be done in realigning Web services around users and their needs in different contexts.

Technology has continued to advance rapidly even as this book was being written. New forms of social search have emerged, and the mobile Web is becoming increasingly important. We believe that the Personal Web is a core principle that reflects human needs, and thus we expect that future technologies, however they emerge, will converge on the kinds of Personal Web functionality envisioned here. It is an exciting time for researchers interested in the Web and we expect that there will be more books that will build on the foundation laid by this book and the previous Smart Internet book that we edited.

The symposium that launched this book would not have been possible without the generous support of the IBM Canada Centre for Advanced Studies Research, and we are grateful for its support. A number of people at IBM Canada put in considerable effort into organizing the Personal Web symposium that led to this book, and we would particularly like to thank Emilia Tung, Debbie Kilbride, and Jimmy Lo for their help. Finally, we would also like to thank Siobhan Cordy for doing the front cover illustration.

May 2013

Mark Chignell
James R. Cordy
Ryan Kealey
Joanna Ng
Yelena Yesha

Organization

Program Committee

Marsha Chechik	University of Toronto
Mark Chignell	University of Toronto
Karuna Joshi	University of Maryland, Baltimore County
Ryan Kealey	University of Toronto
Patrick Martin	Queen's University
Margaret-Anne Storey	University of Victoria
Eleni Stroulia	University of Alberta
Jens Weber-Jahnke	University of Victoria

About the Editors

Mark Chignell is a professor of Mechanical and Industrial Engineering at the University of Toronto, where he has been on the faculty since 1990. Prior to that he was an assistant professor in Industrial and Systems Engineering at the University of Southern California from 1984 to 1990. He has a PhD in Psychology (University of Canterbury, New Zealand, 1981), and an MSc in Industrial and Systems Engineering (Ohio State, 1984). Mark is currently President of Vocalage Inc., a University of Toronto spinoff company, director of the Interactive Media Lab, and a visiting scientist at both the IBM Centre for Advanced Studies and Keio University in Japan.

James Cordy is a professor and past director of the School of Computing at Queens University, Kingston, Canada, where he has been on the faculty since 1985. From 1995 to 2000 he was Vice President and Chief Research Scientist at Legasys Corporation, a software technology company specializing in legacy software system analysis and renovation. Cordy received his PhD from the University of Toronto. He is the author of more than 130 refereed contributions in programming languages, software engineering and artificial intelligence. Cordy is an ACM Distinguished Scientist, a senior member of the IEEE, and an IBM Visiting Scientist and Faculty Fellow.

Ryan Kealey is currently a doctoral candidate in the Mechanical and Industrial Engineering Department at the University of Toronto focusing on optimizing the design and development of healthcare tools for patients and caregivers. He also holds an MSc in Psychology (McMaster University, 2009). Ryan works as a usability and statistical consultant for Vocalage Inc. and has had a variety of clients including Toyota and Wolters-Kluwer Health. In 2011 he was awarded a Strategic Training Initiative in Health Research (STIHR) fellowship as a trainee with KT Canada and has been invited to give presentations and workshops on usability evaluation.

Joanna Ng is currently the Head of Research at IBM Canada Software Laboratories, Centre for Advanced Studies. She is also a Senior Technical Staff Member of the IBM Software Group. She has held various senior management and architect positions in product development teams and software strategy division. Joanna is a an IBM Master Inventor with a long track record of profitable innovations. She has been granted over 25 patents from various countries in research areas such as mobile commerce; voice-enabled portal; commerce portal; retail industry solutions; service-oriented architecture (SOA); asset repository; and semantic and Web technologies.

Yelena Yesha received a BSc degree in Computer Science from York University, Toronto, Canada, in 1984, and MSc and PhD degrees in Computer and Information Science from The Ohio State University in 1986 and 1989, respectively. Since 1989 she has been with the Department of Computer Science and Electrical Engineering at the University of Maryland Baltimore County, where she is currently a professor, and Director of the UMBC NSF Center for Hybrid Multicore Productivity Research. Yesha served as the Director of the Center of Excellence in Space Data and Information Sciences at NASA (1994–1999).

Table of Contents

The Personal Web 1
  Joanna Ng

PWWM: A Personal Web Workflow Methodology 11
  Marsha Chechik, Jocelyn Simmonds, Sotirios Liaskos, Shiva Nejati,
  Mehrdad Sabetzadeh, and Rick Salay

Service Subscription and Consumption for Personal Web
Applications.. 49
  Chunyang Ye, Young Yoon, and Hans-Arno Jacobsen

A Framework for Composing Personalized Web Resources 65
  Bipin Upadhyaya, Hua Xiao, Ying Zou, Joanna Ng, and Alex Lau

A Privacy Framework for the Personal Web 87
  Reza Samavi, Mariano P. Consens, and Thodoros Topaloglou

Intelligence for the Personal Web 113
  Marie Matheson, Patrick Martin, Jimmy Lo, Joanna Ng,
  Daisy Tan, and Brian Thomson

Communities, Artifacts, Interaction and Contribution on the Web 131
  Eleni Stroulia

The SMARTERCONTEXT Ontology and Its Application to the Smart
Internet: A Smarter Commerce Case Study........................ 151
  Norha M. Villegas and Hausi A. Müller

Simplifying the Task of Group Gift Giving 185
  Shadi Ghajar-Khosravi, Louisa Holub, David Canella,
  William Sharpe, and Mark Chignell

Author Index 221

The Personal Web

Joanna Ng

IBM Canada Software Laboratory CAS Research, Toronto, Canada

Abstract. The world-wide-web was originally intended to be a global distributed information space for publishing and sharing of information. The concept of the Personal Web is to extend the design of the web beyond a global information space into a global platform for personal services that provides first class support from the perspectives of users. The objectives of the Personal Web include extending its architecture to provide support for the prospective memory tasks of users; reduction of working cognitive load; facilitation of engagement in users web tasks and ubiquitous web interactions across users computing ecosystem of devices. Building on recent advances in mobile and cloud technologies, the Personal Web will set a people-centric agenda for web technology advancement that will fundamentally change users experience with web.

1 Introduction

The world-wide web was originally conceived of as a hypermedia network where browsing would be dominant, as envisaged by Vannevar Bush [1] in his Memex proposal. However, after the Web was established, search soon became the main means of navigation, as users found it impractical to browse over long distances in the rapidly expanding Web, and as search engines adapted to find what people were interested in, even when their queries were terse and often poorly formulated.

Over the past two decades the Web has evolved into far more than the storehouse of knowledge envisioned in the Memex. Increasingly it is becoming a place to carry out tasks such as travel planning, shopping, accounting, and so on. The current Web interface (as of this writing) largely reflects the requirements of searching for information in a very large repository. The research reported in this book was motivated by the insight that a new kind of Web interface is needed to reconfigure the users view of the Web, so that it facilitates the tasks that the user needs to perform. The Personal Web is a new approach, where the focus is on web users as individuals, bringing control of web elements from across the web into the hands of end users for their own purposes and from their own perspectives.

The focus of technical advances in the Personal Web is on collections of web functions as a transparent, integrated and instrumented, intelligent and social, system for individual web users to accomplish tasks and attend to their matters of concern. The functioning of this system should happen as part of simple everyday activities, without unwieldy programming requirements. The idea is to implicitly discover, gather, aggregate, deliver and recommend data, resources and services from across the web as Integrate-able web elements, to support the users personal situation and needs. Associated cognitive support should then be offered in a way that is contextually, and socially, relevant as well as being intuitive from the users perspective.

M. Chignell et al. (Eds.): The Personal Web, LNCS 7855, pp. 1–10, 2013.

In the Personal Web, the many silos of web domains are melded into a unified web platform within which web users can easily craft their own web integrations. New user interaction patterns should then transfer the burden of initiating web requests for fulfilling user tasks to automated web agents working on behalf of users. Web users could then set up reminders and guide task automation at a high level, assisted by tools aware of their professional, social and personal context and history. We believe that the development of such a Personal Web is inevitable in the long term, but may be slowed in the short term by the prerequisite need to create a number of enabling technologies such as those discussed in this book.

The rest of this paper is organized as follows: Section 2 calls out the core objectives of the Personal Web. Section 3 discusses related work and highlights shortfalls in meeting the goals of the Personal Web with existing methods. Section 4 outlines two proposed scenarios for how the Personal Web would work. Section 5 introduces some key requirements for the Personal Web. Section 6 discusses design considerations relating to the enabling infrastructure for the Personal Web. Section 7 discusses future research possibilities and associated research challenges in the Personal Web. This paper ends with a discussion on the potential significance of the Personal Web.

2   The Personal Web Objectives

This section attempts to call out the initial set of core objectives that govern the designs and evolution of the Personal Web.

2.1   Prospective Memory Tasks Support

What will the Personal Web enable for general Internet users that are not possible without it? First, Personal Web users should be able to count on the web as a platform that *supports prospective memory tasks* (remembering to remember or pending tasks) [2] online. Prospective memory tasks usually impose a large mental burden. In offloading prospective memory tasks, the Personal Web will transform web users from web workers to web supervisors. For example, Jo may set her Personal Web to initiate a response to online bill payments for bills that arrive over the web that are less than a certain amount and she will be able to do this in a universal manner despite the diversity of web domains. And the social dimension of the Personal Web enables her to include her husband as a participant. This type of response initiation needs to be done in a way that is contextually appropriate for Jos (and her husbands) real time mode of interactions across multiple devices and channels, and without raising privacy concerns.

2.2   Working Cognitive Load Reduction

Secondly, Personal Web users should be able to count on the web to reduce the cognitive burden as they perform tasks through the web. Reduction in required cognitive effort may come from actionable analytics presented to web users relevant to their tasks at hand. One example of this is information aggregation from diverse web domains to fulfill web users information requirements for their tasks, such as making a decision.

For example, a stock broker might put together the web elements from across several disjoint web domains that need integrated visualization for efficient and effective decision making in stock transactions. This type of agile gathering of relevant and required information would be done without any need for programming.

2.3 Engagement Facilitation

Thirdly, Personal Web users should be able to count on the web to *facilitate engagement* with others as they perform tasks through the web, seeing the web as a virtual, social collaborative platform. For example, as a claimant performs a car insurance claim on line, users of the Personal Web should be able to count on the web service that he uses to present a chat session with his insurance agent if needed, as well as notifying the case manager of the body shop, and notifying his wife.

2.4 Ubiquitous Interactions Enablement

Today, web users as individuals have many smart, web-enabled devices. The Personal Web should work ubiquitously. Thus a given task could be started with one device and could then be seamlessly picked up from where it left off with a completely different device without losing context, with the state of the task remaining up to date regardless of which device was used. Users of the Personal Web should be able to focus on their tasks, with the specifics of devices being used calmly melting into the background. The Personal Web should be seamlessly collaborative in the support of ongoing personal tasks across devices.

3　Related Work

A number of recent initiatives can be seen as steps towards the Personal Web. This section reviews the progress that has been made thus far in enabling the realization of the properties of the Personal Web previously mentioned.

3.1　Mashups

Mashups can be considered as a form of reducing *working memory burden* of web users by providing the capability to integrate disjoint, silos data and services from disjoint domains, into a unified view. Grammel et al. defined mashups as end user driven recombination of web based data and functionality [3]. Mashups integrate data, services and web presentation to solve user needs for information and services not originally anticipated by web programmers [4].

However, constructing mashups typically involves the use of mashup tools that require deep programming skills (which general internet users typically do not have), resulting in a very high barrier for adoption. To lower this barrier, widget-based user models for mashups have been developed (e.g., Yahoo pipes and Popfly). Widgets representing different web sites can be connected together through wiring. However, these mashup widgets are abstractions of necessary programmatic constructs and are not easily understood by general users unless they have prior understanding of programming concepts such as data flow, loops and selection. Such knowledge requirements exceed that of general users. In addition to this skill barrier, the number of widgets for web integration is too large to be manageable. Finding the right widget to use in a particular context is difficult.

Other mashup approaches include the Karma system enables users to extract data from a web site into a data table through demonstration. XPath generation finds similar data and copies into the table as well. However, the functionality is limited to data integration and is good only for ad hoc integration that does not require persistence. The Vegemite system provides a spreadsheet like user interface for direct manipulation [4], but shares the same limitations in persistence and lack of support for service integration.

While mashups are a step in the right direction, they fall short of providing the properties of the Personal Web previously listed. There is no single mashup model available to general users that is easy enough to be used for frequent, every day web integration activities. There is no way to support robust and deep integration of data, services and web content feeds, all within one mashup model with a high degree of personalization.

3.2   Facebook Open Graph

One can argue that Facebooks Like button is the first ever web integration by end users without any programming requirement. Using Facebook Open Graph Protocol, Facebook and partnering Websites provide users with a simple point-and-click user model to establish relationships between real world things and people in the social graph. Objects from enterprise sites can be tagged according to the protocol to enable real-world things from their sites to be integrated into pages in Facebook, thereby attracting the attention of the users contacts through their friend relationships, all with simple Like operations.

However, this capability is limited to the Facebook environment and is not available openly and universally as part of web programming. In addition, no new operators have been added since its introduction of the like operation in April 2010.

3.3   Cloud Infrastructure for Ubiquitous Interactions

Apples iCloud provides cloud based storage and synchronization services. Apples applications such as email, music, photo-stores etc. can be accessed across all of their devices. Changes made by one instance of an application on a particular device can be instantly propagated to another instance of the app running on another device, providing a seamless user experience. Users can move from one device to other completely worry free, enabling users to focus on their tasks at hand, making the diversity of devices a non-issue.

While Apples iCloud provides a great illustration of how devices are not an issue, its functionality is confined to storage and synchronization. Web application programming model has not yet been extended to provide similar device transparency to its users.

3.4   Overall Assessment

Significant progress has been made in direction of the Personal Web vision, but we are a long way from its full realization. As of this writing, there is little or no work done in augmenting the web for prospective memory task support. Working memory burden can be reduced by analytics and informatics integrations, yet these technologies are too complex to be used by end users, nor are the technologies designed to reduce working memory burden reduction. While social computing services and technologies are popular, the control taken by the social computing platforms inhibits their use in broader contexts. However, the adoption of mobile computing is growing in leaps and bounds, increasing the scope for personalization through interactions with personal devices.

In spite of the progress being made, Web technologies are only just beginning to enable web users with tools and services they can count on for prospective memory tasks support; working memory burden reduction; engagement facilitation and ubiquitous interaction enablement.

4   Two Personal Web Scenarios

4.1   Personal Web Online Shopping

One vision of Personal Web online shopping is as follows. Online shoppers employ social computing services to set up their contact network. With the facilitation provided by the Personal Web for social engagement, a given shopper can set up their budget, annual gift giving occasions (such as birthday, Christmas etc.) and the relationships that require gift purchases. The Personal Web would then provide prospective memory task support. The personal web enabled online commerce site would have automated web agents working on behalf of shoppers to crawl the wish lists of the intended gift recipients, presenting relevant offers to meet the shoppers budget setting, which the shopper/user could then choose to accept or not. The shopper would then no longer be burdened by the worries of missing birthdays or anniversaries of the important people in her life. In addition to reducing anxiety, the working memory burden of gift shopping would also be tremendously reduced. Ubiquitous interaction enabled through the Personal Web would support the setting up of gifting in one device, while monitoring the gift schedule and choosing a fulfillment method in other mobile devices. Repeated shopping tasks like replenishment of regularly used household items, such as diapers for a mother with an infant, could be setup as an automated web tasks, so that shoppers would not have to remember to remember to re-order routinely purchased items.

4.2   Personal Web Business Process Management

Personal Web Business Process Management may go something like this. A bank may exploit the engagement facilitation provided by the Personal Web to quickly work with those who will be affected internally and externally when there is an improvement in the pre-qualification in account opening processes. A telecommunication company might use prospective memory task support within the Personal Web to set up a repeated task of sending billing information to customers. Using the capability of working memory burden reduction of the Personal Web, actionable analytics and integrated relevant information are made visible for business users as they execute the approval step of a given business process. Business users can also specify repeatable business tasks and use the Personal Webs prospective memory tasks support to delegate the initiation of these tasks to the corresponding software agents of the Personal Web working on their behalf.

5   Key Requirements of the Personal Web

The objectives of the Personal Web imply the following set of critical requirements.

Asynchronous Web Services
Todays web depends on web users to initiate a web browser session to request web services or web resources. Web services should be asynchronous so that users do not have to remember to be online at specific times. Web agents should act on behalf of web users, managing the conditions and events implied by user preferences and web integrations, so that when subscribed events happen or when conditions are fulfilled, these web agents will initiate web sessions to request web services or web resources on behalf of users (and without requiring their presence or further involvement from them).

Web Task Automation
Currently, the traversal of hyper-media links through http requests and responses depends on human involvement. To reduce working memory burden and to provide prospective memory tasks support, web task automation is a logical requirement. Software agents should traverse hyper-media links on behalf of users, based on some pre-set rules, conditions or logic. With web task automation, users of the Personal Web can set a certain persistent and repeated task sequence in autopilot mode, running in the web platform as batch processes with the user playing the role of a supervisory controller [5].

Actionable Analytics
To reduce working memory burden and to facilitate better engagement with others, actionable analytics is another key requirements for the support of informed decisions and web actions. Web users of the Personal Web should be able to count on crisp analytics presentations and visualizations to inform them about trends and factors that are contextually relevant to their decisions or other actions.

Informatics Integration
Another aspect of reducing working memory burden for users of the Personal Web is to flexibly aggregate disjoint data that are contextually relevant to the users tasks at hand.

The requirement of informatics integration may also include aggregated data about the user as an individual, with auto-fill of required parameters about the user. Working memory burden will be drastically reduced when users no longer need to enter account numbers, user ids and passwords (that they have difficulty remembering) as they carry out their tasks using the web [6].

Context Sensitive Interactions
Dey defines context as any information that can be used to characterize the situation of a person, place or object, in order to select the most relevant content and services, for the users benefit in a particular situation [7]. Users of the Personal Web should expect relevant information rendered appropriately for the interactive device they are currently using. Lightweight semantics may go a long way [8] towards discovering relevant data; services and web feeds for a specific context. In addition, users should also expect rendered content relevant to situational data such as their current location. Context sensitive interactions will be a key requirements for ubiquitous interaction enablement and facilitation of engagement.

Web Services with Native Social Computing Enablement
Personal web services are expected to support engagement facilitation, with the capability to involve the users social network as appropriate to their contexts and their current web tasks. This leads to a key requirement where social computing and networking services should be used natively with the enterprises web services and platform.

6 Design Considerations for Enablement

An Extended Complement of Today's Web
The Personal Web should complement todays web, by extracting elements of the web that are relevant to users as individuals. These elements will often be captured as intermediary web artifacts, so that individual web users can see surrounding data in context, and can manipulate that data appropriately. It should be possible to extract these sub-web elements from todays monolithic web sites so that they can participate in individual instantiations of the Personal Web. A related design consideration involves enabling end user control over their data, while hiding technological complexity associated with the manipulation of that data.

Lightweight Semantics for User-Defined Web Integration
It is important to design sub-web elements to be integrate-able with other sub-web elements, designed to function together in a collaborative manner, entirely under the users control, despite diversity in schema, meta-model and implementation technology platforms.

Another important design consideration is enablement of asserted relation-ship between people and sub-web elements, so that end users can use common operations and their semantics across similar sub-web elements. For instance, an online shopper should be able to have a single unified check out across a set of eCommerce sites, each with a loaded shopping cart.

A Flexible Integration Construct
Choosing a flexible, open integration construct is important, so that the open information model can combine data from multiple disjoint sources while still being processed automatically at the internet scale [9]. Resource Description Framework (RDF) and

linked data [10] are important structuring formalisms in building the infrastructure for the Personal Web.

The notion of developing personal information systems consisting of focused subsets of information, highly relevant to a particular user, in order to deal with information overload of the user from the web platform, dates back at least as far as the personal web space vision of Abrams et al [11] in 1998. While Abrams et al focused on personal bookmarking, others have looked at enhanced forms of search, but still within a linked data approach [11].

Linked representations of services can also be created using the RDF linked data approach. Services may be inferred through planning methods as discussed in the later paper in this volume by Chechik et al. Other approaches to the task of organizing and finding relevant services are also discussed in two further papers in this volume, namely the papers by Ye at al, and by Upadhyaya et al.

A Three-Layered Meta Model

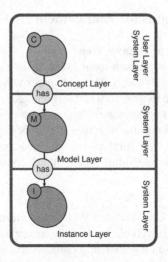

Fig. 1. Three Layer Meta Model for the Personal Web

Establishing a meta-model for the Personal Web is another key design consideration. A meta-model is needed that is universal, open and inter-operative in spite of differences in the way that the same logical entity is represented across various enterprise domains. With an appropriately defined meta-model, automatic discovery of links and relationships through inferences and other means is enabled, and user integrate-able web artifacts can then be developed.

A three-tier meta data model is proposed for the design consideration of the Personal Web infrastructure (Figure 1). The three tiers are respectively: **concept-nodes; model-nodes and instance-nodes**. Users should be able to define Personal web operations at the concept level (e.g. shopper commands, check out all shop carts for these sites) with internal mappings to the model and instance layers.

7   Discussion and Future Work

Further research is needed to bring the vision of the Personal Web to fruition.

Firstly, further work is needed on end-to-end tooling, web application programming models and development environments for the Personal Web. What Personal Web tooling should be provided to Enterprise IT so that they enterprises can identify, adapt and enable existing sub-web elements from todays enterprise sites. How can they enable their users to participate in the Personal Web in simple but effective ways?

Secondly, key characteristics of web services that are required in order to support the objectives of the Personal Web, and how to enable them, need to be identified. How can enterprise IT provide the cognitive optimization by identifying automatable services and resources that their users use?

Thirdly, discussion on infrastructure and server components required to support the runtime operations for the Personal Web is essential. What is the run time architecture and middleware support that the Personal Web requires?

Fourthly, interactions that are ubiquitous and context sensitive and how they can be designed, deployed, monitored and manage is another key dimension. With the diversity and volume of devices, how can Personal Web interactions be designed so that users can experience the intended benefits of the Personal Web?

Fifthly, we need to characterize the life cycle, monitoring and management of the automated, asynchronous tasks of the Personal Web. What role will todays mobile apps and browser paradigm have in the Personal Web? How will users supervise and monitor web tasks that are long running? How should users supervise their tasks across the web from various devices?

Conclusions

The core objectives of the Personal Web is to provide an extension to todays web such that prospective memory tasks are supported; web users working memory burden is reduced; engagement with others is facilitated; ubiquitous interactions across devices are enabled. These objectives provide important guidance in how web architecture and its technologies are being augmented and extended. Asynchronous web services, web task automation, actionable analytics, informatics integration, and context sensitive interactions with native social computing enablement of web services are key requirements of the Personal Web derived from the implications of these core foundational objectives.

The Personal Web is the next step in the short but eventful history of the Internet. I believe the vision of the Personal Web, in part or in whole, will deliver significantly more optimal web experience to web users, not only through improved user interfaces, but also through optimized cognitive efficiency. In this paper I have sketched out a vision of the Personal Web and provided key design considerations to be used in its development. The remaining papers in this volume will provide more detail on some of the themes and research challenges introduced here.

Acknowledgments. Thanks are due to Dr. Mark Chignell and Dr. James Cordy for their reviews, comments and editing of this paper.

References

1. Bush, V.: As we may think. Atlantic Monthly, 101–108 (1945)
2. Brandimonte, M.E., Einstein, G.O., McDaniel, M.A.: Prospective Memory: Theory and Applications. Lawrence Erlbaum Associates Publishers (1996)
3. Grammel, L., Storey, M.-A.: A survey of mashup development environments. In: Chignell, M., Cordy, J., Ng, J., Yesha, Y. (eds.) The Smart Internet. LNCS, vol. 6400, pp. 137–151. Springer, Heidelberg (2010)
4. Lin, J., Wong, J., Nichols, J., Cypher, A., Lau, T.: End-user programming of mashups with vegemite. In: Proceedings of the 14th International Conference on Intelligent User Interfaces, pp. 97–106 (2009)
5. Sheridan, T.B.: Supervisory control. In: Salvendy, G. (ed.) Handbook of Human Factors and Ergonomics, 3rd edn., pp. 1025–1052. John Wiley and Sons (2006)
6. Ng, J., Nigul, J., Litani, E., Lau, D.: End user controlled web interaction flow using service oriented architecture model. In: 2nd IEEE Workshop on Enabling the Future SOA Internet (EFSOW 2008) (2008)
7. Dey, A.K.: Understanding and using context. Personal and Ubiquitous Computing 5(1), 4–7 (2001)
8. Hendler, J.: On beyond ontology – the future of the semantic web (keynote address). In: International Semantic Web Conference (ISWC 2003), Florida (October 2003)
9. W3C: Resource description framework (rdf): Concepts and abstract syntax. W3C Recommendation (February 10, 2004)
10. Bizer, C., Heath, T., Berners-Lee, T.: Linked data: The story so far. International Journal on Semantic Web and Information Systems (IJSWIS) (2009)
11. Abrams, D., Baecker, R., Chignell, M.: Information archiving with bookmarks: Personal web space construction and organization. In: ACM SIGCHI 1998, pp. 41–48. ACM Press (1998)

PWWM: A Personal Web Workflow Methodology

Marsha Chechik[1], Jocelyn Simmonds[2], Sotirios Liaskos[3], Shiva Nejati[4],
Mehrdad Sabetzadeh[4], and Rick Salay[1]

[1] University of Toronto, Toronto, Canada
{chechik,rsalay}@cs.toronto.edu
[2] Universidad Técnica Federico Santa María, Valparaíso, Chile
jsimmond@inf.utfsm.cl
[3] York University, Toronto, Canada
liaskos@yorku.ca
[4] University of Luxembourg, Luxembourg
{shiva.nejati,mehrdad.sabetzadeh}@uni.lu

Abstract. The personal web vision promises to give users a highly personalized
experience on the web. This paper proposes and describes a Personal Web Workflow Methodology, designed to elicit, operationalize and execute a personal web
user's goals. Our approach relies heavily on our prior research in goal modeling
and operationalization, model matching and merging, and web service monitoring and recovery. We integrate this research with the social networking concept
of crowd-sourcing to create a novel methodology for allowing users to produce
customized workflows in order to accomplish their unique goals.

1 Introduction and Motivation

Personal web is ultimately a way to give every user a truly personalized experience
on the web. From remembering her preferences of sites and policies, maintaining her
context, organizing the most essential information, to allowing collaboration and information sharing with her family and friends, the vision of ultimate personalization seems
almost within reach.

In our position paper presented at the Personal Web workshop [1], we proposed the
particular area of our interest in this context as *trying to elicit and execute a personal
web user's goals, through preferred information collection devices and with coopera-
tion of trusted individuals.*

For example, traditional web applications such as commerce and banking offer a
particular interaction with the user and his/her data. Data is stored in the database of a
particular application (e.g., shopping list or wish list), and the user is being offered a
particular workflow that determines the interaction of the user with the system (e.g., on
amazon.com, such things include looking for something, doing a price comparison, determining a particular vendor to go with, choosing the type of shipment and the payment
method).

Instead, as users, we may want to use parts of the different applications which are
useful to us, and then combine them in our own, personal ways. For example, when
buying electronics, a savvy Canadian consumer may want to first check amazon.com to
look at the models and reviews. Amazon.ca has a much smaller product selection, and

M. Chignell et al. (Eds.): The Personal Web, LNCS 7855, pp. 11–48, 2013.
© Springer-Verlag Berlin Heidelberg 2013

very likely will not carry the desired product. Instead, she would look for the equivalent models on other Canadian retail sites. After comparing prices and shipping options, she may want to consult her friends and/or family, and then hit the "pay" button. Wouldn't it be nice if such a process could be stored and repeated whenever the user needs to execute it? This will ensure that steps are not skipped, and our consumer gets the best deal.

Once such workflows are explicated and stored, they may become updated as additional information becomes available. For example, our shopper may hear of additional sites where reliable research can be conducted, additional sources of online coupons to check, or may want to integrate portions of personalized workflows of other Canadian consumers.

Generic workflows can be created as well, and stored on the web in a manner similar to existing customizable phone apps. Some examples of those can be a "web for a Canadian shopper" workflow, or a "Dinner and a Movie" workflow, involving choosing an interesting movie, a time that works and a location which is reasonable to get to and that has a restaurant close by that the person executing the workflow would like to visit and that has seating available in time to catch the movie, all the while coordinating with the persons's date, and restaurant/movie review sites.

In this paper, we propose and describe PWWM – a Personal Web Workflow Methodology that aims to elicit the user's goals for a particular task and create a customizable workflow to accomplish it. Our proposal builds on our areas of expertise: goal modeling and operationalization [2, 3], model matching and merging [4, 5], and web service monitoring and recovery [6]. Specifically, we show how to use and adapt techniques developed in the three areas above in order to elicit user's goals, synthesize possible workflow models, find and merge these with crowd-sourced generic workflows, use planning to produce optimal plans through these workflows, identify relevant web services which can execute various parts of the plan, create custom orchestrations of these services, monitor them dynamically against a variety of user and vendor policies and constraints, and, if a failure is discovered, perform recovery and/or produce an alternate plan. We also rely heavily on a social networking concept of "crowd-sourcing", to help fill the gaps.

We expect our collection of techniques to enable creation of interesting and truly customizable user experiences, while maintaining a degree of quality control over correctness of the execution of the proposed plans and workflows.

While our methodology centers around *customization*, it does not yet address the issue of *collaboration* – where multiple users perform steps towards achieving a common goal.

In the rest of this paper, we describe an example user problem and illustrate a possible user experience with PWWM as she attempts to solve her problem (Section 2), overview our methodology (Section 3), give the necessary background on the three enabling techniques (Section 4), describe assumptions and detail the steps in the methodology (Sections 5-9), outline some research challenges stemming from our proposal (Section 10), discuss related work (Section 11) and finally conclude in Section 12.

2 Motivating Example

To help us motivate our Personal Web vision, we describe a simple example and then show how we envision the user experience with it.

Problem. Consider the following scenario. Our (Canadian) user is six months pregnant and wants to make sure that the baby, once she arrives, will have a safe place to sleep. She is unsure about her preferred options: a bed share? a bassinet (only if she can borrow it!)? but ultimately, she needs to get her baby a crib. Quality cribs are durable but expensive, and take a while to get once ordered. So, she wants to try to buy a second-hand crib. The easiest way to get one is through a local online classified ads, such as craigslist.org, since she can go to the vendor in person and inspect it before making a decision. Our user also knows that quality cribs take 6 weeks to arrive when ordered, so she can only keep looking at used cribs for another 1.5 months. If that (soft) deadline passes, the user will have no choice but to go to a retailer that has cribs in stock and buy whatever they have – clearly not a good choice but might be the only option for meeting the hard deadline – having a crib once the baby arrives. The user can get a crib from a retailer in Canada or the US, but in the latter case should be aware of additional import charges and, most importantly, additional delivery time.

In addition, the user may have a list of preferences: (a) the user prefers a used crib but if none are available within 1.5 months, she will purchase a new one (although what if a perfect used crib becomes available within days of placing an order for a new crib. Can that order be cancelled?); (b) the user wants to avoid shipping from the US in order to avoid customs delays as well as extra taxes.

To accomplish this scenario, the user needs to interact with various services/sites:

- Research: product databases, review sites, user groups and forums.
- Purchase: auction sites, online classified ads, online retailers (and of course the related payment processing).
- Shipping: shipping estimator, shipping, truck rental.
- Utilities: currency converter, online spreadsheet, email, calendar, task lists.

User Experience. Our user aims to find a place for her future baby to sleep by using an online implementation of PWWM. Upon invoking the tool, she enters the *elicitation* step where she can describe her goal. For example, in the screen in Figure 1 she is asked a series of questions using natural language. At this point, some information about the goal is known but it is still too high level for creating an executable flow that calls real web services. For example, there is unlikely to be a service provider that can directly provide a "find a place for a baby to sleep" service, and even the sub-goal "buy a crib" may not have enough detail.

The user then moves to the *refinement* step of the methodology, where she can search the web for information that can elaborate these high-level goals to a greater level of detail. She is presented with a summary of the high level goals and can select one for further elaboration (Figure 2). For example, if she selects "buy crib", then the web is searched for different approaches for achieving this goal (Figure 3). If she selects one of these approaches, she can look at its details and configure or customize it further.

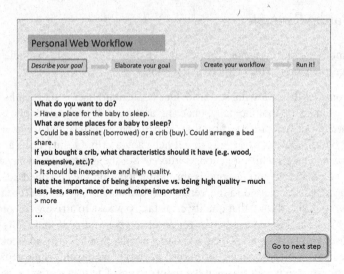

Fig. 1. User view of the PWWM elicitation step

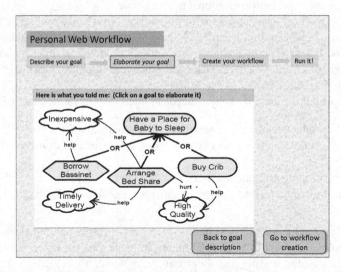

Fig. 2. User view of the PWWM refinement step

This approach is then retained by PWWM and our user can elaborate another goal, and so on.

After the user has elaborated the goal model to a sufficient level of detail, a workflow can be created in the *planning* step of PWWM. The user view of this is illustrated in Figure 4. The workflow creation is automatic and takes into account all the user's preferences and the information she provided in the elicitation and refinement steps. Some preference information comes from a general user profile that we assume exists and contains information about the user's preferred websites, credit cards, etc. Other preference information comes from the elicitation step – for example, in Figure 1, the

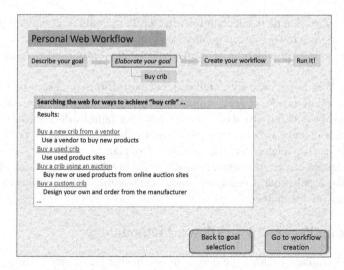

Fig. 3. Web search for crowd sourced goal models

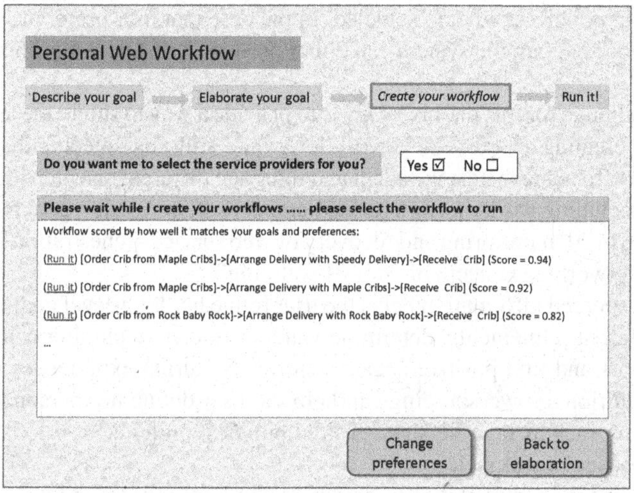

Fig. 4. A rendering of the PWWM planning step

user stated that the crib being "inexpensive" was more important to her than being "high quality".

The user is presented with a ranked list of several workflows. The more a particular workflow satisfies her preferences, the higher is its ranking. The user chooses one (likely the top), which then gets converted into an orchestration of web services to execute it. Alternatively, she can change (i.e., relax or revise) some of her preferences, to produce different workflows. This is accomplished by choosing the appropriate activities in the planning screen (see Figure 4).

Since each step of the workflow requires interaction with different service providers, these providers have to be selected, and the user is given the choice as to whether she wants to be involved in their selection (or whether they should be computed from user preferences and/or crowd-sourced quality ratings). If she does, then she is presented with lists of service providers as needed, dynamically, during the execution of the workflow.

Since the Web is intrinsically unreliable, our best efforts to ensure that the user-produced workflow is correct (i.e., will achieve her goal) may fail. To mitigate that, PWWM actively monitors the workflow for potential failures during execution. If a failure occurs, the framework attempts to recover for the failure either by prompting the user to select another vendor, to choose an alternative plan, to change her preferences so that different plans can be computed. Recovery often involves the use of *compensation*, e.g., cancelling a crib order with one company (and possibly incurring a restocking fee) before placing it with another.

3   Realizing Personal Workflows: Methodology

The PWWM ultimately allows the user to utilize his/her preferences of sites, vendors and policies, as well as to specify and operationalize her goals. The outcome becomes an executable orchestration of web services with a number of monitors checking whether user and vendor policies are being satisfied. In the case that user preferences change or some of the monitors fail, the system can either produce a different workflow or enable recovery.

The key challenge for this methodology is to provide a way to shield the user from the complexity of creating an executable workflow while still guaranteeing that it satisfies the user's goals. To achieve this, we adapt and integrate different research ideas and web technologies including work on configuring personal software using goal models [2,3], model merging [4,5], monitoring and recovery of web service orchestration [6], together with a social networking concept of "crowd-sourcing".

The crowd-sourced information helps the user refine her high-level goals, choose between the different refinements, determine vendor policies (including compensation), rank the vendors and find positive/negative stories capturing experiences with sets of vendors. In addition, crowd-sourcing can help the user define her personal configuration information such as favorite sites, desired policies, preferences (global or defined locally for a particular task), etc.

Figure 5 shows the personal web workflow methodology at a high level. The process begins with the Elicitation step where a high-level goal model representing the user's objectives is elicited from the user. In the Refinement step, this model is elaborated into a detailed goal model by using relevant crowd-sourced models. Then, in the Planning step, the detailed goal model is analyzed and a sequence of web tasks (i.e., a web orchestration) that satisfies the customer's goals is created. Finally, in the Execution step, this sequence of tasks is executed with the user's interaction. As the sequence runs, it is monitored against a potential violation of user or vendor policies, pre- and post-conditions, availability of individual services, etc. As a failure is detected, the system attempts to recover by going back to its previous state or asking the user to choose another plan.

In the remainder of this paper, we discuss steps of the proposed methodology in more detail.

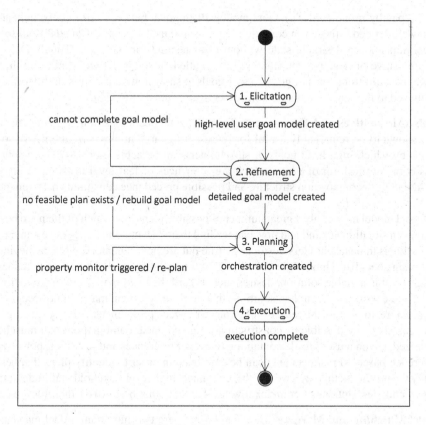

Fig. 5. The high-level steps of PWWM

4   Background

In this section, we provide the necessary high-level background on the techniques used in our methodology: goal modeling and operationalization, model matching and merging, and web service monitoring and recovery.

Goal Models. Goal models are the means by which user needs and preferences are captured and reasoned about. They have been found to to be effective in bridging high-level expressions of stakeholder goals with the low-level human or system activity that is required to achieve those goals [7, 8]. In *i**, the dominant goal modeling framework [9] which we adopt here, this bridging is diagrammatically represented through goal decomposition structures. Thus, high level expressions of stakeholder goals (e.g., "buy a crib") are recursively decomposed into subgoals and eventually into tasks (e.g., "provide credit card information"). Two types of decomposition can be used: AND decompositions where a goal is decomposed into a sequence of simpler goals or tasks (e.g., the goal "buy crib" can be decomposed into the sequence "select crib", "pay for crib", "ship crib") and OR decompositions where a goal is decomposed into alternative ways to achieve it (e.g., the goal "pay for crib" can have alternatives "pay by credit card", "pay by money order".). Goal models distinguish between *hard goals*, indicating a well-defined satisfaction condition (e.g., "crib must be made in Canada") and *soft goals*, indicating a desirable state without clear testing criteria (e.g., "Timely Delivery"). Positive or negative contribution links, called "help" and "hurt" links, are then drawn from different types of goals to soft-goals to show how satisfaction of the former is believed to influence satisfaction or, respectively, denial of the latter.

Goals, Alternatives and Preferences. The AND/OR decomposition structures have been shown to be remarkably useful for representing large numbers of alternative solutions by which high level goals of stakeholders can be achieved [3, 8]. These solutions come in the form of *plans*, which are sequences of leaf level tasks that satisfy the AND/OR decomposition structure and possible precedence constraints between the tasks.

A goal model may imply a great number of possible plans, but which of them are best for a given situation at hand and how can we find them? Using *preferences*, we can represent things that stakeholders desire to be true but are not mandatory, while achieving their main goal [10]. Thus, while "buy a crib" is a mandatory goal and no plan that does not satisfy it is a viable solution, desires such as "crib be hand-made" or "timely delivery" may be preferences, in that, solutions that don't satisfy them may still be accepted. Furthermore, to express the relative importance between preferences, *priority* specifications over them are possible by constructing weighted linear combinations that must be optimized. Given a user profile containing relevant preferences and priorities, powerful preference-based AI planners [11] can be employed in order to identify plans that best satisfy the profile. In this way, we are able to connect high level stakeholder attitudes and desires with descriptions of complex low-level activity that best satisfy those desires.

Model Matching and Merging. *Match* and *Merge* are two important model management operators with a key role in supporting the distribution and coordination of modeling activities [4, 12]. The Match operator (sometimes also referred to as Map) is used to find commonalities between models. The resulting relationship is an explicit statement of how two models overlap in their content. For most types of models, it is a heuristic operator, meaning that the relationship produced by Match may miss some correct correspondences between model elements or identify some incorrect correspondences. As a result, the matching outcome typically needs to be adjusted by a user.

In our context, Match is used mainly as a prerequisite for the Merge operator, whose purpose is to unify the overlaps between a set of models and create a single holistic model. Model merging often becomes necessary when one wishes to gain a unified perspective over a set of models, to analyze the relationships between the models, or to check that models fit together in a consistent manner. In addition to the unification of overlaps, the Merge operator is often expected to satisfy several additional criteria. Some of these criteria are (1) *Completeness*: If a concept appears in one of the source models, it is represented in the merged model as well [13]; (2) *Minimality*: Merge shall not introduce new information that is not already present in or implied by the source models; and (3) *Logical Preservation*: Merge shall support the expression and preservation of logical properties. For example, for goal models, one may want to preserve the dependencies between the goals, to ensure that the intended meaning of the source models is properly captured in the merge. The Merge operator that we apply to goal models in this article (developed previously in [14]) meets all the above criteria.

Runtime Monitoring and Recovery. The goal of *runtime monitoring* is to check whether an application violates a given specification of its behaviour during execution. In this work, we assume that this behaviour is specified as a set of *desired* (what the system should exhibit) and *forbidden* (what the system should not exhibit) behaviours. Specifications of such behaviours come from a variety of sources: positive and negative user stories in crowd-sourced models, desired workflows defined by service providers, user preferences, pre- and postconditions of individual web services, user goal models, etc.

To create monitors, we translate these specifications into deterministic finite state machines (FSMs) and then *register* these with the execution environment. Monitors can become dynamically enabled (e.g., to monitor new properties) and disabled (e.g., to reduce the monitoring overhead or when a particular property is no longer relevant). During execution, the monitoring environment captures events as they pass between the application and its environment and uses these to update the state of the registered monitors. When any of the monitors reach their *accepting state*, this signifies that the application has executed an undesired scenario, and a violation needs to be reported. In our pictorial notation, accepting states are colored red and shaded horizontally. For example, state 3 of monitor M_1 in Figure 14 is red, indicating that the sequence pay, cash is forbidden. Self-loop in state 1 indicates that if the system sees any event in its alphabet (denoted Σ) other than pay, it should remain in the same state.

In addition, monitors can be used to detect *desired* sequences of events, which we pictorially represent using green states shaded vertically (not all states need to have these). For example, state 4 of monitor M_1 is green, indicating that sequences pay, credit are desirable. In order to reason about the unexpected termination of desired sequences of events, we have added a new system event TER, produced when the application terminates (regardless of the reason). For example, monitor M_7 in Figure 15 goes from state 1 to 2 on a TER event, indicating that the application terminated before the receiveDelivery event occurred.

Once an error is detected at runtime, our method can propose recovery plans [6]. Availability of these plans is contingent on vendors providing provisions for *compensating* the effects of the call to their web services. Compensation mechanisms are available in many web service frameworks, e.g., BPEL [15]. This mechanism is used to specify application-specific ways of reversing completed activities, where a service invocation is compensated by invoking additional services (to be determined by the service provider). For example, a vendor that offers a pay service may provide compensation which involves updating the inventory and reversing any charges made to the client's credit card, encapsulated in a cancel_unshipped service. However, once the item has been shipped, the client must pay a restocking fee, so a different service (cancel_shipped) must be used. Compensation might not leave the application in its original state, as some actions have irreversible side-effects, and sometimes compensation might not be available at all.

Given a violation, a *recovery plan* may involve "going back" – compensating the occurred actions until an alternative behaviour of the application is possible. For other violations, such plans include both "going back" and "re-planning" – guiding the application towards a desired behaviour. For example, if our user bought a used crib and decided to ship it using FedEx without consulting with the vendor (who only works with UPS), recovery simply means cancelling the FedEx shipping order and creating one with UPS. On the other hand, if our user purchased a used crib but later got a notice that delivery will be delayed (violating the "Timely Delivery" preference), then recovery means both compensating executed activities (such as returning the used crib when it finally arrives and getting money back) and carrying out new activities (such as buying a new crib). Recovery plans are ranked based on length, as well as the cost of the compensation actions in them.

5 Assumptions

In this section, we describe and exemplify assumptions that our methodology places on the user configuration environment, vendors, and the web.

5.1 Individual User Environment

In order to create and maintain effective personalized workflows, users are encouraged to create and maintain individual environment configurations. Such configurations include information about favourite sites and vendors, desired vendor policies and preferences, as well as additional configuration options. Information about favourite sites and vendors is used to discover web services that can execute part of the personalized workflow. Desired vendor policies are turned into monitors, thus enabling runtime monitoring of these policies. Finally, users can configure additional options, such as the maximum number of vendors to be displayed during workflow configuration, whether or not to enable checking vendor service invocation preconditions, as well as which policy monitors to enable.

In our example, our user prefers different online shopping sites depending on the type of product she is looking for: craigslist.org for used products, and sears.ca or toysrus.ca for new products. Our user also maintains a ranked list of preferred shipping companies, banks, etc. The following are some examples of vendor policies that our user prefers:

- P_1: Never pay cash if the vendor accepts a credit card.
- P_2: Always prefer slower but cheaper shipping to faster but more expensive.
- P_3: Whenever her credit card is charged, check back for a week to make sure that the charge went through and only once.
- P_4: Prefer to receive the merchandise first and be billed for it later.

Policies $P_1 - P_3$ are examples of behaviour that the user wants us to monitor at runtime, while P_4 is a preferred task ordering that can be used to guide the planning phase. With this in mind, users can add preferred (but not mandatory) ordering constraints, such as simple precedence and response properties, as well as occurrence properties, like the presence or absence of certain activities, to their high-level property specification. This can be done using simple templates, as in the Specification Pattern System [16].

```
webService _"http://example.org/pay"
   capability processPayment
      sharedVariables ?item ?creditCard ?order ?x ?y

      precondition pre_pay
         nonFunctionalProperties
            description hasValue "check that the item is still in stock and
               that the given credit card has enough credit for the transaction"
         endNonFunctionalProperties

         definedBy
            ?item memberOf Item and ?creditCard memberOf CreditCard and
            ?item[sku#inStock hasValue _boolean("true")] and
            ?item[price hasValue ?x] and
            ?creditCard[limit hasValue ?y] and
            ?x <= ?y

      postcondition post_pay
         nonFunctionalProperties
            description hasValue "check that a valid order has been placed and
               that the given credit card has been charged"
         endNonFunctionalProperties

         definedBy
            ?item memberOf Item and ?creditCard memberOf CreditCard and
            exists ?order
               (?order memberOf Order and
               (?order[sku] hasValue ?item[sku]) and
               (?order[client] equivalent ?client))
               and ?client[limit hasValue ?y - ?x]

      annotations
         compensation hasValue "if ?item[shipped hasValue _boolean('true')]
                                 then cancel_shipped else cancel_unshipped"
      endAnnotations
```

Fig. 6. WSML definition of the pay service

Finally, our user indicates that the maximum number of vendors to be displayed is five, and that all policy monitors and service preconditions should be checked during runtime. Clearly, these and other assumptions should "follow the user" from a computer to a computer and from one environment to the next, so they should be naturally stored in the cloud.

5.2   Vendor Registry and Configuration

Turning the Web into Services. In our workflow-based vision, users invoke web services in order to accomplish their goals, instead of browsing the web. We assume that vendors publish the APIs for these services in a publicly accessible registry, and a search protocol is available that allows these to be queried based on their metadata. This assumption follows from the evolving standards (e.g., UDDI [17], WS-Discovery [18], etc.) regarding web service discovery.

Service Specification. It is essential to have some notion of specification for services, at least to determine whether a particular service can be invoked at a particular step of the workflow and to discover services. Personal web is not unique in this challenge – good specifications are essential for creating quality web service applications under existing technologies. We think that the semantic web research community has a lot to offer on this topic.

Service interfaces are predominately specified using the Web Services Description Language (WSDL) [19], where the vendor indicates a service's URL and the syntax of its input/output messages. In this work, we need richer interface descriptions, since we also want vendors to specify service compensation and pre- and postconditions.

The Web Service Modeling Language (WSML) [20] allows the specification of such interfaces, so we will use it in this work.

In WSML, services are declared using the **webService** keyword; the URI argument indicates where the service can be accessed. Each web service can declare at most one **capability**, i.e., the task that it carries out. Each capability has a **sharedVariables** block, which is used to indicate the variables that are available to the pre- and post-conditions of the capability, which are defined using **precondition** and **postcondition** definitions, respectively. Each pre- and postcondition definition consists of an optional **nonFunctionalProperties** block, where the condition is described informally, and a logical expression preceded by the **definedBy** keyword, that formally defines the condition to check (which can be used to monitor the service). Pre- and postconditions about service ordering can also be specified in these blocks. Finally, since WSML does not have a specific keyword for specifying compensation, we added the definition of the service's compensation in the **annotations** block.

For example, Figure 6 shows the WSML definition of the pay service discussed in Section 4. This service can be accessed at http://example.org/pay, and has one capability, processPayment. The pay service has shared variables ?item, ?creditCard, ?order, ?x and ?y, as well as one pre- and one postcondition, pre_pay and post_pay, respectively. The precondition pre_pay checks that the item being bought is still in stock (represented by the expression ?item[sku#inStock hasValue _boolean("true")] in the **definedBy** block) and that the item's price is less than the available credit on the credit card (the rest of the expression in the **definedBy** block). Similarly, the postcondition post_pay has two parts, the first one checking that the pay service created a valid order (exists ?order . . .), while the other – requiring that the client's credit card was charged. The pay service is compensatable, since the vendor specified a compensation strategy in the **annotations** block: if the item has already been shipped, invoke the service cancel_shipped; otherwise, invoke cancel_unshipped.

Architectural Support. Given that users define personalized workflows by "stringing" together services, determining if services are compatible is an important issue [21, 22]. There seems to be a lot of success in existing technologies for creating web service compositions: the Semantic Web community mainly relies on AI planning techniques to automatically create service compositions [23, 24]; and service compositions can also be created manually using services like Yahoo! pipes and Google App Inventor. Like these initiatives, we assume that services "talk the same language" w.r.t. input and output messages (ensured through the creation and use of service interface ontologies).

An orthogonal question is that of where the state of a workflow should be stored during execution. To simplify presentation, we assume that workflow data "lives in the cloud", freely available to any service that may need it. We also assume that the cloud deals with data management, format, and storage issues.

5.3   Availability of and Search for Crowd-Sourced Models

In our work, we do not expect users to directly create detailed goal models; instead, we rely on "crowd-sourcing" them from the web. To do so, we make the assumption that the web community (users and/or vendors) publishes goal models representing ways to elaborate and accomplish common goals. For example, some of these models may express the offerings of particular service providers such as the goal model for Amazon.com's services, while others are "good ideas" on how to accomplish common tasks on the web such as finding a good place to eat. We refer to these as *crowd-sourced models* – elaborations of goal models published by web users. Crowd-sourced models are *complete* if their leaf notes are queries to the registry, resulting in lists of vendors which implement the tasks described by those nodes.

We envision the crowd-sourced goal models to be another resource type alongside HTML documents, images, etc. that can be published on the web and be accessible via web search engines – we call such a search engine *super-google* later in this paper. The search uses community rankings of the quality of the model together with information available in the user context (see Section 5.1) and individual vendor contexts to discover most suitable models.

We also assume the availability of a *common ontology* which represents a set of concepts within our domain, (i.e., the online shopping domain) and the relationships between those concepts. It plays a pivotal role in unifying the terms in different contexts and in dealing with potential differences in levels of abstraction as well as any inconsistencies. For example, using ontological relationships between words (e.g., the ontology provided by WordNet [25]), one can infer that a crib is a type of furniture. Thus, super-google can search not only for crib buying scenarios, but also how to buy furniture.

6   Step 1. Elicitation

Elicitation refers to the activities concerned with understanding the personal web user's objectives and preferences and expressing them in a suitable notation. The intended outcome of the elicitation phase of PWWM is a goal model that covers: (1) the user's high-level goals, (2) alternative means for realizing the goals, and (3) the main selection criteria for alternatives. Additionally, the user can provide information on how each of the alternatives are evaluated against her selection criteria.

We assume that a typical user might be unable to construct goal models directly, and we use a simplified approach for eliciting high-level goals. First, the user is asked to describe the web transaction workflow using natural language, and lexical analysis based on keyword search is used to extract high-level goal model elements from the description. The underlying justification for keyword search is that *a goal* is a statement of intent. Table 1, adapted from [26], lists several useful goal-related keywords that might drive goal search in the early stages of elicitation. Then, a wizard is used to elicit elaborations of these high-level goals by asking the user to state "how" to achieve the goals. For example, if a goal is to "have a place for baby to sleep", then asking "how?" might yield alternative approaches such as "Arranging bed share" or "Buying a crib". This process is iterated on these subgoals until the user can no longer elaborate them.

The selection criteria such as "should be inexpensive" are also elicited using a wizard and added to the goal model as soft goals. Such criteria constitute *user preferences* – desires that are not mandatory but nice-to-have when achieving the mandatory goals. Some of these are goal-independent and are described in Section 5.1, whereas others are elicited just for the current task. Focusing on OR-decompositions, the user assesses the

Table 1. Useful keywords for goal search

Prescriptive	shall, should, must, has to, to be, may never, may not, should never, should not
Intentional	in order to, so as to, so that, objective, aim, purpose, achieve, maintain, avoid, ensure, guarantee, want, wish, motivate, expected to

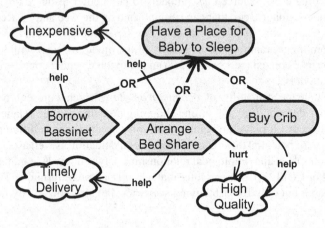

Fig. 7. User's initial goal model for the crib purchasing example

impact of each alternative on each of the identified criteria, wherever applicable. Well-known priority elicitation techniques (see more about them in Section 7.4) can be used to both quantify the impact of alternatives to preferences and (if this is desired at this early stage) to acquire a general sense of which of the criteria are by default more important to the user. These preferences pertain to the general characteristics of preferred workflows (rather than particular preferred vendor instances such as Sears vs. Walmart), and thus we refer to these as *workflow-level preferences*. They get updated and become more specific as the model is further elaborated, as we illustrate in Section 7.4.

Thus, the result of the elicitation process is a well-formed goal model containing the high-level expression of the user's objectives for the web transaction, as well as some general preferences as to what is important for the user. For our crib buying example, we synthesize the goal model (Figure 7), capturing the high-level alternatives suggested by the user for handling the crib shopping scenario. The soft-goals that appear in that model constitute initial expressions of preferences, subject to prioritization in later stages.

7 Step 2. Goal Refinement

The objective of the Goal Refinement step, depicted in Figure 8, is to enable the user to elaborate the high-level goal model produced in Step 1 by showing how these goals can be refined into lower-level ones and, conversely, how lower-level goals contribute to higher-level ones. The refinement continues until the model is *complete* (see Section 5.3), by iterating through the following steps:

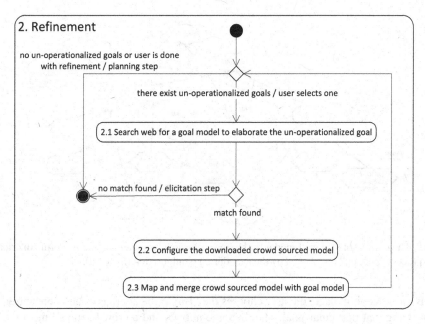

Fig. 8. A Refinement step of PWWM

1. **Step 2.1 (Search):** The user selects a high-level un-operationalized goal and searches the web for a list of crowd-sourced models that can elaborate and/or operationalize the selected goal. She then goes through the list to pick and download one of the crowd-sourced models that best fits her expectations.
2. **Step 2.2 (Configure):** Subsequently, the user may modify and configure the downloaded crowd-sourced model to customize it to her specific needs.
3. **Step 2.3 (Match and Merge):** Then, she attempts to integrate the crowd-sourced model and her initial goal model, developed during elicitation (see Section 6). This, in turn, involves finding a mapping between the crowd-sourced and the initial goal model, and then merging the two models.
4. **Step 2.4 (Preference Refinement):** Finally, the user refines her original general preferences by adding more detail and by defining priorities among them.

If the search in step 2.1 fails to produce satisfactory results, the process shifts back to the elicitation step to get the user's assistance in revising the selected node. The refinement process is repeated as long as there are un-operationalized nodes that the user wishes to elaborate and/or operationalize. Also, in principle, the user can take the crowd-sourced model and add her own tasks to it, which means that she may need to iterate over steps 2.1 and 2.2 multiple times. In the remainder of this section, we discuss each of the activities in more detail.

7.1 Searching for Crowd-Sourced Models

In this step, the user first chooses one of the un-operationalized goals in her initial goal graph. For our example in Figure 7, among the three proposed alternative for handling

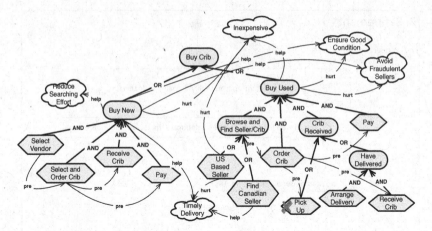

Fig. 9. The crowd-sourced goal model for buying a physical large item online in North America. The process "pick up" is removed by the user during configuration (Step 2.2).

the baby's sleeping place, the user chooses the "Buy crib" alternative and concentrates on refining that particular goal. She then attempts to find a crowd-sourced model describing how that goal can be decomposed into smaller steps, and what alternative scenarios exist on the web to carry it out.

The search engine – super google – returns a ranked list of crowd-sourced goal models describing how the "Buy Crib" process can be carried out on the web. The user has the option of going through the list and reviewing the ratings and comments to make her final decision. In our example, the final crowd-sourced goal model chosen by the user is shown in Figure 9. As shown in the figure, the crowd-sourced model suggests to decompose the "Buy Crib" goal into two main subgoals: "Buy New" and "Buy Used". Each subgoal is then decomposed into sequences of tasks. Specifically, the "Buy New" is decomposed into the sequence of tasks: "Select Vendor", "Select and Order Crib;", "Receive Crib", and "Pay". The "Buy Used" goal is decomposed into a similar sequence, except that there are two options for finding a vendor, since the user is free to choose a vendor from Canada or the US, and the user can receive the crib either by picking it up herself or by arranging it to be shipped to her place.

7.2 Configuring Found Models

The crowd-sourced goal models are generic descriptions with several alternatives and thus are highly configurable. Of course, not all alternatives are applicable to all users. Hence, we expect the user to configure the crowd-sourced goal model based on her needs and according to her personalized scenario, and then integrate it with her personal model.

For example, the user may remove the "Pick up" alternative from the goal model in Figure 9 because she does not have a car and therefore cannot pick up the crib herself. While not illustrated in our example, the configuration could be more advanced. In particular, it could involve choosing values for a number of configurable parameters, e.g., the shipping insurance amount if the shipment is to be insured. Also note that the

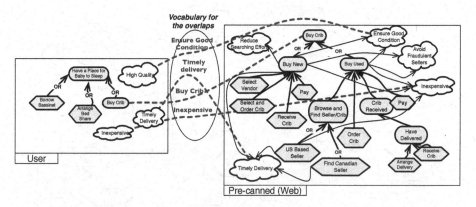

Fig. 10. Relationship between the personal goal model in Figure 7 and the crowd-sourced one in Figure 9

user may decide to extend the crowd-sourced goal model by adding her own tasks to it. In our example, the user may add an "ensure partner agreement before a purchase is made" task, involving sending an email to her spouse and awaiting a confirmation.

7.3   Mapping and Merging of Goal Models

Once the crowd-sourced goal model has been configured, it needs to be merged with the user's (personal) goal model. This in turn requires the relationship between the two models to be specified. When the models are developed in a centralized manner, the relationship can be left implicit and defined through conventions, e.g., name equivalence if models have a common vocabulary, or identifier equivalence if models have common ancestors. In the context of personal web, it is very hard to put such conventions in place as the models are developed independently and often without any prior coordination. The relationships between independently-developed models have to be specified explicitly instead [27]. These relationships are often established through a combination of manual and automated matching based on heuristics [4].

In our example, both the personal and the crowd-sourced models are small, and the matching can be done manually. Figure 10 shows the relationship that the user has defined between hers and the crowd-sourced model. The relationship defines the overlaps between the concepts in the two models: "Buy product" is mapped to "Buy Crib". "Get in a definite time" is mapped to "Timely delivery". "Inexpensive" to "Inexpensive". "Ensure good quality" to "Ensure good quality". The relationship is expressed as a set of labelled mappings between concept pairs. The labels on the mappings specify the vocabulary that should be used for the shared concepts in the merge. The result of merging the personal and the (configured) crowd-sourced models is shown in Figure 11.

Alternatively, we can use automated matching techniques when the models are large or when the user is not certain about her manually built relationships and would like the system to provide her with some recommended matchings. Our automated matcher uses the common ontology discussed in Section 5.3 to unify the terms in different models and discover potential matches in a similar way that the common ontology can be used by super-google for searching the web.

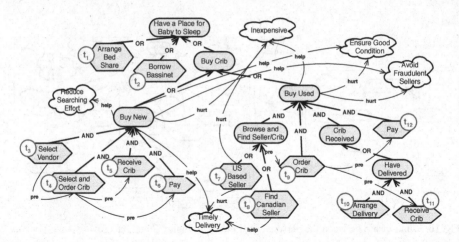

Fig. 11. Merge of the personal goal model in Figure 7 and crowd-sourced one in Figure 9 with respect to relationships in Figure 10

7.4 Preference Refinement and Prioritization

As shown in Figure 11, the merged goal model includes workflow preferences – things that the user generally likes to see satisfied – in the form of soft goals. Examples of these are "Ensure Good Condition", or "Inexpensive". In addition, while the model in Figure 11 does not prescribe whether payment (task t_{12}) precedes delivery (task t_{11}), the user may want to express preferences pertaining to the ordering of tasks. In Section 5.1, such preference was given using P_4, indicating that shipping should precede payment, if possible.

The goal model together with those preferences constitute a relatively stable representation of stakeholder desires and alternative requirements. In practice, in different situations or based on new information that arrives while our user already attempts to fulfill her goal, the relative importance of preferences changes. Specifying *priorities* amongst user preferences allows us to describe their relative importance at a given point in time. These come in the form of weighted linear combinations of individual preferences – the weight being a measure of the relative importance of the corresponding preference. The linear combination can then be seen as an *objective function* to be optimized: from the large number of plans that are implied by the goal model, we are interested in those that satisfy as many of the important preferences as possible.

Elicitation of the weights is possible through a variety of techniques from simple ad-hoc assessment (e.g., [28]) to methods based on pairwise comparison, such as the Analytic Hierarchy Process (AHP) [29–31]. Back to our example, assume that an "Inexpensive" purchase is "strongly more" preferred to "Reduce Searching Effort". Applying AHP, which involves assigning the corresponding preference values to a comparison matrix and estimating its eigenvector, gives us priority weights 0.83 and 0.17, respectively. In practice, a preference profile can include more than two components and more detailed relationships between them, e.g., vendor-level preferences like "Use services by Speedy Delivery Inc." or even vendor-specific temporal properties like "If you purchase from Maple Cribs Inc., use their delivery service as well".

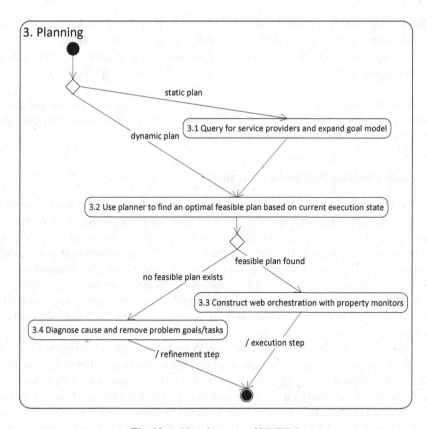

Fig. 12. A Planning step of PWWM

8   Step 3. Planning and Web Service Creation

During this step, state-of-the-art preference-enabled planning algorithms [11, 32] read
the goal models and preference prioritization – automatically translated into a planning
specification language – and compute ranked plans within the detailed goal model that
satisfy the customer's prioritization, by means of maximizing the given priority as expressed in the value of an objective function (see Section 7.4). Picking plans lower in
the ranking indicates relaxing preferences. If the user does not like any of the produced
plans, she may want to change the preferences, resulting in the planner computing a
different set of plans.

Recall that a detailed goal model is fully operationalized if its leaf tasks contain
queries allowing us to discover appropriate web service calls that can execute them.
Models get fully operationalized in the Refinement step. The Planning step allows finding web services before the plan is generated (*static planning*) or as the plan is being
executed (*dynamic planning*). The advantage of a static plan is that it guarantees that
vendor policies, expressed through the pre- and postconditions of their service invocations, are taken into account. However, compared to dynamic planning, it is much
more expensive for the planner to generate and also does not give the user a complete

flexibility in service provider selection. In either case, failure to complete execution of the plan may result in having to change the vendors while the actual plan stays the same, or in relaxing or changing the the workflow-level preferences to get a new plan, or, less likely but possibly, going back to the refinement step in order to update the goal model itself.

In the rest of this section, we provide more detail on static vs. dynamic planning, describe how each method allows for creation and composition of actual services, and how runtime monitoring is possible and beneficial in each case.

8.1   Static Plan and Web Service Creation

Step 3.1. Query for Service Providers and Expand Goal Model. The *static* approach to generating a plan requires that the leaf-level tasks of the goal model be expanded with lists of providers offering the service of interest. Thus, we begin by executing the service registry query associated with each task of the operationalized goal model. The outcome of the query returns a number of services (the maximum number can be controlled by the user – see Section 5.1), with a potential (crowd-sourced) ranking of how well they perform the service in question. Some of the services may also explicitly specify their precise pre- and postconditions, as offered by the providers themselves (see Section 5.2).

For example, consider generating a static plan for the goal model in Figure 11. First, we query the service registry to produce a list of particular services offered by providers to accomplish these goals. For example, one of the services associated with task t_9 is a placeOrder service offered by a Canadian crib vendor, Maple Cribs Inc. This service has a precondition (P_5) that the selection service offered by the same vendor (selectByType) must be invoked first. This vendor also offers a delivery service, arrangeDelivery, which presumes that their service pay, associated with task t_{12}, has been performed. In other words, the arrangeDelivery service has the following precondition (P_6): "pay precedes arrangeDelivery". The arrangeDelivery service also has a postcondition (P_7): "the user should eventually receive the item (receiveDelivery)".

The same tasks can also be accomplished by the corresponding services of a US-based company, Rock Baby Ltd. However, their delivery service (accomplishing t_{10}) presupposes the use of their own order service (associated with t_9). This is also a service precondition (associated to the delivery service): the Rock Baby order service must be invoked before its delivery service can be used.

Step 3.2. Static Plan Generation. Given the expanded goal model produced as a result of Step 3.1, the planner can readily find sequences of steps based on concrete services that vendors provide. Moreover, the fact that a plan is found *guarantees* that there exists a service composition that satisfies the user's goal – at least if provider-specified pre- and postconditions are complete and correct. Furthermore, the user-maintained vendor-specific preferences, if any, can also be used by the planner to produce rankings or service composition possibilities.

If the planner fails to find a plan with higher ranked vendors it will attempt to find one with lower ranked vendors, which may correspond to the same sequence of requirements-level tasks but with different service bindings. Alternatively, the user may change her preferences, resulting in the planner calculating new rankings. Either way, while the exact choice of vendors used in the resulting service composition is *affected* by the user, it is not fully *controlled* by the user.

Returning to our crib-buying example, the planner can produce a number of plans which satisfy the vendor pre- and postconditions while taking user preferences into account. If it is more important to pay after delivery (see P_4 in Section 5.1), the combined order+delivery package offered by Rock Baby may be unavoidable. If a higher preference is given to a Canadian vendor (or to Maple Cribs specifically, reflecting a pre-existing vendor-specific preference resulting from an earlier crib purchase), a delivery service can still be arranged through a third party since the use of the Maple Cribs ordering service does not require that their own delivery service is used as well.

Assume that the user's preference profile is "Inexpensive [Crib]" (with weight 0.5) "Use services by Speedy Delivery Inc." (weight 0.3) and "If you purchase from Maple Cribs Inc., use their own delivery service as well" (weigh 0.2) – in practice, preference profiles can be much richer than this one. The following are the three top scoring statically generated plans that use Maple Cribs Inc services (score value in parenthesis):

$sp_1(0.8) = \{\text{selectByType, placeOrder, pay, arrangeShipment, updateShipment}\}$
$sp_2(0.8) = \{\text{selectByType, placeOrder, pay, arrangeShipment, receiveDelivery}\}$
$sp_3(0.7) = \{\text{selectByType, placeOrder, pay, arrangeDelivery, receiveDelivery}\}$

Services selectByType, placeOrder, pay, arrangeDelivery, receiveDelivery are offered by Maple Cribs Inc, whereas arrangeShipment and updateShipment are offered by Speedy Delivery. For example, in plan sp_1, the user buys the crib from Maple Cribs Inc., but ships it with Speedy Delivery since it offers a better delivery experience than Maple Cribs Inc and thus occurs in the user's preference profile with a higher weight (0.3) than shipping with Maple Cribs (0.2).

Step 3.3. Web Orchestration and Property Monitors (Static). Since a static plan is just a simple sequential orchestration of web services, we can make it executable using BPEL. Figure 13a shows the BPEL implementation of the top-ranked plan sp_1. The workflow begins with the receiveInput activity, which stores the workflow input parameters on the cloud in order to make them available for other services (as discussed in Section 5.2). Each task in plan sp_1 is carried out by invoking a web service (the corresponding activities in the BPEL diagram are preceded by a 🕭 symbol). We attach compensation handlers to the activities that invoke compensatable services (not visible in the BPEL diagram). Figure 13b shows an example of a BPEL compensation handler – the one attached to the pay service invocation. As indicated in Section 5.2, the pay service is compensated by executing the cancel_unshipped service, since the item is paid for before shipping in plan sp_1. Finally, since we assumed that services "speak the same language" w.r.t. input and output messages (see Section 5.2), we do not deal with data management/formatting/storage issues which exist between today's web services.

Since this orchestration can fail at runtime, at this point we also generate monitors for this orchestration. For statically-generated plans, these monitors come from the following sources:

1. User workflow-level preferences, including high-level order and occurrence properties. These are used during construction of a static plan but the user

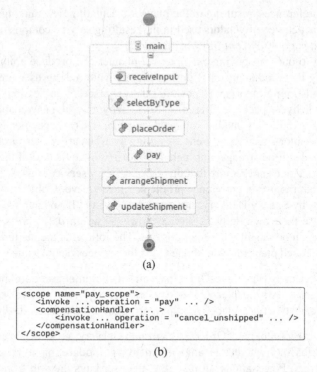

(a)

```
<scope name="pay_scope">
    <invoke ... operation = "pay" ... />
    <compensationHandler ... >
        <invoke ... operation = "cancel_unshipped" ... />
    </compensationHandler>
</scope>
```

(b)

Fig. 13. (a) Static BPEL implementation of plan sp_1 (see Section 8.1) and (b) BPEL compensation handler for pay invocation

may choose to register for the corresponding monitors anyway, to check for runtime failures. For example, some monitors corresponding to user preference policies P_1 and P_4 (see Section 5.1) are shown in Figure 14. The monitors for P_2 and P_3 are very similar to M_1 and thus are not shown. In the case of policy P_1, we first check if the chosen vendor supports both cash and credit actions, i.e., we check whether $\{\text{cash}, \text{credit}\} \subseteq \Sigma_v$ is true, where $\Sigma_v \subseteq \Sigma$ is the set of actions offered by the vendor. If so, then payment using cash is a forbidden behaviour (pay followed by cash), and leads to the bad state 3. On the other hand, payment via credit (pay followed by credit) is a desired behaviour, leaving the monitor in a good state 4. Monitor M_4 checks that the user receives the item before paying for it (leaving the monitor in the good state 4). If payment occurs before the user receives the item, the monitor ends up in the bad state 2, indicating a violation.

2. Vendor-specified pre- and postconditions and expected workflows. Service providers may assume that their services are invoked in a particular order, or work with others in a particular way. While these workflows are used in static plan construction, monitors can still check if stated postconditions achieved by individual invocations hold, or whether various failures affected the expected vendor workflow. For example, since plan sp_1 uses Maple Crib's placeOrder service, precondition P_5 is turned into a monitor (see Figure 15a). Since plan sp_1 does not use Maple Crib's arrangeDelivery service, we do not add the monitors M_6 and M_7 (see Figure 15) to the set of active monitors. Finally, plan sp_1 also invokes the pay service defined in Section 5.2, so the

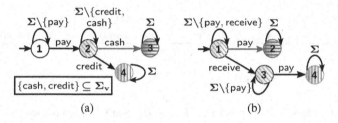

Fig. 14. User preference monitors: (a) M_1 and (b) M_4, corresponding to policies P_1 and P_4 (see Section 5.1), respectively

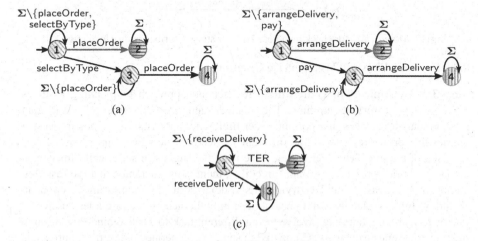

Fig. 15. Vendor monitors: (a) M_5, (b) M_6, and (c) M_7 corresponding to preconditions P_5, P_6 and postcondition P_7 (defined earlier in this section), respectively

pre- and postcondition expressions specified in the WSML file become assertions that should be checked before and after service invocation, respectively.

3. User goal models produced by the Refinement step. There are many reasons why a started plan does not finish, mostly due to the internet being unreliable and/or failure of individual vendor services. At runtime, we aim to check that the entire chosen plan completes successfully. For example, if plan sp_1 runs to completion, monitor M_8- in Figure 16 is left in a good state 6 (coloured green and shaded vertically). On the other hand, if the workflow unexpectedly terminates at any step of the plan, the monitor ends up in a bad state 7 (coloured red and shaded horizontally).

4. User stories from crowd-sourced models. Crowd-sourced models used during the Refinement step may optionally come with user stories, positive or negative, e.g., some users reported that Maple Cribs Inc. products shipped with Speedy Delivery arrive in bad condition. This property is checked using M_9, shown in Figure 17: the monitor is left in a bad state 3 if arrangeShipment (Speedy Delivery's service) is invoked after placeOrder (Maple Cribs' service). Our methodology allows users to register monitors to check whether their own workflows are subject to such desired or undesired behaviours.

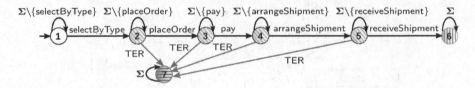

Fig. 16. Monitor M_8 to check that plan sp_1 (Section 8.1) is run to completion

Fig. 17. Monitor M_9 for checking a negative user story described earlier in Section 8.1

8.2 Dynamic Plan and Web Service Creation

Step 3.2. Dynamic Plan Generation. The second approach to planning assumes dynamic task-to-service binding. The planner generates a sequence of abstract requirements-level tasks that optimize user preferences. At runtime, a post-processor queries the service registry to find different service providers that implement the current step of the plan. The user chooses one from the suggested set to call. Since each choice of service providers is done "greedily", there is no guarantee that the resulting composition is feasible, and verifying this is deferred to the monitoring component. Failure to fulfill a plan does not necessarily imply the need to choose a less preferred one or re-planning, but may involve trying different task-to-service bindings, through querying the repository again. Compared to statically-generated plans, this approach is computationally cheaper (on the planner) and gives users more control in the process of choosing their preferred set of vendors. However, the likelihood of the initial failure and the need to try the process multiple times increases.

Let us return to the example of Figure 11. Assume that the preference profile includes the quality preferences "Inexpensive" and "Timely Delivery" as well as the temporal preference "Pay after Delivery", with weights 0.4, 0.4 and 0.2, respectively. The planner generates two top-ranked plans:

$dp_1 = [t_8, t_9, t_{10}, t_{11}, t_{12}]$ with score 1.0 (optimal)
$dp_2 = [t_8, t_9, t_{12}, t_{10}, t_{11}]$ with score 0.8

Thus, the highest ranked plan allows for both an inexpensive purchase and a timely delivery, as it allows buying a used crib from a Canadian seller. It also prescribes that payment must happen after delivery. Thus, all components of the preference profile are satisfied. The second plan satisfies the first two components but not the third one, hence the lower score.

Both plans are descriptions of desired workflows at a high level, without any information about the particular services that will implement it. In what follows, we assume that the user picked plan dp_1 to execute.

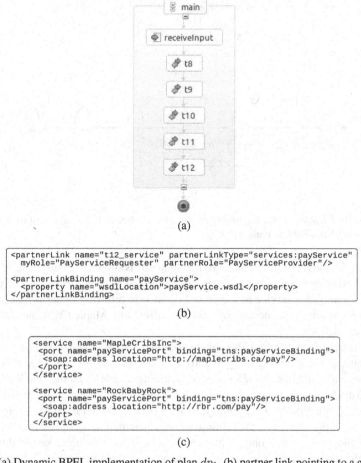

(a)

```
<partnerLink name="t12_service" partnerLinkType="services:payService"
  myRole="PayServiceRequester" partnerRole="PayServiceProvider"/>

<partnerLinkBinding name="payService">
  <property name="wsdlLocation">payService.wsdl</property>
</partnerLinkBinding>
```

(b)

```
<service name="MapleCribsInc">
  <port name="payServicePort" binding="tns:payServiceBinding">
    <soap:address location="http://maplecribs.ca/pay"/>
  </port>
</service>

<service name="RockBabyRock">
  <port name="payServicePort" binding="tns:payServiceBinding">
    <soap:address location="http://rbr.com/pay"/>
  </port>
</service>
```

(c)

Fig. 18. (a) Dynamic BPEL implementation of plan dp_1, (b) partner link pointing to a generic t_{12} service, and (c) snippet of the WSDL file where the concrete pay services are defined

Step 3.3. Web Orchestration and Property Monitors (Dynamic). The dynamic web orchestration used by this approach to planning requires explicating queries to the service registry in order to find appropriate bindings at each step of the plan.

While BPEL engines augmented with aspects [33] can be used for implementing this approach, there are provisions to do this in native BPEL as well, which we follow here. In BPEL, services are made available through partner links which use the information in the referenced WSDL definition files to determine which services are available. BPEL supports dynamic binding of partner links, making it possible to modify various partner link parameters, like service URIs (host, port and path) and target service names at runtime. This means that dynamically generated plans can also be implemented using BPEL, as long as the concrete services are defined in the linked WSDL files. The contents of the WSDL file for each dynamic binding is generated right before the binding is used. Compensation is defined the same way as for static plans.

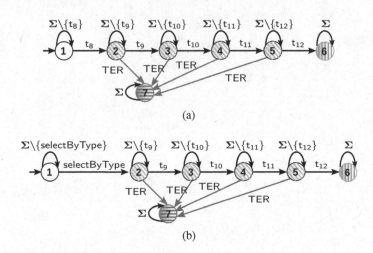

Fig. 19. Monitor M_{10}: (a) initial version where no tasks are bound to services, and (b) after user picks service selectByType to realize task t_8.

For example, the BPEL implementation of plan dp_1 is shown in Figure 18a, where all invocation activities point to generic services instead of concrete services. The partner link for the generic t_{12} service is shown in Figure 18b, referring to the WSDL snippet in Figure 18c where two concrete pay services, offered by Maple Cribs Inc. and Rock Baby Ltd, are defined.

When the user executes the BPEL orchestration in Figure 18a, the runtime environment first queries the service registry to find candidate services for activity t_8. The query results in several Canadian and US vendors, including Maple Cribs Inc. and Rock Baby Ltd. We assume that vendors can be ranked in a variety of ways, e.g., using the notion of crowd-sourced "quality" of a vendor or the user's personal vendor-specific preferences. At each point in the execution, the runtime environment maintains the current "state" of the system and thus displays only those vendors whose pre-conditions satisfy this state.

Unlike the static case where all monitors are generated before execution begins, here monitors are generated on-the-fly as plan steps become operationalized. For example, Figure 19 shows two versions of monitor M_{10}, which checks that plan dp_1 defined earlier in this section is run to completion. The transition labels of the initial monitor (Figure 19a) are placeholders, set as the user chooses particular services. Suppose the user selects Maple Cribs Inc. and attempts to execute service selectByType provided by this vendor (which we suppose includes browsing products, adding them to a cart, etc.). Monitor M_{10} is updated to reflect this choice, resulting in the monitor shown in Figure 19b. In addition, vendor-defined pre- and postconditions are turned into *automatically-registered* monitors since these are no longer satisfied by plan construction. Otherwise, the sources of monitors are the same as discussed in the static case but registered and invoked on-the-fly.

Once the order is placed (t_9), the user proceeds with arranging a delivery (t_{10}). The service registry is queried again, this time returning two alternative services: arrangeDelivery and arrangeShipment, offered by Maple Cribs Inc and Speedy Delivery, respectively. Our user decides to keep shopping with Maple Cribs Inc., so monitor

M_6 (see Figure 15b) is added to the set of active monitors. This monitor is immediately violated, since Maple Cribs' pay service has not been invoked on this execution trace. The runtime environment notifies the user that a monitor violation occurred, prompting her to pick an alternative service for t_{10} (e.g., arrangeShipment) to continue executing dp_1.

The stepwise find-and-execute process described above continues either until all the tasks in the plan are performed (success), or until no services satisfying the existing state of the system can be found (failure). In the latter case, a *recovery process* is initiated (see Section 9), allowing the user to try to execute the same plan but with a different choice of vendors. For example, she may want to withdraw her order from Maple Cribs Inc. if she cannot find an affordable delivery option later on.

In the end, if suitable bindings are not found, the user may choose to relax her preferences and move on to the next plan in the ranking or change her preferences and replan, effectively choosing in both cases a different general workflow and start querying for services step-by-step all over again (see Section 8.3).

8.3   Step 3.4. Replanning

Replanning happens if the user changes her preferences. This step can be entered both from the plan generation step (Step 3.2) and from the execution step (Step 4). In the latter case, the current state of the plan being executed becomes another input to the planner, to give higher rank to those plans that include already executed steps.

Returning to the example of Figure 11, assume that the user follows the dynamic planning approach having the preference profile "Inexpensive" (0.4), "Timely Delivery" (0.4) and "Pay after Delivery" (0.2). While the plan $[t_8, t_9, t_{10}, t_{11}, t_{12}]$ is optimal for this profile, suppose that the user consistently fails to find a suitable binding allowing her to pay after delivery, as the plan requires. Some time passes; she becomes increasingly more impatient and willing to pay more just to finish her purchase. She thus updates her preference profile, adding "Reduce Searching Effort" as a relevant and important goal, with weight 0.5, while the weights of all other preferences are reduced to half their original ones. Without knowing the current state of execution of the user's original plan, the planner would suggest a brand new plan $dp_3 = t_3, t_4, t_5, t_6$ involving purchase of a new crib. However, if some steps of the original plan have already been performed, e.g., placing an order on a used crib as a result of executing t_8, they would now need to be cancelled, and compensation for t_8 – returning the crib – contributes negatively to the "Reduce Searching Effort" goal; thus, the planner will consider alternative plans, some of which involving getting a used crib (but paying before the delivery).

9   Step 4. Execution and Recovery

The Execution step allows the user to register a number of monitors and then run the generated BPEL, executing the plan step-by-step and updating the states of all the registered monitors until one of the following events happens: (a) some monitor fails – at which point PWWM starts a *recovery step*; (b) the user decides to change her preferences (e.g., because the next step of the dynamic plan does not yield any service

provider choices) – at which point PWWM enters Step 3.4; (c) the complete plan suc-
ceeds, satisfying the goals of the user – at which point PWWM concludes successfully;
and (d) the user abandons her plan altogether and decides to start again, e.g., with the
Elicitation phase.

The Recovery step uses semantic information about services involved in the workflow to attempt to fix the problem discovered with the orchestration using runtime monitoring. We explored such *property-guided recovery* in the context of traditional web
applications in [6,34], where both the orchestration and its properties are defined by the
application developer, but recovery plans are computed for individual execution traces.
The recovery process is easily adapted to reasoning about personal web, as we illustrate
below.

We discuss handling static and dynamic plans separately.

Execution and Recovery: Static Plans. For the static plan, execution just involves
running the generated BPEL orchestration. The only monitors activated by default are
those that check that the entire plan executes successfully. Other monitors, such as those
checking for positive or negative user stories obtained from the web, or checking vendor workflows, user preferences or vendor pre- and postconditions can be activated
optionally.

For example, if our user decides to execute the static plan sp_1 defined in Section 8.1,
only monitor M_8 (see Figure 16) is automatically added to the set of active monitors.
Violations of this monitor indicate that the chosen plan could not be executed to completion. Monitors $M_1 - M_4$ (see Figure 14), as well as monitors $M_5 - M_7$ (see Figure 15),
corresponding to user preferences and pre-, postconditions, respectively, represent properties that were taken into account during plan generation and are thus satisfied by construction. However, the user could still decide to register these monitors, since physical
problems, like a server crash, can affect the outcome of the selected plan. Finally, the
user selects whether or not to register monitor M_9 (see Figure 17), corresponding to a
crowd-sourced user story.

Suppose the user is executing the static plan sp_1. She successfully interacted with
Maple Cribs' services (leaving monitor M_8 in state 4), and she now invokes the
arrangeShipment service provided by Speedy Delivery. However, a power outage in
Ottawa knocked Speedy Delivery's data center off the grid, and PWWM timed out
(sending a TER event) while waiting for arrangeShipment to respond. This leaves M_8
in the bad state 7, signalling that sp_1 could not be completed; thus, PWWM attempts to
recover from this error.

We cannot modify statically created plans, since we do not know how these changes
affect all the constraints taken into account when generating the plan. So recovery entails getting the user to try a lower-ranked static plan. In our example, the next best
ranked plan was sp_2; however, sp_2 also invokes arrangeShipment and so may not be
a good recovery plan candidate. The next plan, sp_3, while ranked the lowest, does not
invoke arrangeShipment. It also has the same first three steps as sp_1. Picking this plan
during recovery entails minimal compensation, making it an excellent candidate. If none
of the statically computed plans can replace the current one (according to the user), she
needs to change her preferences or return to te Elicitation phase, to generate new static
plans.

Execution and Recovery: Dynamic Plans. Execution of dynamically generated plans entails running a query to the service registry, getting the user to choose among the list of potential service providers and then continuing. In addition to a number of monitors created to make sure that the plan is executed successfully, dynamic planning also includes activating, at runtime, monitors which check that pre- and postconditions of the user-chosen service providers are correctly satisfied. And, as in static plans, the user may optionally decide to invoke monitors to check for positive or negative user stories which are obtained from the web and associated with a particular service provider they chose to use.

For example, suppose our user decides to execute the dynamic plan dp_1 defined in Section 8.2. Thus, the monitors $M_1 - M_4$ and M_{10} are automatically registered. Monitors $M_5 - M_7$, on the other hand, are registered only if the associated service is invoked. As in the static case, the user can choose whether or not to register M_9.

During execution, suppose the user picked services selectByType and placeOrder to realize tasks t_8 and t_9, respectively (leaving monitor M_{10} in state 3). Since she picked placeOrder, monitor M_5 is also registered and then updated to reflect the current execution trace. This leaves M_5 in the good state 4, which means that placeOrder's precondition is met by the current execution trace. Also, since state 4 of M_5 is a sink state, this monitor can now be unregistered. In the next step, the user must pick a service to operationalize task t_{10}. She decides to use Maple Cribs' arrangeDelivery service, so monitors M_6 and M_7 become registered. Again, we update the state of these new monitors using the current execution trace, so M_6 (M_7) is left in state 2 (1). State 2 of M_6 is bad, indicating that arrangeDelivery's precondition does not hold on the current execution trace.

Recovering from the above error can be done in a variety of ways. The simplest recovery plan is to switch arrangeDelivery for another service, like arrangeShipment (similar to the static recovery case). Another option is to switch to plan dp_2 (see Section 8.2, which is a permutation of dp_1. Since payment occurs before arranging delivery in dp_2, our user can continue using the arrangeDelivery service. If the user is not satisfied with these recovery options, PWWM also offers *replanning* (see Section 8.3), aimed to suggest new plans while taking into account compensation for tasks already carried out.

10   Discussion and Challenges

The Personal Web Workflow vision is just what it is – a vision. We are yet to implement it and experiment with its effectiveness, even though we believe that such an implementation is possible with existing web technologies. This experience would also explicate cases where our framework assumptions, described in Section 5 are too strong. Ideally, they can be addressed using some of the techniques offered in this book.

Regardless of the technological challenges, we believe that the ultimate success of Personal Web Workflow vision described in this paper critically depends on successfully solving three major research problems: (a) effective elicitation of goals and a variety of other properties that can be used to help produce usable plans and monitor for their successful execution; (b) scalability of the various analyses performed "behind the

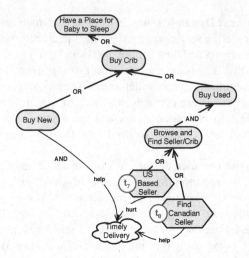

Fig. 20. Model slice relevant to the "Timely Delivery" soft goal

scenes" in this framework, from relationship identification to planning to monitoring and recovery; (c) creating provisions for collaboration of multiple users in order to accomplish a particular goal (e.g., the crib can be bought not only by the user but by her parents who reside in the US, and now the framework needs to ensure not only that the crib arrives on time, but also that two cribs are not bought accidentally). In what follows, we discuss several proposals related to these issues.

Goal and Preference Elicitation. In this paper, we proposed to rely on non-intelligent keyword search to help turn user narrative into goal models. Although simple and useful, this approach may lead to plenty of false positives which need to be filtered manually by the user. This can be ameliorated by using templates that place restrictions on how natural language can be used. In particular, the user may be asked to use a wizard-like environment that permits only certain sentence patterns. Such patterns have been widely studied in behavioural verification for temporal properties [16]. While the general ideas apply to goal models as well, further research is required to identify, classify and evaluate these patterns.

Web 2.0 provides various opportunities to increase the level of sophistication in goal search. For example, if the user owns a blog, the starting point for keyword search could be this blog. Moreover, goal search can take advantage of previous queries that the user placed on the search engine. Some interesting work on this topic has already been done by M. Strohmaier and his colleagues [35, 36].

We also need to experiment further with techniques for elicitation, capture, review and maintenance of user preferences, since these are paramount for the success of our proposed methodology.

Multiple Users: Refinement Step. Recall that our merge example in Section 7 required integration of only two models. In practice, the integration step may involve more models, for example, when the user uses multiple crowd-sourced models to operationalize her desired scenario, or when the notion of "user" represents a group of people rather than just one individual. In this case, the "viewpoints" [37] of the different group members and any pre-existing models used by them need to be combined together, before a desired scenario can be operationalized. This in turn requires the specification of a *collection* of inter-related models. A particularly interesting abstraction that can be used for describing such a collection is that of an *interconnection diagram* adapted from category theory [38]. Interconnection diagrams allow the merge operation to be defined over an arbitrarily large number of models and relationships rather than just pairs of models related by a single relationship. In our previous work, we have already described a model merging operator that works over interconnection diagrams [14].

Scalability: Refinement Step. When multiple models are involved, the merge outcome may become too large and thus too complex for the end-user to comprehend. To address scalability, the modeling environment where goal models are constructed and manipulated needs to provide mechanisms for *slicing* of goal models [39]. The purpose of slicing is to extract the fragments of a model that are relevant to a particular task. For example, the personal web user in our example may be interested in only viewing the goals and tasks that help or hurt the satisfaction of the "Timely Delivery" soft goal, in which case the slice should include three core elements: the "Buy New" goal as well as the two leaf tasks t_7 and t_8 from Figure 11. In addition, since non-root goals and tasks cannot be understood outside their context, the slice should further include the higher level goals and tasks related to the core elements. The slicing process should thus yield the model shown in Figure 20. This slice helps the user narrow down her investigation to a small fragment of the overall model, thus reducing cognitive load and improving comprehension. Leica [39] provides a detailed treatment of slicing for goal models, enabling users to extract slices for various types of reviewing activities often performed on goal models.

Scalability: Planning Step. Planning techniques have advanced significantly over the past years, allowing for efficient reasoning about real problems, even despite the complexity of the underlying computational problem [40]. The planner infrastructure we are considering [11] actually benefits from the presence of explicit preferences and a recomposition structure given by the goal model. In its current state, its performance is practical for models involving tens of goal and task elements [10]. Of course, the planning step can become more efficient if we attempt to minimize goal interactions or remove unnecessary non-determinism [41].

Also, whenever we believe that static planning takes too long, we can always switch to dynamic planning, trading off guarantees of satisfaction of pre- and post-conditions and vendor preferences for planner efficiency.

Finally, a replanning step seems like a natural candidate for application of *incremental planning techniques* [42–44] which take into account the existing state of the plan and look at best ways of continuing it to achieve the (possibly augmented) goal under (possibly augmented) preferences.

Multiple Users: Execution and Recovery. When multiple users collaborate to achieve a common goal, properties of interest involve the state of all of their workflows, since we want to check properties such as "exactly one crib should be bought". Since each user has a local view of the collaboration, it is not clear who should specify such properties.

Another issue is checking them since monitors must now "talk" to one another, i.e., include events from all workflows. Techniques for turning a centralized monitor into a set of distributed ones, running in different process servers, have been investigated by the DESERT project [45]. We believe that these results can be used to distribute monitoring in the collaboration scenario.

Scalability: Execution and Recovery. Currently, our framework permits the definition of properties that depend only on the order and occurrence of system events. By monitoring the actual *data* exchanged by conversation participants, we could check richer properties that depend on such data, e.g., ensuring that the merchant charged the user credit card exactly the cost of the crib purchase. Of course, checking such properties is computationally expensive [46]. Another problem is that since PWWM allows the creation of highly customized applications, we cannot use techniques like caching to reduce the monitoring overhead of multiple applications running on the same server. However, we can reduce these times by doing client-side monitoring, as proposed in [47, 48].

11 Related Work

In this section, we look at approaches related to the three techniques we used here to realize our personal web vision: goal modeling and operationalization, model merging and matching, and web service monitoring and recovery.

Goal Modeling and Operationalization. Goal modeling has been used extensively in the context of early requirements engineering for software design [8, 49] to express stakeholder goals at different levels of abstraction and to show the impact of different software design alternatives on these goals. This includes work on acquiring such variability [3], selecting alternatives based on user skills and preferences [50], using goal-models to reason about software configurations [3] as well as incorporating end-user preferences [51]. A variety of techniques for performing automated reasoning about such goal models have been proposed [52–54]. Some of these, e.g., [55–57], use planners – the reasoning framework we adopt in our work [11, 51]. Planner-based approaches have the benefit of distinguishing between preferences and mandatory goals. Researchers have also attempted to connect goals with services in a variety of ways, including using intentional-level services [58, 59], generating service oriented architectures from *i** models [60], or reasoning about service compositions or adaptations thereof using goals [61, 62]. The modeling of how web service orchestrations impact end-user goals is therefore a natural adaptation of this work. Our approach also extends this work in a novel direction by integrating it with model merge and web service monitoring and recovery.

Model Matching and Merging. A significant body of research has been developed on model merging over the years. In their survey [63], Darke and Shanks identify model merging as one of the core activities in viewpoints-based development [64]. Several papers study model merging in specific domains including database schema design [65, 66], use cases [67], goal models [14], class diagrams [68], state machines [4, 69–71], graph transformation systems [72], and web services [73]. Model merging has also attracted considerable attention in ontology research for handling ontologies originating from different communities. Kalfoglou and Schorlemmer provide a survey of existing approaches to mapping, aligning, and merging ontologies [74].

Our application of merge in the context of personal web borrows from our previous work on merging goal models and state machines. The main prerequisite for a successful application of merge is a precise statement of the overlaps between the models. To assist with this task, we provide in [27] a classification of the different types of model overlaps and the applicability of these overlap types to different modeling notations.

As we discussed in the example in Section 7.3, model merging often requires model matching, i.e., a model management operator for defining relationships between models, as a prerequisite step. Matching is addressed either explicitly or via various forms of thesauri and naming conventions. Applications of matching in software engineering go beyond model merging. In particular, matching may be employed to facilitate reuse of artifacts [75, 76] or to detect inconsistencies [77, 78]. In addition, matching techniques have been used to identify candidate services to replace a service in use when it becomes unavailable or unsuitable due to a change [79, 80].

Web Service Monitoring and Recovery. Monitoring techniques for web services can be roughly divided into *offline*, e.g., [81–83], that analyze system events *after* execution, and *online* [33, 84–87] that monitor the system as it runs. Offline techniques have access to the entire trace and thus can check more complex properties, but do not allow to perform recovery, since errors are detected after the execution has finished. We use online monitoring here.

The approach we use in designing PWWM adapts our previous work on recovery and planning [6, 10], allowing us to create recovery plans *dynamically*, after analyzing an application path that led to an error. Several works [88, 89] have suggested "self-healing" mechanisms for web-service applications that rely on predefined recovery strategies. We intend to investigate whether existing self-healing techniques can be extended to handle the level of dynamism associated with personalized workflows.

12 Summary

In this paper, we proposed a vision of personalizing user experience on the web by allowing users to create and execute their own workflows. The vision, which we call the Personal Web Workflow Methodology (PWWM), is based on using three sets of technologies developed as part of our prior research: goal modeling and operationalization, model matching and merging, and web service monitoring and recovery. PWWM enables (1) elicitation of user goals and preferences, (2) creation of high-level goal models, (3) use of crowd-sourcing to find and put together suitable refined goal models, (4) creation of plans that best accomplish these goals, (5) turning them into executable BPEL orchestrations, (6) using user-, vendor- and community-defined preferences, policies and constraints for runtime monitoring, and (7) user-controllable recovery and replanning in case the desired workflow fails. Our approach combines a high degree of automation with ultimate personalization – the user can be very involved with every step of the process, or customize her environment ahead of time so that the framework takes care of choosing the most suitable workflows, or rely heavily on crowd-sourced information. While our methodology centers around *customization*, it does not yet address the issue of *collaboration* – where multiple users perform steps towards achieving a common goal.

The proposed methodology creates a number of challenges, some of which are technological (and likely solvable in a very near future), whereas others likely requiring advanced techniques and new research.

References

1. Chechik, M., Simmonds, J., Ben-David, S., Nejati, S., Sabetzadeh, M., Salay, R.: Modeling and Analysis of Personal Web Applications: A Vision. In: Proc. of CASCON 2010 Personal Web Wkshp (2010)
2. Liaskos, S., Lapouchnian, A., Wang, Y., Yu, Y., Easterbrook, S.: Configuring Common Personal Software: a Requirements-Driven Approach. In: Proc. of RE 2005, pp. 9–18 (2005)
3. Liaskos, S., Lapouchnian, A., Yu, Y., Yu, E., Mylopoulos, J.: On Goal-based Variability Acquisition and Analysis. In: Proc. of RE 2006, pp. 76–85 (2006)
4. Nejati, S., Sabetzadeh, M., Chechik, M., Easterbrook, S., Zave, P.: Matching and Merging of Statechart Specifications. In: Proc. of ICSE 2007, pp. 54–64 (2007)
5. Sabetzadeh, M., Easterbrook, S.: Analysis of Inconsistency in Graph-Based Viewpoints: A Category-Theoretic Approach. In: Proc. of ASE 2003, pp. 12–21 (October 2003)
6. Simmonds, J., Ben-David, S., Chechik, M.: Guided Recovery for Web Service Applications. In: Proc. of FSE 2010, pp. 247–256 (2010)
7. Dardenne, A., van Lamsweerde, A., Fickas, S.: Goal-Directed Requirements Acquisition. Science of Computer Programming 20(1-2), 3–50 (1993)
8. Mylopoulos, J., Chung, L., Liao, S., Wang, H., Yu, E.: Exploring Alternatives During Requirements Analysis. IEEE Software 18(1), 92–96 (2001)
9. Yu, E.: Towards Modeling and Reasoning Support for Early-Phase Requirements Engineering. In: Proc. of RE 1997, pp. 226–235 (1997)
10. Liaskos, S., McIlraith, S., Sohrabi, S., Mylopoulos, J.: Representing and Reasoning about Preferences in Requirements Engineering. Requirements Eng. J. 16, 227–249 (2011)
11. Sohrabi, S., Baier, J., McIlraith, S.: HTN Planning with Preferences. In: Proc. of IJCAI 2009, pp. 1790–1797 (2009)
12. Brunet, G., Chechik, M., Easterbrook, S., Nejati, S., Niu, N., Sabetzadeh, M.: A Manifesto for Model Merging. In: Proc. of GaMMa 2006, co-located with ICSE 2006 (2006)
13. Batini, C., Lenzerini, M., Navathe, S.: A Comparative Analysis of Methodologies for Database Schema Integration. ACM Computing Surveys 18(4), 323–364 (1986)
14. Sabetzadeh, M., Easterbrook, S.: View Merging in the Presence of Incompleteness and Inconsistency. Requirements Eng. J. 11(3), 174–193 (2006)
15. OASIS: Web Services Business Process Execution Language Version 2.0, `http://docs.oasis-open.org/wsbpel/2.0/OS/wsbpel-v2.0-OS.html` (accessed August 2011)
16. Dwyer, M., Avrunin, G., Corbett, J.: Patterns in Property Specifications for Finite-State Verification. In: Proc. of ICSE 1999, pp. 411–420 (May 1999)
17. OASIS: Universal Description Discovery and Integration Version 2.04, `http://uddi.org/pubs/ProgrammersAPI_v2.htm` (accessed August 2011)
18. OASIS: Web Services Dynamic Discovery Version 1.1, `http://docs.oasis-open.org/ws-dd/discovery/1.1/wsdd-discovery-1.1-spec.html` (accessed August 2011)

19. W3C: Web Services Description Language (WSDL), `http://www.w3.org/TR/wsdl/` (accessed August 2011)
20. ESSI WSML working group: Web Services Modeling Language (WSML), `http://www.wsmo.org/wsml/` (accessed August 2011)
21. Srivastava, B., Koehler, J.: Web Service Composition - Current Solutions and Open Problems. In: Proc. of ICAPS 2003, pp. 28–35 (2003)
22. Rao, J., Su, X.: A Survey of Automated Web Service Composition Methods. In: Cardoso, J., Sheth, A.P. (eds.) SWSWPC 2004. LNCS, vol. 3387, pp. 43–54. Springer, Heidelberg (2005)
23. Hoffmann, J., Bertoli, P., Helmert, M., Pistore, M.: Message-Based Web Service Composition, Integrity Constraints, and Planning under Uncertainty: A New Connection. J. Artif. Intell. Res. (JAIR) 35, 49–117 (2009)
24. Sohrabi, S., McIlraith, S.A.: Preference-Based Web Service Composition: A Middle Ground between Execution and Search. In: Patel-Schneider, P.F., Pan, Y., Hitzler, P., Mika, P., Zhang, L., Pan, J.Z., Horrocks, I., Glimm, B. (eds.) ISWC 2010, Part I. LNCS, vol. 6496, pp. 713–729. Springer, Heidelberg (2010)
25. Fellbaum, C. (ed.): WordNet: An Electronic Lexical Database (Language, Speech, and Communication). The MIT Press (1998)
26. van Lamsweerde, A.: Requirements Engineering: From System Goals to UML Models to Software Specifications. Wiley (2009)
27. Chechik, M., Nejati, S., Sabetzadeh, M.: A Relationship-Based Approach to Model Integration. J. Innovations in Systems and Software Engineering 8(1), 3–18 (2012)
28. Wiegers, K.: First Things First: Prioritizing Requirements. J. Soft. Development 7(9) (1999)
29. Karlsson, J., Ryan, K.: A Cost-Value Approach for Prioritizing Requirements. IEEE Software 14(5), 67–74 (1997)
30. Avesani, P., Bazzanella, C., Perini, A., Susi, A.: Facing Scalability Issues in Requirements Prioritization with Machine Learning Techniques. In: Proc. of RE 2005 (2005)
31. Saaty, R.W.: Decision Making with the Analytic Hierarchy Process. Int. J. of Services Sciences 1(1), 83–98 (2008)
32. Bienvenu, M., Fritz, C., McIlraith, S.: Planning with Qualitative Temporal Preferences. In: Proc. of KR 2006 (June 2006)
33. Baresi, L., Guinea, S.: Towards Dynamic Monitoring of WS-BPEL Processes. In: Benatallah, B., Casati, F., Traverso, P. (eds.) ICSOC 2005. LNCS, vol. 3826, pp. 269–282. Springer, Heidelberg (2005)
34. Simmonds, J., Ben-David, S., Chechik, M.: Monitoring and Recovery of Web Service Applications. In: Chignell, M., Cordy, J., Ng, J., Yesha, Y. (eds.) The Smart Internet. LNCS, vol. 6400, pp. 250–288. Springer, Heidelberg (2010)
35. Strohmaier, M., Prettenhofer, P., Kroll, M.: Explicit User Goals from Search Query Logs. In: Proc. Web Intelligence/IAT Workshops 2008, pp. 602–605 (2008)
36. Kroll, M., Strohmaier, M.: Analyzing Human Intentions in Natural Language Text. In: Proc. of K-CAP 2009, pp. 197–198 (2009)
37. Sabetzadeh, M., Finkelstein, A., Goedicke, M.: "Viewpoints". In: Laplante, P. (ed.) Encyclopedia of Software Engineering, pp. 1318–1329. Taylor & Francis (2010)
38. Barr, M., Wells, C.: Category Theory for Computing Science, 3rd edn. Les Publications CRM Montréal, Montreal (1999)
39. Leica, M.: Scalability Concepts for i* Modeling and Analysis. Master's thesis, University of Toronto (2005)
40. Bylander, T.: Complexity Results for Planning. In: Proc. of IJCAI 1991, pp. 274–279 (1991)
41. Barrett, A., Weld, D.S.: Characterizing Subgoal Interactions for Planning. In: Proc. of IJCAI 1993, pp. 1388–1393 (1993)

42. Marzal, E., Onaindia, E., Sebastia, L.: An Incremental Temporal Partial-Order Planner. In: Proc. of AIPS 2002 Wksp. on Planning for Temporal Domains, pp. 26–32 (2002)

43. Williams, B.C., Nayak, P.P.: A Reactive Planner for a Model-Based Execution. In: Proc. of IJCAI 1997 (1997)

44. Giacomo, G., Lespárance, Y., Levesque, H., Sardina, S.: IndiGolog: A High-Level Programming Language for Embedded Reasoning Agents. In: Multi-Agent Programming, pp. 31–72. Springer (2009)

45. Inverardi, P., Mostarda, L., Tivoli, M., Autili, M.: Synthesis of Correct and Distributed Adaptors for Component-Based Systems: an Automatic Approach. In: Proc. of ASE 2005, pp. 405–409 (2005)

46. Hallé, S., Villemaire, R.: Runtime Monitoring of Message-Based Workflows with Data. In: Proc. of ECOC 2008, pp. 63–72 (2008)

47. Choudhary, S.R., Orso, A.: Automated Client-Side Monitoring for Web Applications. In: Proc. of WEBTEST 2009, pp. 303–306 (2009)

48. Hallé, S., Villemaire, R.: Browser-Based Enforcement of Interface Contracts in Web Applications with BeepBeep. In: Bouajjani, A., Maler, O. (eds.) CAV 2009. LNCS, vol. 5643, pp. 648–653. Springer, Heidelberg (2009)

49. Van Lamsweerde, A.: Goal-Oriented Requirements Engineering: A Guided Tour. In: Proc. of RE 2001 (2001)

50. Hui, B., Liaskos, S., Mylopoulos, J.: Requirements Analysis for Customizable Software: A Goals-Skills-Preferences Framework. In: RE 2003, pp. 117–126 (2003)

51. Liaskos, S., McIlraith, S., Mylopoulos, J.: Integrating Preferences into Goal Models for Requirements Engineering. In: Proc. of RE 2010, pp. 135–144 (2010)

52. Horkoff, J., Yu, E.: Analyzing Goal Models – Different Approaches and How to Choose Among Them. In: Proc. of SAC 2011 (2011)

53. Sebastiani, R., Giorgini, P., Mylopoulos, J.: Simple and Minimum-cost Satisfiability for Goal Models. In: Persson, A., Stirna, J. (eds.) CAiSE 2004. LNCS, vol. 3084, pp. 20–35. Springer, Heidelberg (2004)

54. Fuxman, A., Liu, L., Mylopoulos, J., Pistore, M., Roveri, M., Traverso, P.: Specifying and Analyzing Early Requirements in Tropos. J. Requirements Eng. 9(2), 132–150 (2004)

55. Gans, G., Lakemeyer, G., Jarke, M., Vits, T.: SNet: A Modeling and Simulation Environment for Agent Networks Based on i* and ConGolog. In: Pidduck, A.B., Mylopoulos, J., Woo, C.C., Ozsu, M.T. (eds.) CAiSE 2002. LNCS, vol. 2348, pp. 328–343. Springer, Heidelberg (2002)

56. Wang, X., Lesperance, Y.: Agent-Oriented Requirements Engineering using ConGolog and i*. In: Proc. of AOIS 2001 (2001)

57. Bryl, V., Massacci, F., Mylopoulos, J., Zannone, N.: Designing Security Requirements Models through Planning. In: Martinez, F.H., Pohl, K. (eds.) CAiSE 2006. LNCS, vol. 4001, pp. 33–47. Springer, Heidelberg (2006)

58. Kaabi, R.S., Souveyet, C., Rolland, C.: Eliciting Service Composition in a Goal Driven Manner. In: Proc. of ICSOC 2004, pp. 308–315 (2004)

59. Rolland, C., Kaabi, R.S., Kraiem, N.: On ISOA: Intentional Services Oriented Architecture. In: Krogstie, J., Opdahl, A.L., Sindre, G. (eds.) CAiSE 2007. LNCS, vol. 4495, pp. 158–172. Springer, Heidelberg (2007)

60. Castro, C.B., Franch, X., Astudillo, H.: From i* Models to Service Oriented Architecture Models. In: Proc. of ACT4SOC 2010, pp. 52–63 (2010)

61. Chopra, A.K., Dalpiaz, F., Giorgini, P., Mylopoulos, J.: Modeling and Reasoning about Service-Oriented Applications via Goals and Commitments. In: Pernici, B. (ed.) CAiSE 2010. LNCS, vol. 6051, pp. 113–128. Springer, Heidelberg (2010)

62. Baresi, L., Pasquale, L.: Live Goals for Adaptive Service Compositions. In: Proc. of SEAMS 2010, pp. 114–123 (2010)

63. Darke, P., Shanks, G.: Stakeholder Viewpoints in Requirements Definition: a Framework for Understanding Viewpoint Development Approaches. Requirements Eng. J. 1(2), 88–105 (1996)

64. Finkelstein, A., Kramer, J., Nuseibeh, B., Goedicke, M.: Viewpoints: A Framework for Integrating Multiple Perspectives in System Development. J. Soft. Eng. and Knowl. Eng. 2(1), 31–58 (1992)

65. Pottinger, R., Bernstein, P.: Merging Models Based on Given Correspondences. In: Proc. of VLDB 2003, pp. 862–873 (2003)

66. Melnik, S., Rahm, E., Bernstein, P.: Rondo: a Programming Platform for Generic Model Management. In: Proc. of SIGMOD 2003, pp. 193–204 (2003)

67. Richards, D.: Merging Individual Conceptual Models of Requirements. Requirements Eng. J. 8(4), 195–205 (2003)

68. Alanen, M., Porres, I.: Difference and Union of Models. In: Stevens, P., Whittle, J., Booch, G. (eds.) UML 2003. LNCS, vol. 2863, pp. 2–17. Springer, Heidelberg (2003)

69. Uchitel, S., Chechik, M.: Merging Partial Behavioural Models. In: Proc. of FSE 2004, pp. 43–52 (2004)

70. Nejati, S., Chechik, M.: Let's Agree to Disagree. In: Proc. of ASE 2005, pp. 287–290 (2005)

71. Fischbein, D., D'Ippolito, N., Brunet, G., Chechik, M., Uchitel, S.: Weak Alphabet Merging of Partial Behaviour Models. ACM Transactions on Software Engineering and Methodology 21(2) (March 2012)

72. Engels, G., Heckel, R., Taenzter, G., Ehrig, H.: A Combined Reference Model- and View-Based Approach to System Specification. J. Soft. Eng. and Knowl. Eng. 7(4), 457–477 (1997)

73. Liu, N., Grundy, J.C., Hosking, J.G.: A Visual Language and Environment for Composing Web Services. In: Proc. of ASE 2000, pp. 321–324 (2005)

74. Kalfoglou, Y., Schorlemmer, M.: Ontology Mapping: The State of the Art. In: Semantic Interoperability and Integration. Number 04391 in Dagstuhl Seminars (2005)

75. Maiden, N., Sutcliffe, A.: Exploiting Reusable Specifications Through Analogy. Communications of the ACM 35(4), 55–64 (1992)

76. Ryan, K., Mathews, B.: Matching Conceptual Graphs as an Aid to Requirements Re-use. In: Proc. of RE 1993, pp. 112–120 (1993)

77. Spanoudakis, G., Finkelstein, A.: Reconciling Requirements: A Method for Managing Interference, Inconsistency and Conflict. Annals of Software Engineering 3, 433–457 (1997)

78. Egyed, A., Medvidovíc, N.: A Formal Approach to Heterogeneous Software Modeling. In: Maibaum, T. (ed.) FASE 2000. LNCS, vol. 1783, pp. 178–192. Springer, Heidelberg (2000)

79. Lohmann, N.: Correcting Deadlocking Service Choreographies Using a Simulation-Based Graph Edit Distance. In: Dumas, M., Reichert, M., Shan, M.-C. (eds.) BPM 2008. LNCS, vol. 5240, pp. 132–147. Springer, Heidelberg (2008)

80. Zisman, A., Spanoudakis, G., Dooley, J.: A Framework for Dynamic Service Discovery. In: Proc. of ASE 2008, pp. 158–167 (2008)

81. Mahbub, K., Spanoudakis, G.: A Framework for Requirements Monitoring of Service Based Systems. In: Proc. of ICSOC 2004, pp. 84–93 (2004)

82. Mahbub, K., Spanoudakis, G.: Run-time Monitoring of Requirements for Systems Composed of Web-Services: Initial Implementation and Evaluation Experience. In: Proc. of ICWS 2005, pp. 257–265 (July 2005)

83. van der Aalst, W.M.P., Pesic, M.: Specifying and Monitoring Service Flows: Making Web Services Process-Aware. In: Baresi, L., Nitto, E.D. (eds.) Test and Analysis of Web Services, pp. 11–55. Springer (2007)

84. Lazovik, A., Aiello, M., Papazoglou, M.P.: Associating Assertions with Business Processes and Monitoring Their Execution. In: Proc. of ICSOC 2004, pp. 94–104 (2004)

85. Baresi, L., Ghezzi, C., Guinea, S.: Smart Monitors for Composed Services. In: Proc. of IC-SOC 2004, pp. 193–202 (November 2004)

86. Pistore, M., Traverso, P.: Assumption-Based Composition and Monitoring of Web Services. In: Baresi, L., Nitto, E.D. (eds.) Test and Analysis of Web Services, pp. 307–335. Springer (2007)

87. Simmonds, J., Gan, Y., Chechik, M., Nejati, S., O'Farrell, B., Litani, E., Waterhouse, J.: Runtime Monitoring of Web Service Conversations. IEEE Tran. on Service Computing 2(3), 223–244 (2009)

88. Baresi, L., Guinea, S., Pasquale, L.: Self-Healing BPEL Processes with Dynamo and the JBoss Rule Engine. In: Proc. of ESSPE 2007, pp. 11–20 (2007)

89. Fugini, M.G., Mussi, E.: Recovery of Faulty Web Applications through Service Discovery. In: Proc. of SMR-VLDB 2006, pp. 67–80 (2006)

Service Subscription and Consumption for Personal Web Applications

Chunyang Ye, Young Yoon, and Hans-Arno Jacobsen

Middleware Systems Research Group
University of Toronto

Abstract. Web services have played a vital role in our daily life for some time now. A wide spectrum of online applications have been developed in diverse domains such as banking, shopping, gaming, and video streaming. However, the end-user does often not have the means to tune the applications to her personal needs and interests, especially not across services from different providers. Moreover, the end-user can not take full advantage of the myriad of useful resources and services available on the Web, as interoperation among different services is often not given. Hence, the new Web application paradigm called *Personal Web* has emerged. The key idea behind the Personal Web is to have Web services exploit Web data that is collected and organized automatically according to the end-users' context and preferences. This paper introduces a new concept that enables Personal Web applications, namely, *service subscription and consumption*. This new concept is driven by events exposed from Semantic Web resources and Web services through PADRES, a distributed content-based publish/subscribe messaging substrate, and POLARIS an approach for event exposure at service interfaces. We explain service subscription and consumption based on a comprehensive scenario and design a framework and architecture that realizes the approach.

1 Introduction

In 1976, Niklaus Wirth presented the insight that in computer programming, algorithms and data structures are inherently related [1]. Since then programming has evolved, embracing distribution and the Web. Complex applications are formed with Web services [2] following the service-oriented architecture (SOA) paradigm. Also, data structures are represented as linked data catering towards the vision of a Semantic Web [3].

In this chapter, we build on Wirth's philosophy, proposing a new interpretation of Web applications as combinations of SOA principles and Semantic Web ideas. This novel perspective motivates us to devise a holistic framework for automatically composing personal Web applications based on individual end-users' interests and needs.

The basic idea behind our framework is as follows: We make Web services aware of personal data published as linked data to the Semantic Web. Here, personal data such as comments on a movie and product wish lists are produced through personal Web applications that are shared with others across social networking platforms such as Facebook. Today, it is not uncommon to subscribe to the updates of personal linked data and to get notified about others' activities of interest. We take this user experience to the next level. That is personal Web application users can also *subscribe* to Web services

M. Chignell et al. (Eds.): The Personal Web, LNCS 7855, pp. 49–64, 2013.

that are triggered upon the update of others' personal linked data. For example, a user may first subscribe to movie recommendations made by her Facebook friends. Then, this user subscribes to an online box office service that is automatically triggered to reserve movie tickets based the user's calendar data and her friends' recommendations about current movies.

To make this vision of a *Personal Web* a reality, there are several technical challenges to overcome. First, SOA and Semantic Web adopt different standards and protocols to share and exchange data. Thus, interoperability between both technologies poses a problem. Second, data and services usually belong to different organizations that are beyond the end-users' control. Hence, coordinating data and services across organizational boundaries is a further challenge. In the rest of this paper, we lay out how we address these challenges with a novel approach we refer to as *service subscription and consumption*.

2   Service Subscription and Consumption Overview

In this section, we present an overview of our methodology, namely *service subscription and consumption*, that overcomes the obstacles in jointly harnessing SOA and Semantic Web concepts.

In order to enable the interoperability between SOA and Semantic Web, we have to first enable Web services to access linked data from Semantic Web resources. The difficulties in achieving this are as follows: (1) The data from the Semantic Web resources and Web services may not belong to the same organization; (2) the data may have different formats and semantics. Therefore, existing Web services cannot access and manipulate the linked data directly.

Our solution is to bridge the gap between the Semantic Web and Web services based on *"events"*. An event is defined as a state change [4]. We view the linked data in Semantic Web as states. Any modification to the linked data is regarded as a state change. For example, the update of a user's online calendar is an event indicating that the state of the calendar has changed. Such an event can be propagated to Web services that are interested and authorized to receive such updates, even if they are administratively separated from one another. Upon the notification via events, Web services can determine individual end-users' personal contexts. For instance, a box office service could become aware of the changes in availability of end-users.

In order to enable this event-driven solution, exposing contents of events is imperative. We do this through a novel concept called *event interfaces* [5,6]. An event interface declares what events should be exposed at runtime and what events Web services want to subscribe to. For example, Figure 1 shows an event interface for an end-user's calendar. This interface declares the events that are raised upon the update of particular linked data elements. Similarly, a Web service can also declare in its own event interface what kinds of events it is interested in. For instance, a booking service subscribes to events from the user's calendar and box office through the respective event interfaces.

The interaction between the Semantic Web and Web services through event interfaces requires a communication mechanism. Here, we use the publish/subscribe (in short pub/sub) communication paradigm [7]. In pub/sub, loosely-coupled clients communicate in an asynchronous fashion. Figure 1 gives an example of how pub/sub is

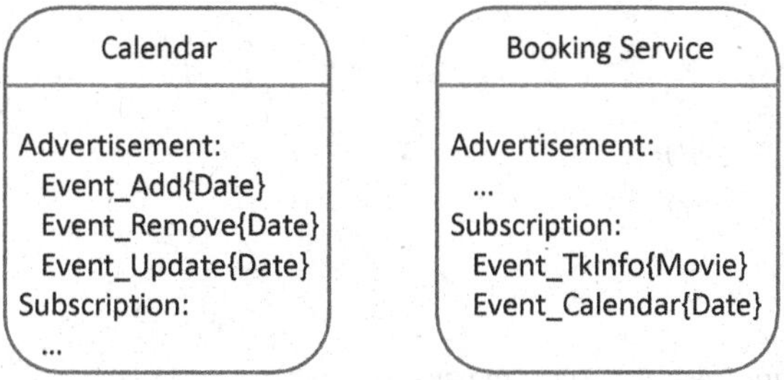

Fig. 1. An example event interface

applied in this example. The online calendar *advertises* what it intends to *publish* in the future. The booking service *subscribes* to the events the online calendar may publish. Whenever the calendar is updated, an event is exposed and propagated to the booking service. Upon the receipt of events, the booking service keeps a copy of the updated linked data. Later, the booking service can also update the copy of the linked data. Upon this update, the booking Web service can generate events and expose them in its own event interface. For example, the booking service reserves a time slot for watching a movie, based on the event received from the online calendar of a given user. Subsequently, the online calendar can be updated to block the time slot reserved for the movie, if the online calendar also subscribed to the events published by the booking service.

The pub/sub and event interface approaches solve the interoperability problem between Web services and Semantic Web. However, we are still left with the issue that linked data may not be under the control of Personal Web users. To address this issue, we devise an interface for Personal Web users to subscribe to Web services. This is to invoke a subscribed service automatically whenever it acquires the required linked data. For example, an end-user may issue its subscription to a box office service. The box office service is invoked automatically to reserve tickets for the user when a movie recommended by the user's friends is currently playing. More specifically, a Personal Web user subscribes to a Web service based on Event-Condition-Action (ECA) rules. In the ECA rules, the *Event* component describes what the subscribed service should listen to. The *Condition* component describes the conditions for invoking the subscribed services. The *Action* component describes what the services do when triggered. For example, the following ECA rule is defined for the example in Figure 1:

Event = Recommended movie is currently in theatre.
Condition = There is an available time slot in the end-user's calendar.
Action = Box office service automatically reserves the ticket for the end-user.

The event interface can be implemented through the POLARIS framework [8]. For exchanging the events through event interfaces, we employ the brokered PADRES content-based pub/sub system [7]. The details of the implementation using the the above described building blocks are presented in Section 4.

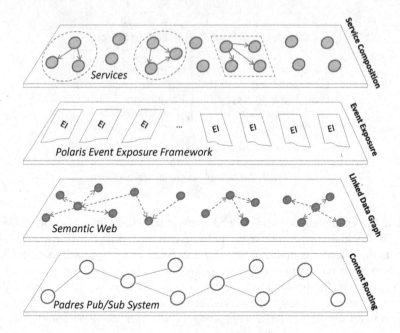

Fig. 2. Methodology overview

3 A Sample Use Case

This section illustrates our solution based on an online Personal Web movie recommendation and booking scenario.

John is a movie fan who closely follows the review of his friends Ebert and Roeper in some social networking application. As shown in Figure. 3, John would like to use an application that can automatically reserve a ticket whenever both Ebert and Roeper recommend a newly released movie as long as John's personal schedule permits. We describe how our service subscription and consumption concept applies to satisfy John's need.

First, John has to subscribe to recommendations by Ebert and Roeper. Since the recommendations are conveyed via a social networking application, the data is usually represented as linked data inside the application. In order to subscribe to updates of recommendations, events are defined to represent the change of recommendations (*e.g.*, recommendations added or updated). As shown in Figure 4, federated content-based publish/subscribe brokers route the recommendation events of Ebert and Roeper towards John.

Recommendation events are abstracted and represented as linked resources in a standardized RDF format and are added to Semantic Web repositories. A Semantic Web repository implements the event exposure interface [5] that can convert an update to the repository (*e.g.*, a recommendation by Ebert or Roeper) to a publication message which is forwarded to interested subscribers. The consumption of the event

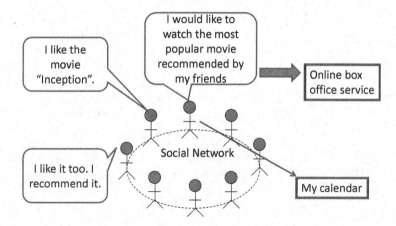

Fig. 3. Automatic ticket booking system in the Personal Web

(contained in a publication message) is represented as linked data and added into a Semantic Web repository, as shown in Figure 5.

We now introduce the novel concept of subscribing and consuming a service. So far, what John can only do upon receipt of the recommendation event is to reserve tickets manually, *i.e.*, examine his personal calendar and search for a ticketing service. Instead, with service consumption and subscription, a composition of services executes desired tasks upon receipt of events on behalf of John. As shown in Figure. 6, triggering and executing of a task is based on Event-Condition-Action (ECA) rules which are declared by end-users.

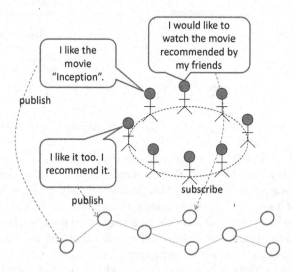

Fig. 4. Event-based subscriptions to linked data updates

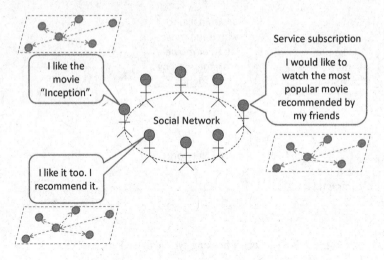

Fig. 5. Semantic Web repository update as an event

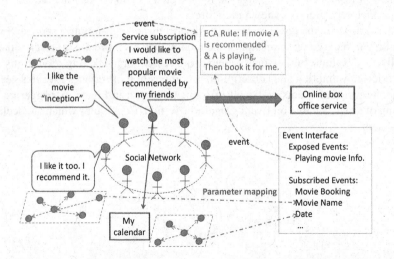

Fig. 6. Event routing through federated content-based publish/subscribe brokers

The *condition* of the ECA rule represents the current state. For example, a service may check the condition of whether the recommended movie John wants to watch is available in the nearest theater or not. This condition is advertised as an event in the event interface of a service, e.g., the booking service. The *event* (e.g., recommendation by Ebert and Roeper) triggers an action (e.g., a reservation process). It is highly likely that an action can be triggered by multiple events that are in conjunction or disjunction. This is handled through *composite subscriptions*. Also, as shown in Figure 7, an action is actually a process which can be composed with other services in a distributed fashion given additional end-user specific constraints, for example, John's preferred payment option and delivery date preference.

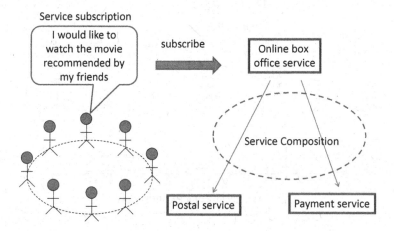

Fig. 7. A service composition for the execution of a process to satisfy the end-user constraints

The critical components to support service subscription and consumption are a content-based publish/subscribe messaging system, event-exposure interfaces, composite subscriptions, and a process planning framework, which we discuss in the following section.

4   Prototype Implementation

In this section, we present the key components that enable our service subscription and consumption concept, presented in the previous section.

4.1   The PADRES Event Dissemination Substrate

In the previous section, we described how the Semantic Web and Web services can interact by publishing and subscribing to events. Since Semantic Web and Web service data sources are distributed, we need a event dissemination substrate that can route events in a distributed and scalable manner. PADRES [7] developed by the Middleware Systems Research Group at the University of Toronto satisfies these requirements. PADRES is a content-based publish/subscribe system that routes publications to interested subscribers through an overlay network of brokers.

The architecture of the PADRES broker is presented in Figure 8. The broker is mainly responsible for matching events (i.e., publications) against subscriptions and relaying the publications to the next destination according to the outcome of the matching process. The broker is equipped with an efficient matching engine for filtering historic and future events based on subscriptions and correlating events from multiple data sources [9,10,11].

A publisher issues an *advertisement* before it can publish. Advertisements are disseminated to all brokers in the overlay network. Subscriptions are routed based on

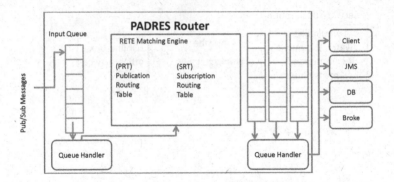

Fig. 8. Architecture of a PADRES broker

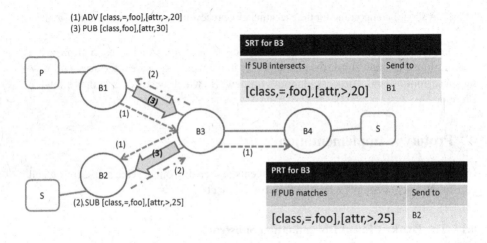

Fig. 9. PADRES Broker Network

the Subscription Routing Table (SRT). The SRT is essentially a list of [advertisement,last hop] tuples. If a subscription matches an advertisement in the SRT, it is forwarded to the last hop broker the advertisement came from. In this way subscriptions are routed towards the publisher along the reverse-path of the advertisement the publisher issued. Subscriptions are used to construct the Publication Routing Table (PRT). Like the SRT, the PRT is a list of [subscription,last hop] tuples, which is used to route publications. If a publication matches a subscription in the PRT, it is forwarded to the last hop broker the subscription came from. This process continues until the publication reaches the subscriber. Figure 9 illustrate an example of content-based routing. In Step *1)*, in the figure, an advertisement is published at B_1. In Step *2)* a matching subscription enters from B_2. Since the subscription matches the advertisement at broker B_3, it is sent to B_1. In Step *3)* a publication is routed along the path established by the subscription to B_2.

4.2   The POLARIS Event Exposure Framework

POLARIS is an event exposure framework for Semantic Web and Web services. It is built on top of PADRES, which we described in the previous section. The architecture of the POLARIS framework is shown in Figure 10. The framework consists of the following three components: Event listeners, pub/sub adapters and a rule engine.

Event Listener. The event listener module is designed to monitor state changes over the Web. Different data sources may have different event listeners. For example, one can design an event listener to monitor the data change inside an online calendar application. Similarly, we can define another event listener to monitor the update of linked data about movie information. Note that the update of data generates many raw events, some of which may not need to be exposed. Also, some events may need to be transformed before being exposed. For example, an event indicating the update of a Lunar calendar needs to be transformed into the data format of a Gregorian calendar. Therefore, mapping rules can be specified to filter and transform events. In other words, events that do not conform to the mapping rules are not exposed.

Pub/Sub Adapter. The pub/sub adapter serves to publish and subscribe to events over the Web. If an event listener wants to expose an event, the pub/sub adapter is invoked to publish the event to the underlying pub/sub system. The event is then propagated to interested subscribers. The pub/sub adapter can be used to subscribe to particular

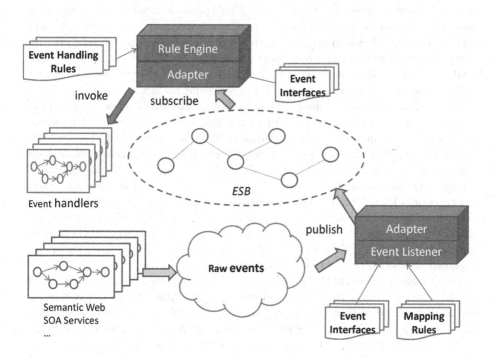

Fig. 10. POLARIS architecture

events. Upon the notification about an event, the pub/sub adapter invokes the rule engine to handle the event. PADRES provides APIs to implement pub/sub adapters.

Rule Engine. The rule engine is responsible for managing and maintaining ECA rules. On being notified about an event, the rule engine checks and evaluates the registered ECA rules. If the conditions for an ECA rule is satisfied, then the action in the rule (e.g., the invocation of a subscribed service) is executed. To describe the service subscription, a description language about the subscribed service is needed. The description language can include functional and non-functional descriptions of the subscribed services. Many existing languages have been devoted to describing and searching services [12,13,14]. In our framework, we focus on functional descriptions of a service based on its behavior. Other aspects of the service subscription language can be extended based on the application requirements.

4.3   Service Composition

The final component for implementing the service subscription and consumption concept is the service composition framework. Revisiting the movie ticket booking example from Section 3, the booking service may involve Web services for ticketing, delivery and payment as shown in Figure 11. Note that the customized booking service for a particular person may not be readily available since the user-specific constraints can be transient and even implicit. For example, John's personal schedule can change over time and John may not be able to watch the recommended movie on certain dates and times. The technical challenge is to infer the implicit constraints and successfully find compatible services that can satisfy those constraints. Also, since there can be thousands of users like John on the Web with various constraints, our framework must be able to compose customized services in a highly scalable manner.

In order to address the technical challenges above, a distributed service composition technique can be used [15]. Suppose John's constraints are as follows: (1) John wants a ticketing service that guarantees to provide online ticketing for AMC Theaters; (2) John wants overnight delivery; (3) John wants to pay with his Visa credit card and (4) John wants to watch the movie at a date and time Mary plans to watch it as well. Interestingly, the last constraint does not explicitly specify the exact date, since John does not necessarily know whether Mary has booked the movie or not. Given these personal constraints, Figure 11 describes how the distributed service composition realizes a personalized workflow just for John. Figure 11 shows a directed acyclic graphic (DAG) that represents the transition between different services to fulfill John's request. We briefly explain how this DAG is constructed in a distributed way.

John's request consists of an input and output. The input constitutes the user-specified constraints such as ticketing options and the output constitutes the results of the service request execution such as delivery status. In our framework, all participating services subscribe to these service requests published by personal agents. For example, the MovieTicket.com Web service subscribes to constraints pertaining to payment, ticketing, delivery options, date preferences, and delivery status specified by a personal agent. The MovieTicket.com service does not completely fulfill John's request, because this service does not yield the delivery status [15]. Also the UPS delivery

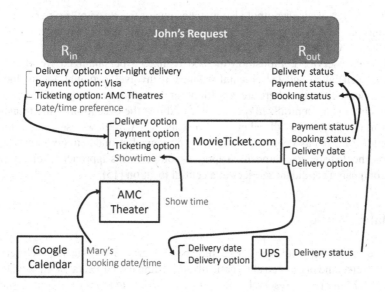

Fig. 11. Distributed service composition

service does not fulfill John's request either, as it does not accept a ticketing option as an input. Hence, the participating services have to concurrently and incrementally search for services that can satisfy John's request on behalf of John's personal agent. For example, the `MovieTicket.com` service has to find a service that can accept a delivery date as input. The `MovieTicket.com` service internally publishes another service request with the delivery date as an input which the UPS delivery service subscribes to. When the delivery service receives this internal publication, it adds the `MovieTicket.com` service as a service that executes a preceding task, so that it knows it can later output a delivery status upon processing the delivery date event issued by the `MovieTicket.com` service. Every service follows this procedure concurrently until services that satisfy John's request are found. Recall that ECA rules govern the processing of events at the POLARIS event-exposure interface as explained in the previous section. For example, an ECA rule can be specified to express that the update of Mary's calendar regarding the movie booking triggers a Google Calendar service to notify the update to the AMC Theater service, which in turn yields the remaining seat availability information for the particular show time Mary booked.

Note that John's preference on date and time is implicitly given as alluded to earlier (John wants to watch the movie at the same date his friend Mary plans to.) Thus, the `MovieTicket.com` service has to infer the exact show time, which is the required input. Our framework extracts John's preferences involving Mary's booking information which is available through the Google Calendar service shared with John.

With the concurrent and distributed service matching process we briefly described above, a transition is added between the Google Calendar service and the `MovieTicket.com` service in the DAG. Also, available seats can be obtained when the Google Calendar service's output (e.g., the show time booked by Mary) is connected to the AMC Theater service that yields the remaining seats for the particular show time.

The AMC Theater service's output also matches one of the `MovieTicket.com` service's inputs, *i.e.,* the availability of a particular show time. Hence, a transition is added between the AMC Theatre service and the `MovieTicket.com` service.

In short, this service composition method realizes a personalized workflow in a concurrent, distributed and incremental manner. It involves personal agents and distributed services, given that there are constraints and an objective declared by end-users. Moreover, there is no centralized orchestrator to direct the execution of the transitions specified in the DAG. This distributed processing of a workflow resembles prior approaches [16,17]. It has been experimentally proven, that under many experimental conditions, the distributed composition approach outperforms approaches for determining and composing candidate services at a central location [15].

5   Related Work

The key idea of the Personal Web is to exploit and integrate Web data and Web services that are collected and organized automatically according to end-users' context and preferences [18]. Many recent research efforts have been devoted to related issues, such as information integration frameworks [19], data sharing [20], privacy concerns [21], and information filtering [22], to just name a few. In our work, we introduce a new paradigm to develop Personal Web applications by integrating linked data concepts with Web services. The newly proposed concept, service subscription and consumption, not only complements the spectrum of Personal Web applications, but also enables end-users to customize the Web applications in an easy to manage manner.

In our solution, one of the key components of POLARIS are the ECA rules that are dynamically specified by end-users. A system that can infer an appropriate action upon receipt of events has already been seen in production systems such as OPS5 [23]. Recently, more flexible declarative approaches for specifying constraints in business processes have been proposed [24,25]. Also, it has been shown that a Dynamic Call Graph (DCR) [26], which formalizes ECA-like rules as Event Structures [27], can be distributed to multiple participants for efficient collaboration. These prior works have been the basis for POLARIS that allows users to specify constraints dynamically and to impose constraints to services participating in the collaboration.

Recently, a number of works about exploiting data for SOA technologies have also been introduced. For example, a *Business Artifact* [28] is a declarative process definition framework that is based on the notion of guard-stage-milestones which are similar to ECA rules. Events are triggered to achieve a milestone. The events can be shared across different tasks, thus the life cycle of a given process can be governed transparently and consistently. However, a Business Artifact cannot be adopted for Personal Web applications for a couple of reasons. The process defined with a Business Artifact is not flexible enough to incorporate end-users' dynamic constraints. Most importantly, event notification is done in a centralized fashion, limiting scalability to a large user base, a critical requirement for Personal Web applications, since they have the potential to involve many services and users from all around the world.

Another similar concept, "Event-driven SOA", also known as SOA 2.0, has been proposed from the perspective of event-based business process execution and collaboration [29]. The purpose is to define and trigger business applications based on event-driven rules instead of describing the business logic in a procedural manner. The advantage is that business applications can be executed dynamically and can react quickly to changing requirements. In our work, an event is not only a medium to trigger subscribed services asynchronously, but also a way to bridge the gap between the linked data of the Semantic Web and Web services.

Event-driven business process management has been widely adopted in enterprise applications due to the needs for increased flexibility and adaptability of business processes [30,15,16,4,31,32,33,34,35,17]. This requires effectively integrating business logic with the generation, exposure, propagation, detection and handling of events in business applications. Frei *et al.* [36] proposed to use aspect-oriented program (AOP for short) techniques to extract and expose events from legacy enterprise applications. Developers can make use of these events for refactoring legacy applications. In addition, industry standards like BPEL [12], also support two kinds of events, namely a timeout alarm and the receiving of a message, which are local to a BPEL process and are not propagated to other partners. The notification mechanism in BPEL is similar to event notification, but it is based on messages. BPEL processes interact through messages only. In our work, we do not make any assumption about how events are generated. Instead, different web services and Semantic Web linked data can define their own event listeners using the aforementioned solutions and deploy them into our POLARIS framework.

6   Conclusions

In this paper, we introduced a new paradigm to develop Internet applications for Personal Web leveraging Web services and Semantic Web concepts. We integrated PADRES and POLARIS, our content-based publish/subscribe middleware and event exposure framework, to provide a comprehensive solution for service subscription and consumption in the context of the Personal Web. Moreover, we employed composite subscriptions and distributed service composition techniques to support complex and dynamic user-specific rules and constraints. These techniques extend the spectrum of Personal Web applications, allowing end-users to subscribe to Web services and consume services asynchronously and automatically without the need of any designated centralized coordinator.

The current prototype implementation provides some basic functionality to prove the concept of service subscription and consumption for Personal Web applications. The following features complement the work described in this chapter.

- **Selective Service Discovery and Matching.** The given service subscription and consumption framework can be developed further by extending the matching algorithm of PADRES to filter various preferences over services. For example, a user may want to subscribe to services used and recommended by friends. These preferences can impose additional overhead to the service composition we discussed in Section 4.3. This motivates the development of heuristics for determining the best match satisfying a user's needs and interests.

- **Service Wrapper.** In order to make use of linked data, services need to provide an event interface to specify how the data internal to the service and the linked data outside the service is exchanged. This task however is tedious and error-prone. This motivates the development of a tool for services to generate wrappers automatically to map between the data exposed by Web services in event interfaces and the linked data from the Semantic Web.
- **Linked Data Advertisement and Subscription.** In Semantic Web, data from different locations is linked. The linking relationship between data forms linked data graphs. In some applications, if one piece of data is changed, some other data, that is linked to the changed data, may also have to be changed. For example, if a user updates the linked data about his/her favorite movies, the user's friend may want to know the details of the movie that may be available in another location. Therefore, it is interesting to explore the linked data graph to generate the related advertisements and subscriptions automatically. In this way, users can get notification of related data transparently.

Acknowledgments. This research was in part supported by IBM's Center for Advanced Studies, an IBM Faculty Award, a Discovery Accelerator Supplement and a Discovery grant from the Natural Sciences and Engineering Research Council of Canada, an Ontario Early Researcher Award, and a grant from the Mathematics of Information Technology and Complex Systems research network.

References

1. Wirth, N.: Algorithms + Data Structures = Programs. Prentice Hall PTR, Upper Saddle River (1978)
2. Papazoglou, M.P., Traverso, P., Ricerca, I., Tecnologica, S.: Service-oriented computing: State of the art and research challenges. IEEE Computer 40 (2007)
3. W3C: Semantic web, http://www.w3.org/RDF/FAQ
4. Luckham, D.C.: The Power of Events: An Introduction to Complex Event Processing in Distributed Enterprise Systems. Addison-Wesley (2001)
5. Ye, C., Jacobsen, H.A.: The smart internet, pp. 197–215. Springer, Heidelberg (2010)
6. Ye, C., Jacobsen, H.A.: Whitening soa testing via event exposure. IEEE Trans. Softw. Eng., 1–25 (April 2013) (preprint)
7. PADRESweb site, http://padres.msrg.org
8. Ye, C., Jacobsen, A.: Polaris: a framework to compose and evolve smart web services via event exposure. In: IBM CASCON Exhibits (2010)
9. Li, G., Jacobsen, H.A.: Composite subscriptions in content-based publish/subscribe systems. In: ACM/IFIP/USENIX International Middleware Conference, pp. 249–269 (2005)
10. Li, G., Muthusamy, V., Jacobsen, H.A.: Adpative content-based routing in general overlay topologies. In: ACM/IFIP/USENIX International Middleware Conference, pp. 1–21 (2008)
11. Li, G., Muthusamy, V., Jacobsen, H.A.: Subscribing to the past in content-based publish/subscribe. Technical Report CSRG-585, Middleware Systems Research Group, University of Toronto (January 2008)
12. OASIS: BPEL 2.0, http://docs.oasis-open.org/wsbpel/2.0/wsbpel-v2.0.html

13. W3C: Web Service Description Language, `http://www.w3.org/TR/wsdl`
14. W3C: Web Services Choreography Description Language,
    `http://www.w3.org/TR/2004/WD-ws-cdl-10-20041217/`
15. Hu, S., Muthusamy, V., Li, G., Jacobsen, H.A.: Distributed automatic service composition in large-scale systems. In: DEBS, pp. 233–244 (2008)
16. Li, G., Muthusamy, V., Jacobsen, H.A.: A distributed service-oriented architecture for business process execution. ACM Trans. Web 4(1), 1–33 (2010)
17. Yoon, Y., Ye, C., Jacobsen, H.A.: A distributed framework for reliable and efficient service choreographies. In: Proceedings of the 20th International Conference on World Wide Web, WWW 2011, pp. 785–794. ACM, New York (2011)
18. Abrams, D., Baecker, R., Chignell, M.: Information archiving with bookmarks: personal web space construction and organization. In: Proceedings of the SIGCHI Conference on Human Factors in Computing Systems, CHI 1998, pp. 41–48. ACM Press/Addison-Wesley Publishing Co., New York (1998)
19. Ng, J.: The personal web: smart internet for me. In: Proceedings of the 2010 Conference of the Center for Advanced Studies on Collaborative Research, CASCON 2010, pp. 330–344. IBM Corp., Riverton (2010)
20. Geambasu, R., Cheung, C., Moshchuk, A., Gribble, S.D., Levy, H.M.: Organizing and sharing distributed personal web-service data. In: Proceedings of the 17th International Conference on World Wide Web, WWW 2008, pp. 755–764. ACM, New York (2008)
21. Mannan, M., van Oorschot, P.C.: Privacy-enhanced sharing of personal content on the web. In: Proceedings of the 17th International Conference on World Wide Web, WWW 2008, pp. 487–496. ACM, New York (2008)
22. Somlo, G.L., Howe, A.E.: Filtering for personal web information agents. In: Proceedings of the 27th Annual International ACM SIGIR Conference on Research and Development in Information Retrieval, SIGIR 2004, pp. 588–589. ACM, New York (2004)
23. PCAI: OPS5, `http://www.pcai.com/web/aiinfo/pcaiops.html`
24. Pesic, M., van der Aalst, W.: A Declarative Approach for Flexible Business Processes Management, pp. 169–180 (2006)
25. Pesic, M., Schonenberg, M.H., Sidorova, N., Van Der Aalst, W.M.P.: Constraint-based workflow models: change made easy. In: Meersman, R., Tari, Z. (eds.) OTM 2007, Part I. LNCS, vol. 4803, pp. 77–94. Springer, Heidelberg (2007)
26. Hildebrandt, T., Mukkamala, R.R., Slaats, T.: Safe distribution of declarative processes. In: Barthe, G., Pardo, A., Schneider, G. (eds.) SEFM 2011. LNCS, vol. 7041, pp. 237–252. Springer, Heidelberg (2011)
27. Winskel, G.: Event structures. In: Advances in Petri Nets, pp. 325–392 (1986)
28. Hull, R., Damaggio, E., Masellis, R.D., Fournier, F., Gupta, M., Heath, F.T., Hobson, S., Linehan, M.H., Maradugu, S., Nigam, A., Sukaviriya, P.N., Vaculín, R.: Business artifacts with guard-stage-milestone lifecycles: managing artifact interactions with conditions and events. In: DEBS, pp. 51–62 (2011)
29. Wiki: SOA 2.0, `http://en.wikipedia.org/wiki/Event-driven_SOA`
30. Chau, T., Muthusamy, V., Jacobsen, H.A., Litani, E., Chan, A., Coulthard, P.: Automating sla modeling. In: CASCON 2008, pp. 126–143. ACM, New York (2008)
31. Muthusamy, V., Jacobsen, H.A.: BPM in cloud architectures: Business process management with SLAs and events. In: Hull, R., Mendling, J., Tai, S. (eds.) BPM 2010. LNCS, vol. 6336, pp. 5–10. Springer, Heidelberg (2010)

32. Muthusamy, V., Jacobsen, H.A., Coulthard, P., Chan, A., Waterhouse, J., Litani, E.: Sla-driven business process management in soa. In: CASCON 2007, pp. 264–267. ACM, New York (2007)
33. OSOA: SCA event processing, http://www.osoa.org/
34. Papazoglou, M.P., Heuvel, W.J.: Service oriented architectures: approaches, technologies and research issues. The VLDB Journal 16(3), 389–415 (2007)
35. Yan, W., Hu, S., Muthusamy, V., Jacobsen, H.A., Zha, L.: Efficient event-based resource discovery. In: DEBS 2009, pp. 1–12. ACM, New York (2009)
36. Frei, A., Popovici, A., Alonso, G.: Eventizing applications in an adaptive middleware platform. IEEE DSO 6(4), 1 (2005)

A Framework for Composing Personalized Web Resources

Bipin Upadhyaya[1], Hua Xiao[2], Ying Zou[1], Joanna Ng[3], and Alex Lau[3]

[1] Dept. of Electrical and Computer Engineering,
Queen's University Kingston, Ontario, Canada
{9bu,ying.zou}@queensu.ca
[2] School of Computing, Queen's University
Kingston, Ontario, Canada
huaxiao@cs.queensu.ca
[3] IBM Canada Laboratory, Markham, Ontario, Canada
{jwng,alexlau}@ca.ibm.com

Abstract. There are a large number of Web resources available on the Internet. However, only small subsets of Web resources are used to fulfill a user's needs. Due to the heterogeneity and decentralization of Web resources, it is a time-consuming and tedious process for users to identify Web resources to fulfill their needs. For repeated activities, a user has to perform the same process over and over. To support users' recurring online activities, we propose a framework for creating a personalized Web space to manage and orchestrate Web resources. Our framework provides helps to: 1) discover Web resources distributed in different websites despite their format; 2) provide mechanisms to allow users to share their information and resources; and 3) compose Web resources distributed in different websites. As a proof of concept, we designed and developed a prototype to demonstrate the use of our proposed framework for creating a personalized Web space.

Keywords: Web resource composition, Web resource identification, RESTful service, personalized Web space.

1   Introduction

Internet has become one of the major sources for people to obtain information and perform tasks (*e.g.,* online shopping) for their daily activities. Various types of Web resources, such as Web pages, Simple Object Access Protocol (SOAP)-based Web Services [1] and Representational State Transfer (REST) services [2], exist on the Internet to provide various functionalities. Due to the heterogeneity and decentralization of Web resources, it is a time-consuming and tedious process for users to sift through the sheer volume of Web resources to fulfill their needs. The previous accessed Web resources are not automatically tracked. Therefore, if the activities (*e.g.,* planning a trip) need to be repeated, a user has to perform the same process over and over again. Although there are a large amount of Web resources available on the Internet, a very small subset of Web resources is used to fulfill the needs of users' daily activities, such as online shopping and planning a trip. It is a

M. Chignell et al. (Eds.): The Personal Web, LNCS 7855, pp. 65–86, 2013.

time-consuming and tedious process for users to sift through the sheer volume of Web resources to perform their daily activities due to the following limitations of existing technologies to access Web resources.

1) Heterogeneous Web resources hinder search engines and users to discover suitable Web resources for fulfilling users' goal of daily activities. Existing Web resources are described in heterogeneous formats. For example, Web Service Description Language (WSDL) [3] is used to describe SOAP-based Web services that make remote procedure calls. WSDL is designed for programmers. It is difficult to be understood by non-IT professional users. HTTP-based APIs are increasingly used by companies such as Twitter [4] and Flickr [5]. They are chosen over SOAP-based services. However, HTTP-based APIs reveal little information about the functionality of the APIs. It is challenging for existing search engines such as Google [6] to discover the HTTP-based APIs due to the lack of functional descriptions.

2) Replicated information and accounts are across different online services and websites. More and more people use social networking services, such as Facebook [7], MySpace [8] and Twitter [4] to communicate. However, the messages and friends in one social networking service are not easily shared with another social networking service. For example, messages posted on Facebook cannot be viewed by the friends on MySpace although a user may have the same friends in both services. To share a message and communicate with friends in each service, users have to log into each service to post the replicated information across multiple online services. It requires effective tools or platforms help users manage the accounts and replicated information across the boundaries of services.

3) Web resources for fulfilling a user's activity are often distributed in several websites. In today's online experience, users frequently re-visit Web resources distributed across different websites to perform repeated tasks [9]. For example, a person planning a conference trip needs to locate various Web resources to search for transportation, reserve accommodation, and look for local attractions. In current practices, users have to visit multiple websites to find the desired Web resources. The visited Web resources are not recorded. Therefore, users cannot automatically reuse the already performed process for a recurring activity. It is a time-consuming process to manually compose Web resources. The result of service composition may not provide the optimal outcome. For instance, a user may not be able to discover a Web service that provides the most economical air ticket.

To support the user's social, recreational, professional, and other activities, it is essential to create a personalized Web space that provides the following functionalities:

1) Discover available Web resources from websites to fulfill a user's goal (*i.e.*, activities), despite the formats of Web resources. For example, when a user needs to buy a flight ticket, we can return appropriate Web resources related to the flight ticket purchasing. The Web resources could be a SOAP-based service, a HTTP-based API, a website or even a message with a coupon code for buying flight tickets.

2) Provide mechanisms to allow users to share their information and Web resources over different websites and online services. For example, a user only needs to post a message one time and the personalized Web space can

automatically share the message across multiple social networking services that a user registered.

3) Help users compose Web resources distributed over different websites to fulfill their activities. For instance, when a user plans a trip, we can automatically provide and organize the related Web resources from heterogeneous websites to the user and help her/him plan the trip.

To achieve these functionalities, we propose a framework for building a personalized Web space that assists a user in managing various Web resources and composing Web resources for automatic reuse. We create a unified description schema to describe heterogeneous Web resources. A unified description schema can facilitate our framework to discover functionally similar Web resources regardless of the formats. We provide an approach to describe relations among different Web resources forming a resource graph. The relations specified in such a resource graph enable users to manage various Web resources easily. Moreover, we provide techniques to compose coarse granular Web resources using a resource graph. The composite Web resources are represented as an ad-hoc processes which capture user's dynamic needs. Similar to traditional business processes, an ad-hoc process captures a set of activities (*i.e.*, work items) and the control and data flows among the activities. Different from the business processes, work items within an ad-hoc process do not follow strict order. For example, "planning a night out" can be described as an ad-hoc process. It involves several work items, such as going for a movie, and reserving a table in a restaurant in any orders based on a user.

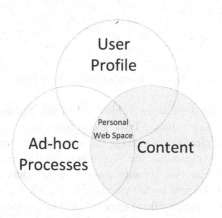

Fig. 1. Overview of a personalized Web space

The remainder of this paper is presented as follows. Section 2 gives an overview of the proposed personalized Web space. Section 3 describes the schema for representing various Web resources in a unified format. Section 4 proposes a resource graph for modeling the relations among Web resources. Section 5 presents the technique for constructing ad-hoc processes. Section 6 discusses our prototype for demonstrating the proposed framework. Section 7 discusses the related work. Finally Section 8 concludes the paper and explores the future work.

2   The Proposed Personalized Web Space

We envision that a personalized Web space is an interaction of three major components: user profiles, content and ad-hoc processes as shown in Figure 1. A user profile contains data related to a user including profession, interests, online behaviors, frequently visited Web resources and his/her social peers. Content refers to the information delivered by Web resources, such as subscribed RSS feed, bookmarks and Web services. Ad-hoc processes denote a set of recurring user's activities. An ad-hoc process involves activities that are frequently performed in the past and might be interested to a user in the future. More specifically, each activity can be fulfilled by one or more Web resources.

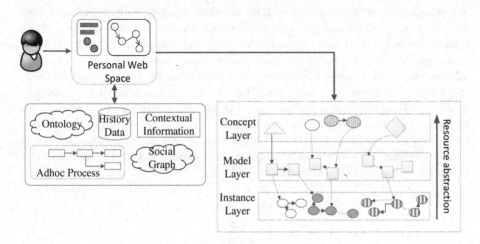

Fig. 2. Architecture of a Personal Web Space

In Figure 2, we present three layer architecture of the proposed personalized Web space including instance layer, model layer and concept layer. The architecture treats Web resources as a key element to manage the data involved in a personalized Web space. The instance layer represents the Web resources distributed over the internet. Web resources with similar functionality can be implemented by various types of services (*e.g.*, RESTful services or SOAP-based services) in different websites. The model layer represents the Web resources in our proposed unified schema. The concept layer contains the semantic concepts that are used to describe the functionality of Web resources available in the instance layer.

The semantic concepts of the Web resources are annotated by the users in the personal Web space. Instance layer represents the physical Web resources hosted by different service providers. Based on their usages by the users, the semantic relations can be established among Web resources. For example a "restaurant" resource and a "review" resource in different Websites can have the "hasReview" relationship. We identify relations among different Web resources and construct a resource graph in the model layer. Resource Description Framework (RDF) [10] is designed specifically for exchanging and integrating Web data. In the proposed architecture, we migrate various Web resources into RESTful services, and then adopt RDF to describe RESTful services and their relations. In concept layer, we allow a user to annotate semantic concepts to the Web resources using keywords. Concept layer provides a high level overview of the functionality of Web resources. For example a flight booking service has concepts: flight and city. The concepts are then linked to resources in the model layer and instance layer. Web resource providers can specify the categories of their Web resources using the concepts defined in the concept layer. Concept layer defines relations among different Web resources based on concept shared. We use open database such as WordNet [11] and ConceptNet [12] to correlate concepts in the concept layer. Our previous work [13] provides more detail steps on extracting concepts from service description files.

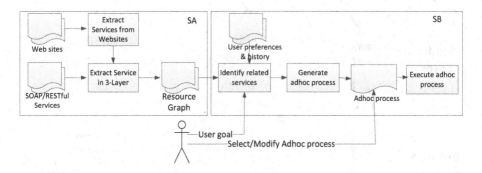

Fig. 3. Overall steps to generate an ad-hoc process

Figure 3 shows the overall steps to generate an ad-hoc process. The framework takes the various Web resources (such as forms defined Websites, SOAP based services and RESTful services) as inputs. We extract Web resources and abstract them in three layer architecture. The resource graph is generated based on the three - layer architecture. Given a user goal, our framework identifies Web resources required to fulfill the user's goal based on his/her preferences and historical data. A user can modify the generated ad-hoc process and then executes the process.

When accomplishing an online activity, a user can simply describe the desired goal using keywords. We map a goal into Web resources described by a resource graph and infer an ad-hoc process to help a user fulfill the goal. Based on the data flow between Web resources, we identify the control flows between Web resources. Figure 4 shows an example scenario of using our proposed framework. A user provides a keyword "travel" to describe his/her goal. Our framework generates an ad-hoc process which maps the activities into the Web resources in the model layer. The concrete Web resources, such as Air Canada web site (*i.e.*, www.aircanada.com) to book flight tickets, are represented in the instance layer. Using the mapping between the model layer and the instance layer, we can find the concrete Web resources to fulfill different work items specified in the ad-hoc process. Meanwhile, a user can interact with the personalized Web space to connect different Web resources and customize the ad-hoc process.

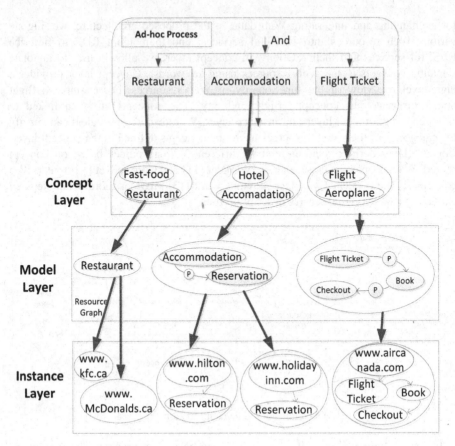

Fig. 4. An example scenario of an application of the architecture for the personalized Web space

3   Modeling Heterogonous Web Resources in a Unified Format

We devise a unified resource schema that represents heterogeneous Web resources (e.g., Web Forms, SOAP-based services, and HTTP-based APIs) in a single format as shown in Figure 5. A service aggregates different Web resources identified using a Universal Resource Identifier (URI). A Web resource represents an entity from the real world. Its state can be exposed and changed via accessing the URI. We represent all the Web resources in REST style.

Web resources are accessed using methods defined in a protocol. In the HTTP protocol, a method can be GET, POST, PUT, and DELETE. A GET method notifies the service provider to retrieve the data. A PUT method updates the data with the ones send in the request. A DELETE method deletes the data of a service. A POST method creates a new resource. A method has at least one request and several optional response messages. A request includes a set of parameters to be sent to the Web resource. A response message is linked with a representation that returns the state of

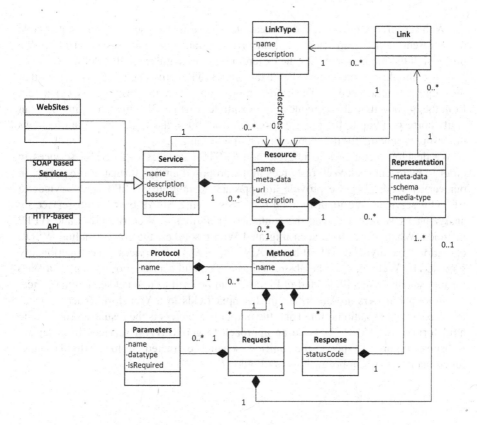

Fig. 5. The unified description schema

```
<xs:element name="Restaurant">
    <xs:complexType>
        <xs:sequence>
            <xs:element name="name" type="xsd:string"/>
            <xs:element name="establishedDate" type="xsd:date"/>
            <xs:element name="lat" type="xsd:Integer"/>
            <xs:element name="lon" type="xsd:Integer"/>
            <xs:element name="address" type="xsd:String"/>
            <xs:element name="phone" type="xsd:String"/>
        </xs:sequence>
    </xs:complexType>
</xs:element>
```

Fig. 6. Excerpt of resource schema of a restaurant resource

the Web resource after a method invocation. The response uses different status code to represent faulty responses (*e.g.,* incorrect parameters, and server errors). The protocol of the method specifies the different types of status code that defines how the response should be interpreted. For example, HTTP status code 200 represents that the request has succeeded. The information returned in the response is dependent from the method used in the request. For example, when a GET method is invoked, an entity corresponding to the requested resource is sent in the response. Figure 6 shows the resource schema for the representation of a restaurant.

We develop techniques to migrate non-RESTful services to RESTful services in order to represent such Web resources in the proposed unified format. For example in our earlier work [14], we provide an approach to migrate SOAP-based services to RESTful services. We identify Web resources from a SOAP-based Web service by analyzing its WSDL and map the contained operations to Web resources and HTTP methods. When a user uses such migrated Web resources, the corresponding WSDL operations are invoked. HTTP-based APIs are RESTful services. The functionality provided by Web sites can be abstracted as a RESTful service. For example, a Web form to search tickets illustrated in Figure 7 can be used as a ticket searching service; the input parameters are described in the input fields in a Web form (such as input text, text area and radio buttons) and the output parameters is the result returned in the html format. In [15] we provide an approach to get RESTful services from legacy websites. Figure 8 shows the unified schema extracted from a flight search functionality of a Web Form shown in Figure 7.

Fig. 7. A Web form for flight search

Figure 8 shows an example of a Web form represented in the unified schema. The Web resource shown in Figure 7 is provided by "Flight Network" and the base URL (http://www.flightnetwork.com/) of the service provider. The resource name is "Flight Search" with meta-data "Search", "Flight" and "Tickets". The resource uses POST method. The resource has request parameters including "Category", "From",

"To", "Departure Date", "Return Date", "Adult (s)", "Child (2-11), "infant (0-23mth)" and "Type". POST method is used by the form. The response has the media-type "txt/html". Converting different types of Web resources to REST style provides a simplified view for users to use and manipulate Web resources. The Web resources are described in RDF to simplify the manipulation of Web resources specified in different languages, such as query languages (*e.g.*, SPARQL [16]), transformation languages (*e.g.*, Gleaning Resource Descriptions from Dialects of Languages [17]), and rule languages (*e.g.*, Rule Interchange Format [18]).

```
<Service>
<Name> Flight Search </Name>
<Description>Search and bok the flight</Description>
<Provider>Flight Network <Provider>
<BaseURL>http://http://www.flightnetwork.com</BaseURL>
<Resource>
        <Name> Flight Search </Name>
        <Meta-data>
                <name= "Search"/>
                <name= "Flight"/>
                <name= "tickets"/>
        <Meta-data>
        <URL> http://www.flightnetwork.com/flights/search</URL>
        <Protocol type="HTTP" ref="http://tools.ietf.org/html/rfc2626">
        <Method name="POST">
        <Request>
                <Parameter>
                        <name="Category" datatype="String" />
                        <name="From" datatype="String" />
                        <name="To" datatype="String" />
                        <name="From" datatype="String" />
                        <name="Departure Date" datatype="Date" />
                        <name="Return Date" datatype="Date" />
                        <name="Adult(s)" datatype="Integer" />
                        <name="Child(2-11)" datatype="Integer" />
                        <name="infant(0-23mth)" datatype="Integer" />
                        <name="Type" datatype="String" />
                </Parameter>
        </Request>
        <Response>
                <media-type> txt/html </media-type>
        </Response>
        </Method>
        </Protocol>
</Resource>
</Service>
```

Fig. 8. A unified schema to represent a Web form illustrated in Figure 7

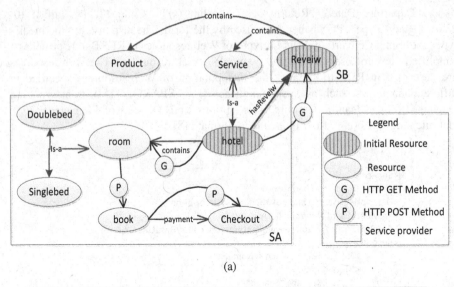

(a)

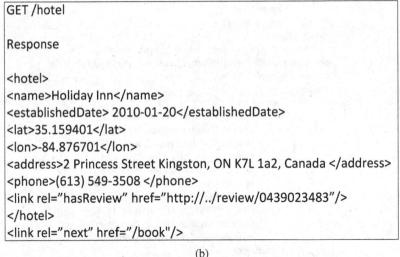

(b)

Fig. 9. An example of Web resources and their relations

4   Representing a Resource Graph

We create a resource graph to represent Web resources and the relations between Web resources. We consider the resource graph as a semantic network model which consists of entities and relationships. Entities in a resource graph denote Web resources identifiable using URIs. A Web resource may be linked to other Web resources by a set of relations. We have identified three types of relations:

Data Flow Based Relations: Data flow relations define the flow of data between two or more resources. The data flow relation is determined by matching the schema between the input and output of methods in Web resources. We use link specification [19] to describe the data flow based relation between Web resources in a resource graph. A "*rel*" attribute defined in the link specification gives the information about the semantics of the link. Figure 8 b. shows two links with "*rel*". We identified the flowing four kinds of data flow relations

i. **See-also** recommends other Web resources. For example a book resource, b1, has *see-also* relation with book resources, b2 and b3, if all the three books are written by the same author a1.

ii. **Same–as** provides the similar Web resources. For example, if flight resources, f1 and f2, fly between two cities at the same time, these Web resources are related by *same-as* relation.

iii. **Is-a** defines is-a relation between the Web resources. For example, a single bedroom, and a double bedroom are the resources of room type. Hence both single bedroom and double bedroom have an *is-a* relationship with the resource room.

iv. **Contains** define different Web resources encapsulated in a composite Web resource. For example, a search result to a book results multiple instance of the resource books.

Transitions Based Relations: The response of a Web resource contains next state transition information. A user agent can decide next state based on the semantics of the relations defined in the links available in the response. The relations are used to recommend new Web resources, identify similar Web resources, and define the relationship between the Web resources. Similar to data flow relations, we use link specification to describe the transition based relations.

Semantic Relations: A semantic relation among Web resources is imposed to Web resources based on the concept relation found in the conceptual layer of three layer architecture. Our approach relates Web resources based on concept shared between them. We identified concepts between resources and then identify the related between the concepts between resources. We propagate this relation down to the resource layer. Figure 9 shows an example resource graph. The concepts in two services are "hotel" and "review". Since Hotel and review are semantically related, this relation can be propagated to the instance layer, connecting the review and the hotel resources. Moreover the analysis of input and output parameters if there is some data flow relation. In this particular case in Figure 9 the review resource requires the name of the hotel and its location as input parameter. The hotel resource is the initial resource. The review resource is not hosted by the same provider, but is linked with "hasReveiw" relation. Double bedroom and single bedroom resources have is-a relationship with room, all semantic relation from the room resource is carried over to those two different categories of the rooms. The small circle represents the method that can be invoked on Web resources from the current state. In our resource graph, the resource from where a user can start consuming a service (a starting point) is defined as the initial node. In Figure 9, the hotel resource is represented in a darker color and it denotes the initial node. When a user requests a service, this node is returned; and from that node, a user can start using the resource. The semantic information embedded in the nodes (*i.e.*, *rel* attribute in link) can substantially increases the user agents' capability to discover Web resources.

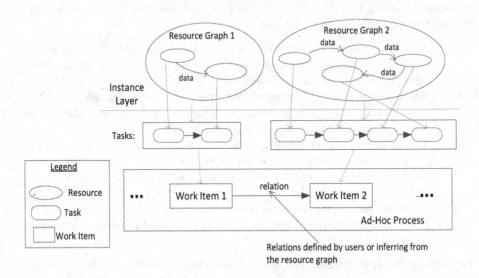

Fig. 10. Definition of an ad-hoc process

5   Generating Ad-Hoc Processes

A resource graph describes the relations among multiple Web resources. However, when a user needs to fulfill the goal of a daily activity, the goal generally only involves a very small subset of Web resources defined in the resource graph. Ad-hoc processes are designed to describe and organize such a subset of Web resources. This section presents the definition of ad-hoc processes. Then we introduce our approach to generate ad-hoc processes based on the input of users, expert knowledge, and the resource graph.

5.1   Definition of Ad-Hoc Processes

An ad-hoc process records the work items that need to be performed for achieving a goal. Figure 10 illustrates our hierarchical definition of ad-hoc processes that can be represented in different levels of abstraction. A task, the lowest level of abstraction, is defined as an operation (i.e., method in the uniform resource schema) on a resource. For example, a task "search for flight ticket" could be implemented as the resource "flight ticket" with the associated operation "GET". There exists a mapping between the methods of Web resources captured in a resource graph and the tasks in the ad-hoc processes.

A transaction often consists of one or more tasks. Therefore, we define the notion of a work item to specify a set of tasks along with their data flow for fulfilling a transaction. For example, to fulfill the transaction of "buy flight tickets", a user needs to perform tasks "searching for ticket", "choosing ticket" then "paying the bill". The data "searching results of tickets" is passed from the first task to the second task, and the data "ticket price" is passed from the second task to the third task. In a higher level of abstraction, a work item can contain one or more tasks. An ad-hoc process aggregates work items and existing ad-hoc processes (*i.e.*, sub ad-hoc processes) performed by a user to fulfill a goal. We define the follow three control relations among work items.

• **And** relation indicates that all the work items have to be executed.

• **Or** relation means that users only need to execute one task from a given set of work items.

•**Optional** is used to recommend related work items after one work item is performed. For example, after a user performs the work item "buying a flight ticket", we may use optional relation to recommend a work item "map of the airport" to a user.

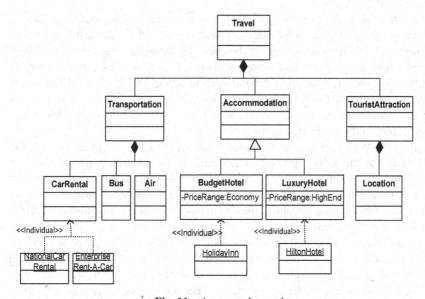

Fig. 11. An example ontology

The methods of the Web resources fulfilling the tasks are connected by data links in the resource graph. The data links make tasks archiving a work item highly coupled. A user needs to execute all the tasks linked by the data in the work item. For example, a work item "buy flight tickets" includes tasks "search ticket", "choose ticket" and "pay the bill". To accomplish such a work item, the user has to perform all three tasks within the work item. The relations among work items are loosely coupled.

Users can choose different work items to perform, add a new work item or remove an existing work item from the ad-hoc process. Therefore, various users can create personalized ad-hoc processes with different work items to achieve the same goal. For instance, when planning a trip, some users may prefer taking flight than driving car; but other users may prefer driving than flying. The ad-hoc processes of planning a trip for these user groups contain different work items since the ad-hoc process for the former group contains the work item "buy flight tickets" and the latter does not have.

5.2   Generating Ad-Hoc Processes

Our framework allows a user to specify a goal using a collection of keywords, and helps a user compose an ad-hoc process to fulfill the goal. We use the goal description to find a matching ontology to extend the semantic meanings of the goal. An ontology represents knowledge as common entities (e.g., people, travel and weather), and the relations among the entities. In ontology, the semantic of a high-level goal is expanded into one or more concrete entities. Figure 11 illustrates an example ontology that defines "travel". The semantic of a high level entity (e.g., "travel") can be further expanded into four entities: "transportation", "accommodation", "tourist Attraction" and "car rental".

In our framework, the entities (*i.e.*, classes, individuals, and attributes) defined in the ontology are used to search for matching Web resources from the instance layer of the architecture of the personalized Web space. However, a large number of Web resources could be returned and mixed together. It is a tedious job for users to manually select and organize their desired Web resources. To facilitate the selection of Web resources and identification of the interaction among Web resources, our framework aggregates the functionally related Web resources into work items based on the structure of the matching ontology.

To group the Web resources with similar functionalities, we design an algorithm to identify tasks for the ad-hoc process. The details of the algorithm are described in described in our earlier paper [15]. In the algorithm, we take an ontology which matches with the goal description as the input. The algorithm uses a stepwise approach to discover and organize the Web resources according to the level of abstraction. The high level entities in an ontology graph convey more abstract meanings suitable for discovering Web resources offering general purpose services. Such services allow users to receive the desired Web resources (*e.g.*, expedia.com) in one place without having to go through multiple servers for visiting different Web resources. For example, expedia.com provides a general service for planning a trip by providing information, such as car rental, flight ticket purchasing and hotel reservation. The low level entities in an ontology graph provide more specific meanings of the goal and therefore indicate the possibility to find concrete Web resources which provide more specialized services or information. For example, to check into a flight operated by Air Canada, a user has to visit more specialized Web resources by going to Air Canada website to print their boarding passes and check fight status.

To satisfy a user with varying needs in different levels of specialization, we use the breadth-first search algorithm to scan the ontology graph. We identify the general purpose Web resources from the top of the graph and the specialized Web resources from the low level of entities in the graph. To identify the control relations between tasks, our framework analyzes the relations of Web resources captured in a Web resources graph to infer the control relations among tasks. Table 1 summarizes the mappings from Web resources in a resource graph to the control relations among tasks.

Table 1. Infer work item relations from resource graphs

Relation in a resource graph	Control relations among tasks	Description
A —See_also→ B	optional, A → B	"See_also" in a resource graph is interpreted as an "optional" relation which recommends another task to a user.
A, See_also→ B, See_also→ C	A optional → B, C	Two tasks followed by the "optional" relation indicate that both tasks can be recommended to users.
A —Same_as→ B	Or → A, B	"Same_as" means two similar Web resources; therefore, the user only needs to perform one of the tasks.
A, Is_a→ B, Is_a→ C	Or → B, C	Web Resources B and C are instance of resource A. Thus, resources B and C are similar. A user only needs to choose one from Web resources B and C
A, contains→ B, contains→ C	And → B, C	Web Resource A contains Web resources B and C. Therefore, to handle A, users might need to perform the work items related to both B and C.

As listed in Table 1, the "See_also" relation in the resource graph is mapped to an "optional" relation in the ad-hoc process which is used to recommend tasks to a user. The user has the option to perform it or ignore it. The "Same_as" relation in the resource graph indicates that two resources are equal. Therefore, we convert the "Same_as" relation into an "Or" relation of tasks. "Is_a" relation shows that one resource is an instance of another and these instances have the same features.

Therefore, the siblings of "Is_a" relation in the resource graph are converted to "Or" relation of tasks. "Contains" relation indicates that one resource is the composite of other Web resources. Therefore, the elements in a "Contains" relation in the resource graph is converted to "And" relation among tasks. We can further segment the tasks into a work item if a set of tasks are related to one transaction. The relation among the work items is inferred from the relations among the segment of tasks.

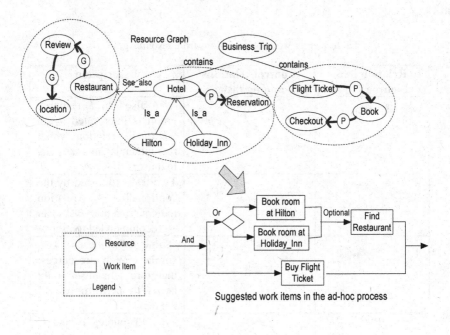

Fig. 12. An example of relation inference

Figure 12 presents an example of mapping the relations defined in the resource graph to the relations of related work items in an ad-hoc process. In Figure 12, the Web resources "Hilton", "Holiday_Inn", "Flight", and "Restaurant" are converted to work items in the ad-hoc process. In this example, if we trace the entire resource graph, these work items can be implemented by several tasks which are associated with more specialized Web resources.

6   A Prototype Implementation

As a proof of concept of our proposed framework, we have designed and developed a prototype personal Web space. We use a Firefox plugin to record a user's Web browsing history. Our prototype analyzes the browsing history and connects different Web resources visited by users to generate ad-hoc processes in order to automate the repetitive tasks. To collect the Web resources of interest, our prototype allows a user to annotate the Web resources of interest using tags. Such Web resources are recorded and converted to the unified schema.

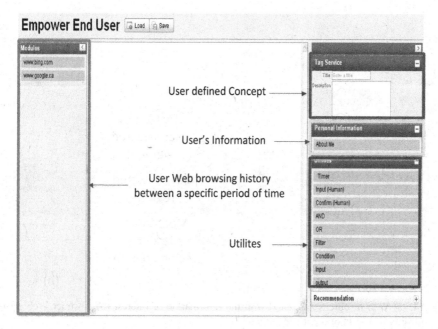

Fig. 13. An annotated screenshot of our prototype

Figure 13 shows the screenshot of the prototype that helps a user compose Web resources. We implement our prototype using WireIT [19] utility which allows the user to wire different Web resources. The left hand side of our prototype illustrated in Figure 13 shows the Web resource interacted with the user. There are three sections on the right hand side of the screen depicted in Figure 13. The top section (*i.e.,* Tag Service) allows a user to tag and describe the functionality of Web resources as concepts. The middle one (*i.e.,* Personal Information) in the right hand side of the screen shown in Figure 13 describes the personal data including address, credit card details, and online accounts. The bottom section (*i.e.,* utilities) contains the utilities that help the user invoke the defined ad-hoc processes following certain criteria, such as timing constraints. The center region enables a user to connect to Web resources.

As an example usage scenario, a user uses Flight Network to search for the flights. The user goes through the returned Web resources and tags the Web resources of interest using the prototype. In the screenshot shown in Figure 14 (a), a user selects a rate, flight departure date and departure time. The bottom of the interface (Figure 14 (a)) shows the tags of selected elements, name of the component and a submit button. Figure 14 (b) shows the input/output interface for fight selection interface. When a user interacts with more than one Web resources to accomplish a certain task, he can connect the selected Web resources to define the flow between Web resources. We represent the connected Web resources using the proposed resource graph.

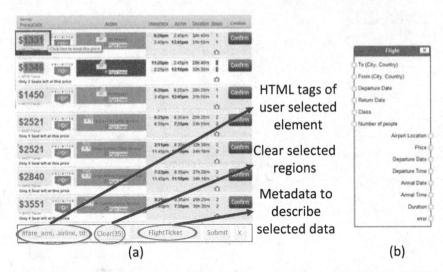

(a)   (b)

Fig. 14. (a) Web resources annotated with the information of interest (b) Abstract Web form functionality in a form of input and output

Let us consider a use case scenario for our prototype. Assume that a user wants to attend a conference. The main activities involve booking a flight ticket and a hotel room. He may also need a taxi to transfer from the airport to the hotel. A user needs to enter flight information, like To (City, Country), From (City Country), Date and time Range. Similarly, a user needs the duration (From Date and To Date) and the type of room as input to reserve a hotel room. The taxi reservation can leverage the input from the Flight and Hotel services. The time to rent a taxi is dependent on the time when a flight arrives. A user manually performs initial the activities. Our prototype records all the events occurred in the browser during the given interval of time. The user can then wire different Web resources to produce an ad-hoc process. The user connects these two Web resources to define the data flow. Furthermore, we abstract the ad-hoc process to allow the process to link with different Web resources of the equivalent functionality. Figure 15 shows an ad-hoc process for managing traveling to attend a conference.

7   Related Work

Our work is related to three different areas: (a) service migration, (b) data extraction, and (c) service composition. The following subsections describe the related work in the corresponding area.

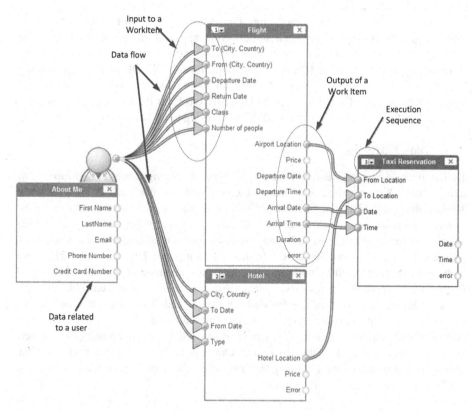

Fig. 15. An annotated screenshot for creating an ad-hoc process by a user

7.1   Service Migration

Migration of legacy systems to Service-Oriented Architectures (SOA) uses both static and dynamic reverse engineering techniques [15, 33, 34]. RESTful services are relatively new in the area of SOA. To the best of our knowledge, there is not much work done in migration towards RESTful services. A few approaches [22, 23, 24] are proposed to model the REST based services. Kopecky et al. [25] present hRESTS as a solution for missing machine-readable Web APIs of RESTful services. They argue that a microformat is the easiest way to enrich existing human-readable HTML documentations. They introduce a model for RESTful services, but with a focus on documentation and discovery. Alarcon et al. [26] introduce a meta-model for descriptions of RESTful services. The meta-model is the basis for the Resource Linking Language. The authors identify links as first class citizens and focus on service documentation and composition. Engelke et al. [27] present an industrial case study to migrate a transportation Web service to a RESTful service and describe issues encountered in designing and implementing a set of RESTful services to extend and replace traditional Web services. Laitkorpi et al. [24] describe an approach of abstracting Application interfaces to REST-like services. There are mainly three major steps: analyzing a legacy API, abstracting it to a canonical form with constraints in place, and generating the adapter code for the abstraction. Athanasopoulos et al. [22] provide a model-driven approach in identifying REST-like resources from legacy service descriptions. Using the information contained in the descriptions of the available functionality (in the form of WSDL or message schema specifications), the authors proposed a way to model service operations signatures into a MOF model called Signature Model. Different from the above approaches, we represent different Web resources in REST style using a unified description schema.

7.2   Data Extraction

Data extraction is a key feature for many user programming tools. Yahoo Pipes [28] and Potluck [29] can extract data from structured data sources, such as Web services, RSS feeds. Sifter [30] and Solvent [31] are tools that work with unstructured data sources, such as the human-readable information on webpages. Mash Maker [32] supports extraction, aggregation, and visualization across multiple websites. The interface in Mash Maker allows users to directly manipulate URLs, but requires some technical expertise, such as understanding URL arguments and regular expressions. Karma [33] allows the users extract data from a website into a data table through demonstration. To extract data, users visit a webpage and click on the sections within the page they want to extract, such as a restaurant name and address. The tool uses an XPath generalization scheme to find similar data on the same page and other related pages, and then copies the data into a table. Our approach of data extraction is similar to Karma's approach as we use the selector to select the data [35]. In addition, we use HTTP events to abstract the resources.

7.3   Service Composition

Service composition is a process to combine collaborating services to obtain more complex functionality. Mashup performs service composition manually in a user friendly way to compose services without following the formal definition of business processes. Yahoo! Pipes [28] is a visual drag and drop environment for fetching and merging data from different sources. Using Yahoo Pipes [28], a user can combine many feeds into one, then sort, filter and translate it and place them on a personal website. Pipes support a variety of output formats such as RSS, JSON, and KML. Our approach is different from Yahoo Pipes as we abstract ad-hoc processes based on the HTTP events and our approach does not depend on the data formats.

Carlson et al. [36] provide an approach to progressively compose Web services based on the interface matching. Given a Web service, Carlson et al. use the output description of the Web service to match the inputs of existing Web services in the repository. Liu et al. [37] propose a Mashup architecture which extends the SOA model with Mashups to facilitate service composition. Similar to the work of Carlson et al. [36], Liu et al. match the input with output to help end-users compose services. They also use tags and Quality of Service (QoS) to select services. Our work enhances service Mashups by providing guidance to end-users as they create their Mashups through the automatic composition of services and abstracting services at concept level.

8   Conclusion

This paper presents a framework for composing Web resources in a personalized Web space. In the framework, Web resources are described by a unified description schema and are wrapped as RESTful services. The unified schema addresses the issues of integration resources and drives the innovation to the user side. We design a resource graph to represent the semantic relationship among Web resources. By analyzing the relations among Web resources and using ontologies, our framework can generate ad-hoc processes for composing Web resources. We have built a prototype to demonstrate that the repetitive tasks in the Web can be automatically tracked and the user can change simple Web resources into reusable services by annotating the data with them.

In future we will improve our framework to allow a user to share ad-hoc processes. In our current implementation, the resource graph is manually created from the user's browsing history, we plan to provide automatic approach to identify the relations among the Web resources and generate the resource graph for a given set of Web resources. We also want to design case studies to evaluate the performance of our framework for generating ad-hoc processes from a user's goal.

References

1. SOAP, version 1.2, World Wide Web Consortium (W3C), http://www.w3.org/TR/soap12-part0/ (last accessed on April 21, 2013)
2. Fielding, R.: Architectural Styles and The Design of Network-based Software Architectures. PhD thesis, University of California, Irvine (2000)
3. Chinnici, R., Moreau, J., Ryman, A., Weerawarana, S.: Web Service Description Language, W3C Recommendation (2007)
4. Twitter, http://twitter.com/ (last time accessed on April 21, 2013)
5. Flickr, http://www.flickr.com/ (last accessed on April 21, 2013)
6. Google, http://www.google.com (last time accessed on April 21, 2013)
7. Facebook, http://www.facebook.com/ (last accessed on April 21, 2013)
8. MySpace, http://www.myspace.com/ (last time accessed on April 21, 2013)
9. Upadhyaya, B., Zou, Y.: Integrating Heterogeneous Web Services from an End User Perspective. In: Proc. the ACM/IFIP/USENIX International Middleware Conference, Doctoral Symposium, Montreal, Canada, December 3-7 (2012)
10. Beckett, D., McBride, B. (eds.): RDF/XML Syntax Specification (Revised), W3C Recommendation (last accessed on April 21, 2013)
11. Miller, G.A.: WordNet: A Lexical Database for English. Communications of the ACM 38(11), 39–41
12. Liu, H., Singh, P.: ConceptNet: A Practical Commonsense Reasoning Toolkit. BT Technology Journal 22 (to appear)
13. Upadhyaya, B., Khomh, F.: A Concept Analysis Approach for Guiding Users in Service Discovery. In: IEEE International Conference on Service-Oriented Computing and Applications (SOCA 2012), Taipei, Taiwan (2012)
14. Upadhyaya, B., Zou, Y., Xiao, H., Ng, J., Lau, A.: Migration of SOAP-based Services to RESTful Services. In: Proc. of International IEEE Symposium on Web Systems Evolution (WSE), Williamsburg, VA, USA (September 30, 2011)
15. Upadhyaya, B., Khomh, F., Zou, Y.: Extracting RESTful Services from Web Applications. In: Proc. the 5th IEEE International Conference on Service-Oriented Computing and Applications (SOCA), Taipei, Taiwan, December 17-19 (2012)

16. SPARQL Query Language for RDF,
    `http://www.w3.org/TR/rdf-sparql-query/` (last accessed on April 21, 2013)
17. Gleaning Resource Descriptions from Dialects of Languages (GRDDL),
    `http://www.w3.org/2004/01/rdxh/spec` (last accessed on April 21, 2013)
18. Link Relations,
    `http://www.iana.org/assignments/link-relations/`
    `link-relations.xhtml` (last accessed on April 21, 2013)
19. RIF In RDF, `http://www.w3.org/TR/rif-in-rdf/` (last accessed on April 21, 2013)
20. WireIt - a Javascript Wiring Library, `http://neyric.github.com/wireit/` (last accessed on April 21, 2013)
21. Almonaies, A., Cordy, J.R., Dean, T.R.: Legacy System Evolution towards Service-Oriented Architecture. In: Proc. International Workshop on SOA Migration and Evolution (SOAME 2010), Madrid, Spain, pp. 53–62 (2010)
22. Athanasopoulos, M., Kontogiannis, K.: Identification of REST-like Resources from Legacy Service Descriptions. In: WCRE 2010 (2010)
23. Vinoski, S.: RESTful Web Services Development Checklist. IEEE Internet Computing 12, 96–95 (2008)
24. Laitkorpi, M., Koskinen, J., Systa, T.: A UML-based Approach for Abstracting Application Interfaces to REST-like Services. In: 13th Working Conference on In Reverse Engineering, pp. 134–146 (2006)
25. Kopeck´y, J., Gomadam, K., Vitvar, T.: hRESTS: An HTML Microformat for Describing RESTful Web Services. In: WI-IAT 2008: Proc. Int. Conf. on Web Intelligence and Intelligent Agent Technology (2008)
26. Alarcón, R., Wilde, E.: RESTler: Crawling RESTful services. In: Proceedings of the 19th International Conference on World Wide Web, WWW 2010, pp. 1051–1052. ACM, New York (2010)
27. Engelke, C., Fitzgerald, C.: Replacing Legacy Web Services with RESTful Services. In: WS-REST 2010 First International Workshop on RESTful Design
28. Yahoo Pipes: Rewire the web, `http://pipes.yahoo.com/pipes/` (last accessed on April 21, 2013)
29. Huynh, D., Miller, R.C., Karger, D.: Potluck: Data Mash-Up Tool for Casual Users. In: Aberer, K., et al (eds.) ASWC 2007 and ISWC 2007. LNCS, vol. 4825, pp. 239–252. Springer, Heidelberg (2007)
30. Huynh, D., Miller, R.C., Karger, D.: Enabling Web Browsers to Augment Web Sites Filtering and Sorting Functionalities. In: Proc. UIST 2006, pp. 125–134. ACM Press (2006)
31. Solvent, `http://simile.mit.edu/wiki/Solvent` (last accessed on April 21, 2013)
32. Ennals, R.J., Garofalakis, M.N.: MashMaker: mashups for the masses. In: Proceedings of the 2007 ACM SIGMOD International Conference on Management of Data. ACM (2007)
33. Ennals, R., Gay, D.: Building Mashups by Example. In: Proceedings of IUI (2008)
34. Sneed, H.M., Sneed, S.H.: Creating Web services from legacy host programs. In: 5th International Workshop on Web Site Evolution (WSE), pp. 59–65 (2003)
35. SelectorGadget: point and click CSS selectors,
    `http://www.selectorgadget.com/` (last accessed on April 21, 2013)
36. Carlson, M.P., Ngu, A.H.H., Podorozhny, R.M., Zeng, L.: Automatic mash up of composite applications. In: Bouguettaya, A., Krueger, I., Margaria, T. (eds.) ICSOC 2008. LNCS, vol. 5364, pp. 317–330. Springer, Heidelberg (2008)
37. Liu, X., Huang, G., Mei, H.: A User-Oriented Approach to Automated Service Composition. In: IEEE International Conference on Web Services (ICWS), Short paper, Beijing, China, September 23-26, pp. 773–777 (2008)

A Privacy Framework for the Personal Web

Reza Samavi[1], Mariano P. Consens[1], and Thodoros Topaloglou[2]

[1] MIE, University of Toronto
[2] Rouge Valley Health System, Toronto, Canada

Abstract. User-centric privacy management is an important component of the Personal Web, and even more so in the context of personal health applications. We describe the motivations behind the development of a personal web privacy framework and outline a layered model for self-management of privacy in the context of Personal Health Record applications. In this paper we provide an overview of our framework. The privacy goals and settings mediator model addresses the understandability problem of privacy agreements and settings by supporting the users' privacy decision-making process. This model provides privacy experts with the tool support to encode their knowledge and fill the gap between the end-users' high-level privacy intentions and what personal health applications offer as privacy features. The second model in our framework, smart privacy model, is an ontological model that supports privacy enforcement. The model provides interoperable and computer interpretable translations of privacy settings, allowing the privacy settings selected by a user, to be translated as enforceable constraints on the data and processes of a personal workflow.

Keywords: privacy model, user privacy preferences, Personal Health Record; goal-oriented modeling, Ontology, Process Specification Language.

1 Introduction

Personal Web is an emerging research topic driven by the transformation of the Internet and web from the way users currently interact with and navigate resources in the web, to a smart paradigm mainly centered on users' experience [1]. The main goal of the Personal Web is to empower users, as individuals, seamlessly and smartly self-manage the vast amount of web resources and services to achieve their personal goals [1]. A user-centric perspective of service utilization requires users to play an active role in the process. The promise of the personal web is to make this shift socially and cognitively viable. Such a perspective brings new challenges into the design and architecture of web applications.

In this paper, we investigate the problem of privacy support in Personal Health Record (PHRs) as an emerging Personal Web application. PHR have been growing toward becoming platforms for an extensible ecosystem of personal health applications. PHRs are open platforms with application-programming interfaces (API). Service providers use these APIs to augment the platform with new applications and services [2]. The main goal of these applications is to empower users to utilize PHR not only for the purpose of storing and retrieving health and life style information, but also as a medium to create personal workflows to accomplish their personal health goals

M. Chignell et al. (Eds.): The Personal Web, LNCS 7855, pp. 87–112, 2013.

[3]. Communicating an individual's health data with clinicians, participating in clinical research, or partially sharing health data on social networks [4], are all examples of leveraging PHR platforms for personal goals [5]. With the shift in the PHR's role, users remain loyal to the platform while the third party applications are easily substitutable [2]. The privacy implications of this new PHR architecture are multifold. In this paper we address two aspects of user privacy management in PHR context, the users' privacy configuration problem and the problem of enforcing the configured privacy settings when multiple services over a web platform are utilized.

1.1 Privacy Configuration

For every health-service there are multiple service providers that can become part of the personal workflow. The decision criteria for users to prioritize one application over another are based on the application's cost, value [2], and more importantly the extent that the service respects users' privacy goals [6]. Thus the users' ability to self-manage their privacy and comprehend the consequences of privacy settings in such workflows becomes a core requirement of the Personal Web. However, supports for the self-management of privacy in existing PHRs platforms are primitive and insufficient. When we start to use a service, the only option offered is often to push the "I agree" button at the end of a long legal privacy text (which in most cases is left unread [7]). A number of other applications offer privacy options based on a growing number of privacy features. Nevertheless, these features usually reflect the system's perspective instead of the privacy desires and expectations that a user would want to achieve. Privacy experts can offer users advice to help configure their privacy settings, but there is a lack of tools to support the task of privacy configuration.

As the comprehensibility of privacy agreements and the configuration of privacy settings have become daunting tasks, we propose a solution that seeks the comfort of conceptual modeling techniques. In this paper, we propose the Privacy Goals and Settings Mediator (PGSM) model, a privacy model that helps users to comprehend the privacy settings when employing multiple services over a web platform. The model is based on the i* multi-agent modelling technique [8]. The i* modeling technique is originated in the software engineering community, where conceptual modeling is regarded as a tool for engineers and designers to promote a common understanding of a subject matter and facilitate a complex design process [9], [10]. We believe that conceptual models and modelling is equally valuable in order to understand and manage privacy.

The i* modeling technique is utilized to model the environment and the goals of agents involved in a privacy sensitive interaction, creating a privacy goals and settings mediator model (PGSM). The parties involved in an interaction within a context are represented as the i* agents who depend on each other to achieve some goals or perform some tasks. Goals are used to express the purpose or utility of an interaction, as well as the qualities associated with a purpose. The users' perception of their privacy are expressed in terms of goal-models of multiple agents. These goal models link the privacy features offered by services to the high-level users goals. The goal-structure allows designers as well as users to reason about how the changes in privacy features affect the users' goals. The achievement or violation of privacy is determined by evaluating the degree of satisfaction of the users' goals.

There is a software tool (OpenOME [11], implemented as an Eclipse plug-in) implementing the i* framework. The software provides a modeler with the ability to check the model in terms of the satisfaction of each agents goals as circumstances change. We leverage the tool in PGSM to demonstrate how the knowledge of the privacy experts can be encoded into the model as part of the system design process (design-time). We conducted qualitative evaluation of the PGSM model in terms of the model contribution to the comprehensibility of the privacy configuration task performed by PHR users when the application is utilized by the users (run-time). We interviewed privacy experts and we found that they see value in using the PGSM model in order to serve end-users needs. The evaluation results have been reported in [12].

1.2   Privacy Enforcement

When a personal workflow is executing, the configured user's privacy settings, needs to be enforced by multiple services. In other words, the precise constraints on resources or actions that a service provider commits to respect need to be determined over the course of a workflow execution. Classical privacy policy languages for policy enforcement (e.g. P3P[13], XACML[14]) are either suffer from insufficient expressive power, semantic incompatibility, or are too cumbersome to be used in a personal workflow [15]. The second model proposed in this paper addresses the problem of privacy settings enforcement when multiple participants are involved in a personal workflow. We propose the Smart Privacy Model (SPM) in which a modular and extensible ontology provides an unambiguous, interoperable and computer interpretable description of the privacy constraints over the data and processes in a personal workflow.

The Smart Privacy Model maps the output of PGSM to a process ontology that provides the underlying semantics for the enforcement of privacy constraints across multiple services. The PGSM model maps the semantics of the users' high-level privacy concerns and desires to a set of system-level privacy settings. However for substitutable services in a PHR platform to be able to consume these settings at run-time, the settings need to be expressed as sharable and reusable knowledge. In SPM the privacy constraints are expressed declaratively as parameterized first order axioms. We built the model by extending the Process Specification Language (PSL) ontology [16]. As a proof of concept, in this paper, we demonstrate by an example scenario that common privacy constructs (e.g. conditional access, obligations, and norms) can be expressed as constraints on run-time sequences of behaviour execution.

1.3   Research Contributions

The contributions of this research are threefold. First, we identify the gap between the PHR users' privacy goals and the system's privacy features and propose the PGSM model and methodology to fill this gap. Second, the model provides a novel solution for capturing the privacy knowledge of experts and sharing this knowledge. Third, by designing the logical privacy model we were able to translate users' goals and concerns to reusable and interoperable rules and constraints in the operational level of a personal workflow at run-time. This model contributes to the users' privacy management task by allowing privacy preferences to be expressed once and used by multiple services. Furthermore, from the systems' perspective, privacy constraints in the SPM are expressed using the same semantics constructs available to express all other general process constraints such as task ordering, task concurrency, and task decomposition. This approach allows the design for privacy to be embedded into the design of the application itself as proposed by the principles of *Privacy-by-Design* [17].

We expect with the support that the PGSM and SPM models provide for explicit representation of multiple actors, their goals and desires, and refinement of those goals in an operationalized level as enforceable constraints, would benefit privacy experts to explore and encode PHR privacy-sensitive usage scenarios. Results of the initial survey of privacy experts (Reported in [12]) has been promising, yet more comprehensive study on usability and usefulness of the model for privacy experts would benefit personalized privacy research community.

The remainder of this paper is organized as follows. In Section 2, we describe the architecture of the personal web privacy framework. A motivating scenario is introduced in Section 3. PGSM model and Smart Privacy models are described using the motivating scenario in Section 4 and 5, respectively. Related work is presented in Section 6. We conclude this paper and provide some future directions in Section 7.

2   Personal Web Privacy Architecture

Existing formal privacy policy languages (e.g. P3P [13], XACML[15], EPAL[15]) and privacy logical models (e.g. [18], [19]) are different in terms of their expressive power and scope. However, the key underlying assumption of these languages is that users' privacy goals and concerns are similar to the system privacy rules and constraints. Thus they can be expressed with the same level of abstraction. This is understandable in the classical web realm, where supports for privacy are mainly provided to protect websites and institutions from being liable in case of breaching the privacy laws and regulations rather than addressing users' privacy needs [20].

We identify two problems in the current privacy architecture of the personal web application (such as PHRs). First, as shown in Fig. 1, in the current architecture users are required to configure their privacy in the system context directly. Second, even at the system level, for every single service users need to interact with the different services repeatedly in order to define their privacy settings.

Users' privacy concerns are usually high-level, informal, and negotiable, while the privacy features offered by a system are detailed, strict, and binding. Systems usually do not offer enough support for ensuring that the choices selected by users will achieve the user's intents and desires. Thus, the first design goal of the personal web privacy architecture is to facilitate the users' privacy configuration task in terms of understanding the privacy features and the consequences of sharing personal information.

When the privacy settings for a given service are realized by a user, the user should not be required to reconfigure the privacy settings of her personal workflow if she decides to substitute a service with another service while nothing has changed in terms of her privacy preferences. Therefore, the second design goal of the personal web privacy architecture is eliminating the repeating task of privacy configuration by providing a run-time support for reusing the semantics of the user's privacy settings.

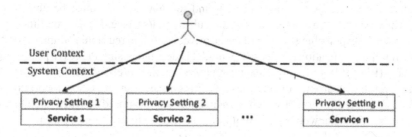

Fig. 1. Current Privacy architecture in PHR

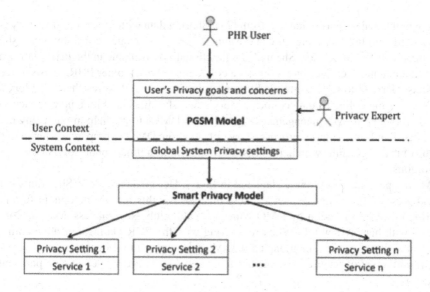

Fig. 2. Proposed privacy architecture for PHRs

In this paper we address these two problems by proposing two privacy models as shown in Fig. 2.

Privacy Goals and Settings Mediator Model (PGSM): PGSM employs i* [8] to model the environment and the goals of participants involved in a privacy sensitive interaction. The users perceptions of their privacy are expressed in terms of goal-models of multiple actors. PGSM links the privacy features offered by a service to the high-level users' goals allowing users to understand how changes in a privacy feature affect the users goals. These goal models encode the knowledge and recommendations of privacy experts as well.

Smart Privacy Model: The output of PGSM is a set of system-level privacy settings. These settings cannot be directly utilized by the personal workflow at run-time for the privacy enforcement purpose due to the lack of semantic interoperability. Multiple services are in a choreography in a personal workflow and each one may have its own privacy enforcement mechanism. Furthermore, in a personal workflow users may substitute a services every now and then and the new service must be able to enforce what the user had configured for the substituted service. Hence, the Smart Privacy Model is responsible to make the user privacy settings reusable and interoperable across multiple application services. The model is designed using Process Specification Language (PSL[16]). PSL allows capturing users' privacy preferences in terms of constraints over the occurrence of activities at run-time execution of personal workflows.

We now describe how two components of the proposed privacy architecture addresses the personal web privacy requirements using a motivating scenario.

3   Motivating Privacy Scenario

In a hypothetical scenario (adapted from [21], Sharing data with fitness coach), Mary is concerned with her blood pressure and wants to actively manage her health; hence she registers with a PHR service. She uses the functionalities available in the PHR platform to augment a new service (blood pressure collecting service) to her PHR. This service collects Mary's blood pressure at different point in time and stores them in Mary's PHR. After the collected data confirms Mary's fear she signs up with a new service in her PHR called disease management organization (DMO) to get help in managing her hypertension. In the sign-up process Mary opts to allow DMO to prepare a referral to a health club and consults with her fitness coach to arrange a fitness plan based on Mary's conditions.

Mary's personal workflow is depicted in Fig. 3. Her goals are clear. She wants her blood pressure to be managed in a timely manner. For this reason she opts in further sharing of her information by DMO with the health club. Nevertheless, Mary is concerned with her privacy too. When registering with the PHR platform or augmenting any of the three services mentioned above Mary is exposed to different privacy agreements and/or set of features that she has to agree or set in order to create her personal workflow.

As indicated in Fig. 3 by this icon (🐷), there are five interactions between these services and Mary's PHR data. What Mary agrees to defines how her PHR data will be used. While Mary is concerned about her privacy, she finds it very difficult to understand these agreements. She simply accepts them in order to achieve her workflow's goals. In other words, while Mary is concerned about her privacy and does not want her data being misused, she is also concerned if her privacy settings delay her from receiving timely treatment. From the users' perspective, these are clear expectations and concerns, although not as concrete as the features and constraints that offered by the services or described in agreements. Mary's expectations and goals are described in Table 1.

In contrast to the Mary's goals, from the PHR and services perspectives, the privacy is supported by a number of features. The user is responsible to pick features as she thinks are matching her needs. Table 2 describes a number of these privacy features. We limited the privacy features to only the ones offered by DMO. By the first feature Mary asks DMO to obtain her explicit consent whenever there is an interaction between DMO and the Health club. The other three features bind the access to PHR data by the Health club to some conditions or commitments. For example, access is limited only if Mary trusts DMO through her personal experience; if DMO is a covered entity under

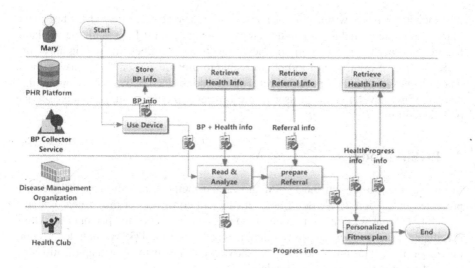

Fig. 3. Mary's personal workflow for blood pressure management

Table 1. User's goals and concerns

Title	Goals
Treatment	I want to receive treatment in an emergency case.
Timely Treatment	I am concerned if my privacy settings affect receiving treatment in a timely manner.
Privacy	I am concerned with my health data being misused.

Table 2. System privacy features

Title	Privacy Features
Explicit consent	I give explicit consent.
Personal experience	DMO is known to me.
Audit log	DMO agrees to log accesses for audit purposes.
HIPPA compliance	DMO is HIPPA compliant.

HIPAA legislation [22] (excluding access to the PHR from other jurisdictions); or if DMO agrees to log accesses for audit purpose.

By comparing the items in Table 1 and 2, we observe that Mary's concerns are high-level and casual while the system privacy features in Table 2 are strict and binding. Mary's concerns are expressed as goals, desires, and intentions. for example, Timely treatment, Privacy protection) and (Treatment). While the achievement of some of these goals (e.g. (Treatment) can be clearly judged, the achievement of the other goals cannot be judged based on a dichotomy of all-or-nothing.

The second observation is the gap between Mary's goals and the system privacy features. Mary can equivocally opt in or out the features described in Table 2. However, it is unclear for her how selecting or not selecting these features may affect her goals. Mary is not able to find answer to questions such as; "what if I opt in all the available features in order to maximize my privacy protection?" or "does this setting allow my PHR being used even when I'm not accessible to provide consent?" To answer these types of questions, we propose to bridge the gap described above with a model that maps the high-level goals of a user to the low-level privacy features of that service providers offer.

4 PGSM Model

In this section we present the PGSM model and methodology through the scenario presented in Section 2. We describe elements and constructs of the i* goal-oriented modeling [8] that we employ in order to address one aspect of the personal workflow specification (i.e. privacy and user preferences [3]). By using PGSM, we hide the complexity of privacy technical details from the users of the personal web applications by filling the gap with i* conceptual models.

i* provides a set of notations and constructs that can be used to model multiple actors' interactions in the intentional level. i* stands for distributed intentionality [8], referring to the premise that actors are social and they achieve their goals through the dependency relationships with the other autonomous actors. i* has been designed to be used by software engineers for requirements analysis, particularly in the early stages of system design, to capture the intentions and expectations of stakeholders of a system. The i* framework is also used in the design process in order to understand stakeholders' expectations with the features of the system to-be.

In this section, we use i* as a conceptual modelling technique to model the participants of a privacy sensitive interaction, their goals and dependencies. We first focus on the external dependencies of the participants. We then describe the internal decision-making rationale of each participant by constructing the goal models of each participant. Using the dependency model and the goal model together, we describe how goals of one participant can be externally attributed to the other participant's' goals. We describe all modeling steps through our example scenario.

4.1 Actors and the Network of Dependencies

In i*, the *actor* (◯) is an abstraction of an active entity that is capable of independent action. Actors can be humans, hardware and software, or combinations thereof. Actors are autonomous, social, and are attributed with motivations and intents [8]. As shown in Fig. 4, the PHR user, the PHR platform, the DMO, and the Health Club (as a secondary user) are some actors in our example scenario. A concrete actor is represented as an *Agent* (◯). Actors depend on each other to achieve *goals*, perform *tasks*, and furnish *resources* [8].

Goals are state of affairs that one or more actors of interest would like to achieve [8]. Goals (◯) are objectives for which there is a clear-cut criterion for their satisfaction. Manage my BP illness in Fig. 4 is a goal that the PHR user wants to achieve. However, the PHR user herself cannot achieve this goal. Therefore, she states it as an assertion that she wants DMO to make it true, without specifying how it is to be achieved. This has been expressed in the model as a directed goal-dependency relationship (——D——, the letter D shows the direction) from the PHR user to the DMO. Using the dependency links, we can create a network of directed dependency relationships among actors (cf. Fig. 4).

If what two actors depend on each other is stated as an activity (or a set of activities) which defines a specific course of action, it is called a *task dependency* (◠). For example, DMO depends on the PHR platform to provide Authentication service.

If the subject of dependency is an entity (e.g. information or material object) the dependency is called a resource dependency (▢). The depender wants the dependee to furnish the entity so that it can be consumed as a resource. In Fig. 4, Partial PHR data is a resource that DMO depends on the PHR platform in order to acquire and utilize the user's health data. This dependency expresses the notion of linking the user's profile to a third party service in the existing PHR platforms.

Softgoals (◠) define the quality of the goal or task need to be achieved or performed. A softgoal is a goal without a clear-cut criterion for its achievement. Softgoals are satisfied to a "good-enough" degree, depending on subjective judgment of the actor and relevant evidence. The PHR user depends on the DMO for the softgoal Timely Treatment.

The dependency network helps in exploring the vulnerabilities of a depender since in each dependency relationship the dependee may fail to fulfill a goal or a task, or furnish a resource. For example, DMO becomes vulnerable to achieving the Timely Treatment goal if the PHR user fails to fulfill the PHR data resource dependency. To see how these dependencies impact a participant's goal, we need to extend our model in order to capture the internal reasoning structure of each actor. In the rest of this paper, we concentrate on the most important aspect of the model which is the interaction between the PHR user (Mary), DMO, and the Health club. Since, we are not investigating the interaction of Mary and PHR platform, we consider these two actors as one actor, Mary in PHR user's role.

4.2   Participants' Internal Rationale

The i* framework offers a set of constructs, as described below, to capture the internal rationale of participants in an interaction. For every actor there is a boundary (the expanded area in Fig. 5) that defines the actor's attributed goals, tasks and resources and their internal relationships. From the PHR user's perspective, in any interaction where personal information is involved, two sets of goals can be identified.

Utility Goals. Utility goals are the reasons and values of an interaction. For example, managing blood pressure is the objective or the utility goal of the interaction between

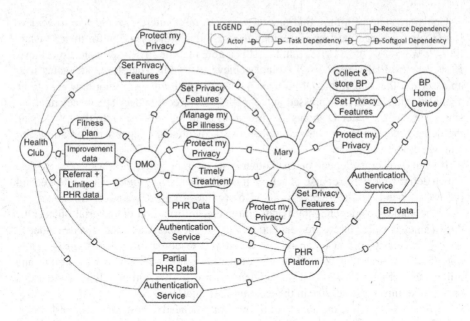

Fig. 4. Actors' dependency model

Mary and DMO. Without this goal the entire interaction would be meaningless. Thus, Mary wants to achieve this value out of the context of interaction with the DMO. In the PHR user's actor model (Fig. 5), we used the goal Manage BP Illness to model the utility goal.

Quality Goals. The second set consists of quality goals associated with the utility goals. In our example scenario, Mary wants her PHR data not being misused, and so, her privacy is protected. She is also concerned if her privacy setting affects the quality of her treatment. For example, if opting-in a feature causes an extra delay in managing her blood pressure illness by DMO. In the model shown in Fig. 5, we used the softgoals Privacy and Timeliness of Treatment to represent the PHR user's quality goals.

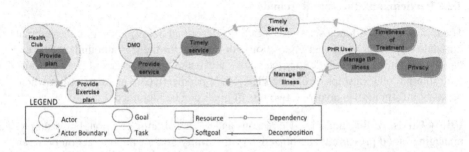

Fig. 5. Actors' internal goals

Back to the dependency network in Fig. 4 Mary depends on the DMO for both Manage BP Illness goal and Timely service softgoal. For the Privacy softgoal however not the external dependency, but the rationale behind the configuration of the privacy features, and the settings the user picks will determine the achievement of this goal.

Privacy Features. The privacy features, that are available to a PHR user, are modeled as tasks at the bottom of the actor's model. For example, the privacy features Explicit Consent or Audit Log each one may impose a specific commitment or obligation to DMO that needs to be compliant with, when access to the PHR is provided or the data is utilized by DMO.

The dependency links between the PHR user and the DMO (cf. Fig. 6) represent the offered privacy options. The semantic of each privacy option determines the direction of the dependency relationship. For example, if the PHR user opts in the Explicit Consent, then DMO depends on the PHR user to provide consent, and consequently further actions of the DMO will be impacted by this choice subject to the internal rationale of the DMO. In contrast, if the user opts in the Audit Log option with two other options (Known to me and Encrypt communication) the PHR user depends on the DMO (and the PHR platform which is not modeled here) to provide the required logs and adhere to specific communication obligations.

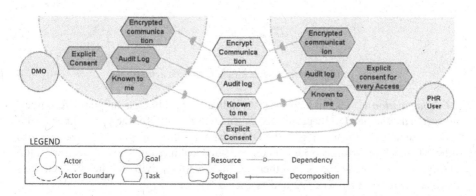

Fig. 6. Privacy features and their dependency directions

4.3 Actors' Goal Models

To see how the selection of each feature impacts the actors' goals, we need to extend our model to capture the internal reasoning structure of each actor. For this purpose, the i* offers three relationship types, *Means-ends*, *Decomposition*, and *Contribution* that combined with the intentional elements introduced before (*goal, softgoal, task, resource*) provides the required notations for a directed goal interdependency graph. Leaf level nodes of this graph are tasks. The roots can be tasks, goals, or softgoals. The graph provides vertical traceability from the high-level concerns to the low-level tasks [22]. In PGSM, the privacy features are modeled as the tasks in the goal-model. The goal-model describes each participant's behavior by relating the high-level goals to the low-level privacy features. We now describe the properties of the new relationships and the goal models.

Means-ends (→) relationship shows a particular way to achieve a goal. In our example (cf. Fig. 7), we used means-ends relationship to show that DMO as an actor in the model has different alternatives to access Mary's partial PHR data subject to what privacy features are being opted in by the PHR user. Since not all these alternatives necessarily have the same impact on the DMO's high-level goals, modeling these alternatives allows us to investigate the impact of each alternative.

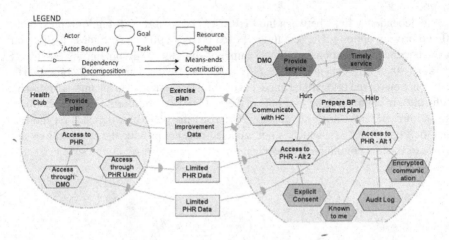

Fig. 7. Internal goal structure of each actor

Decomposition (⎯) links are used to indicate the subtasks, subgoals, resources, and softgoals that need to be performed or satisfied in order for the parent task to succeed. In the model shown in Fig. 7, the DMO cannot achieve its goal (BP treatment) without the task communicating with HC (the Health club). Thus, we defined a top activity as Provide Service and then decompose this activity to other sub-activities such as Communicate with HC and Prepare BP treatment plan. As this example shows investigating the internal rationale of an actor may unravel new tasks, goals, and actors. We also used the decomposition link to show which privacy features need to be opted in for either of the Access to PHR tasks to be performed. For example if a user opts in Explicit Consent privacy feature, this enables the access to PHR in a specific way (i.e. Access to PHR - Alt. 2).

Contribution (⎯⊷⎯) links connect tasks to softgoals or softgoals to other softgoals, indicating how the tasks contribute to achieving the actor's quality goals. Contribution can be positive or negative, with different strengths (*break, hurt, unknown, help, make*). In the model shown in Fig. 7, from the DMO's point of view not all alternative ways of accessing to the PHR data have the same impact on the Timely Service softgoal. If the access to the PHR data is bound to the Explicit Consent privacy feature, this type of access has negative contribution to the Timely Service (*hurt*). However, when access to the PHR data is bound to the Audit log and two other privacy features the impact is positive (*Help*).

Using the set of contributions, decompositions, and means-ends relationships, we were able to create the goal model for the DMO (cf. Fig. 8). With the same methodology, we construct the goal model for the PHR user based on the domain and privacy expert knowledge. In the model in Fig. 8, we combined these two goal models with the actors' dependency network- this allows the rationality of an actor being externally attributed so that the modeler can reason about impacts of other actors' behaviour [8].

4.4 Goal Model Analysis

Goal-models (cf. Fig. 8) support two types of graph-based reasoning, the forward [23] and the backward label propagation algorithms [24]. Therefore the PGSM model is capable of providing a reasoning guide for the PHR end-users to observe how changing a privacy feature may impact their privacy or utility goals.

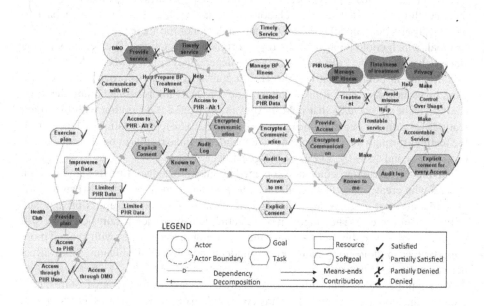

Fig. 8. Internal goal structure of each actor

Five types of qualitative i* labels satisfied ($\checkmark$), denied ($\nearrow$), partially satisfied ($\checkmark$), partially denied ($\nearrow$), unknown (?), and conflict ($\searrow$) are used for this purpose. When a source node receives a label, other nodes will be labeled based on the type of the relationships between the two nodes. The dependency, means-ends and decomposition relationship traverse the source label, however, the propagation of label through contribution links will be different based on the type and the strength of the link. We refer readers to [23] for more details.

In forward reasoning (bottom-up), the privacy options receive the assigned labels and then moving forward in the graph using contribution links, the degree of satisfaction or denial of the high level softgoal will be determined. The following scenario shows how the upward reasoning available in the goal graph can promote the comprehensibility of the privacy features and in turn helps the users to make a wiser decision about their privacy settings.

Assume the PHR user fulfils the resource dependency Provide access and also opts in the Explicit Consent privacy option (note that both tasks in Fig. 8 received satisfied ✓ label). Starting from this feature with respect to the type of the out-going contribution link to the upper softgoal and to the root softgoal (i.e. Privacy) which is *make*, the Privacy softgoal is satisfied. A closer look at the dependency link from the Explicit Consent privacy feature in the PHR user actor model to its counterpart feature in the DMO actor model reveals a more interesting impact on the Timeliness of Treatment softgoal of the PHR user. Through the dependency link and then decomposition link the satisfied label (✓) propagates to a type of access to PHR (Alt. 2) that hurts the Timely Service softgoal (✗) in DMO actor model. This is due to the fact that for DMO, for every interaction asking for Mary's consent and receiving PHR data through Mary makes the process stops until Mary becomes accessible. Propagating the label through the dependency relationship (Timely Service dependum), back to the PHR user's goal model unravels the partial denial of the Timely treatment (✗) softgoal, which could be against the user's original expectations. The denial is partial since if we check the Partial PHR Data dependency link between DMO and the Health club, in both alternatives, the Health club is still able to provide the exercise plan, however in one case it takes longer time for DMO to process it. Using the same analysis technique reveals that if Mary opts in the Audit Log option with two other features (Known to me and Encrypt communication), propagation of labels from the features through the contribution and dependency links results in partial satisfaction of Privacy and Timely service softgoals.

Having this reasoning guide accompanied by the knowledge of privacy and domain experts who create these models allow us to establish logical bridge between the privacy features that a user selects (Table 2) and the impacts on the user's privacy and utility goals (Table 1). The judgment on selecting which privacy features could be still subjective. However, the user now have the support of privacy expert with her and more importantly can judge how change in non-understandable technical features may affect her understandable goals.

We simplified the model with having only two alternatives for privacy features; nevertheless the model allows analyzing any combination of privacy features. Furthermore, the backward reasoning can help the PHR user to find the best privacy features available given her privacy and utility goals. In the next section we demonstrate how the selected features can be utilized by multiple actors in a personal workflow for the privacy enforcement purpose at run-time.

4.5   Evaluation and Generalization of the PGSM Model

We proposed the PGSM model, using the i* notations, in order to demonstrate and understand the alignments of the two privacy perspectives, i.e. users' privacy perspective and systems' privacy perspective. The example scenario, presented in this paper, is a proof of concept, aiming at demonstrating the feasibility of our work. To evaluate the methodology, we employed the method of expert interviews in the qualitative research [25]. The goals of the evaluation were to provide answers to three questions: (i) is the comprehensibility of privacy settings a valid problem? (ii) is the PGSM model useful for privacy experts? (iii) is the settings derived by the expert using the model be of the benefit of PHR end-users?

For this purpose, we prototyped PGSM model using OpenOME [11] , which is the i* modelling and analysis tool implemented as an Eclipse Plug-in. The tool is empowered with a reasoning engine that supports both the forward and backward reasoning. The engine prompts for the human judgment whenever a non-deterministic situation arises [26]. The prototype was then presented to the three privacy analysts who had more than 10 years' experience in designing privacy policies in the health care domain. The details of evaluation process is described in [12]. The results of the evaluation showed that experts found the PGSM model useful in terms of using the model to encode their privacy knowledge. The results also showed that from the privacy experts' point of view, the model would help the PHR end-users if used during the process of privacy configuration. The ease-of-use of the model received the lowest score, suggesting that special consideration of user interface improvements needs to be in place for the model to be used by experts. The comments made by the experts when answering the open-ended questions also confirm the usability concerns.

Our context of utilizing the i* social modelling is similar to the context of using i* for the early requirements analysis in the process of a system design, where the i* technique is used to align the stake holders' goals, desires and intentions with the features of a *to-be* information system. Due to this similarity, the path to the generalization of PGSM model will become easier, since the guidelines that have been designed over the years for utilizing i* for the requirements engineering (e.g. methodologies described in i* wiki [27] and in the other related literature such as [28] and [29]) can also be used for the design and analysis of PGSM models. Using the i* guidelines, we describe the major steps need to be taken to generate PGSM models for the other PHR usage scenarios described in the literature (e.g. [21]). For every step, we make a reference to the PGSM model designed for the motivating scenario described in Section 3.

1. Identify participants in a scenario and model them as i* actors (cf. Section 4.1).
2. Generate the actors' dependency model (cf. Section 4.1).
3. For each actor identify the internal rationale of being in the interaction by identifying the participant's utility and quality goals (cf. Section 4.2).
4. Use the dependency network generated in step 2 to identify form which internal goals the external dependency between actors are originated. Introduce new dependencies if it is required (cf. Section 4.2).
5. Model the privacy features as task dependency between the user and the systems (cf. Section 4.2).
6. Using the privacy experts' knowledge construct the internal goal structure of each actor (cf. Section 4.3).
7. Evaluate the PGSM model using forward or backward reasoning guide (cf. Section 4.4).

The second approach for generalization of the PGSM model is through application of privacy patterns and templates. Using patterns as an approach to facilitate i* modelling has already been studied [30]. The PGSM models designed for the generic PHR usage scenarios can be presented as privacy templates. In the design time of a system, these templates incorporate the privacy and domain experts' knowledge in terms of the norms applicable to a generic context (as we showed for an emergency context in our motivating scenario described in Section 3), the participants in a context and their roles, the canonical activities that occur in that context, and other concepts of the context as described by the concepts of privacy in contextual integrity [31]. When these privacy templates are used in the run-time by a PHR user, they can be personalized with two sets of user-defined parameters as described by Liaskos et. al in [32]: *values for the privacy features* and the *type and strength of contribution links* in the goal models.

When generalizing PGSM model, we are aware of the limitations we may be encountering due to the utilizing i* as the underlying modelling notation. Although, in this thesis our goal was not to test i* expressive power in terms of capturing the privacy requirements of an information system (as discussed in the related literature, e.g. [33], [34]), there are aspects of privacy requirements, such as ownership and custodianship of personal information, delegation of usage right, permission, and trust that could become important when bridging a user's privacy perspective with an information system's one. We discussed a number of these limitations in [35]. Further study is required to investigate if the extensions proposed in [36] and [37] for i* to capture security and privacy requirements are applicable to PGSM when it is used to express more complex privacy scenarios.

5   Smart Privacy Model

Our goal in designing the smart privacy model is to provide seamless integration of privacy constraints in the personal workflow processes. We explain how we achieve this goal through our motivating scenario. Assume Mary, with the help of PGSM model, picks the privacy features that best satisfy her goals. Then the problem would be how she can be confident that DMO and health club will respect what she has selected. For example if Mary picks Audit log as a feature, the workflow processes should guarantee that all the Health Club communications with DMO are being logged in Mary's PHR. Furthermore, if Mary substitutes DMO in her workflow with a more valuable service or DMO wants to send referral to multiple health clubs, the privacy settings should have not been required to be reexamined by Mary since her goals and preferences have not been changed. The Smart Privacy Model offers a solution for this problem by offering a logical model for privacy enforcement that is interoperable and reusable among multiple services.

In this section, we first describe the smart privacy ontology, its components, and how it has been built based on the foundational privacy theory of Contextual Integrity (CI) [31]. We introduce the theory of CI as constraints on activity occurrences of a process. Thus, we describe the smart privacy ontology as an extension to the general process specification theory. We also discuss the static ontology as the second component of the smart privacy ontology. Finally, the antecedents for the privacy reasoning problems are discussed. We use the same example scenario introduced in Section 3 to describe the smart privacy ontology.

5.1 Smart Privacy Ontology

The logical framework for smart privacy is an extensible ontology that has been built using the Process Specification Language (PSL) [16] ontology. In smart privacy, theories of PSL are extended to express required privacy constructs such as pre-access conditions, post-access obligations and other communication behaviors that a workflow needs to adhere in order to respect users' privacy. As shown in Fig. 9, two main components of the Smart Privacy model are the deontic ontology and the static ontology. The deontic ontology represents all privacy constraints by extending PSL theories. Since the extension is definitional, the deontic ontology inherits properties of the consistency and entailment of PSL theories. The static ontology, described in 5.4, characterizes classes of entities and their relationships used in the Smart Privacy Ontology.

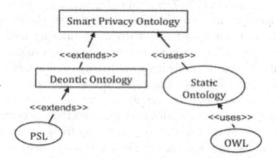

Fig. 9. Ontology-based Smart privacy

Our definition of privacy is based on the theory of Contextual Integrity (CI) [31]. CI provides a normative model and framework, for evaluating an individual's privacy when the information flows between actors [31]. The concept of *actor* in CI defines the participants in an information flow who play different roles and send and receive personal information. The concept of principal actor in CI represents the data subject. i.e. the participant whose personal information is at stake. *Attributes* in CI define the type of information. Two other key constructs of CI are, *contexts* and *norms*. Contexts are structured social settings characterized by the roles that actors play (e.g. Mary in a patient role), by certain values that a context offers (e.g. providing health care), the canonical *activities* and actions in which people in differnet *roles* perform. *Norms* prescribe and proscribe acceptable actions and practices in a particular context ([31], pp. 133-135). Based on CI theory certain patterns of flow of information in a particular context provoke the sense of privacy violation while others not [31]. The goal of the smart privacy ontology is to identify in any point in time which patterns are violating an individual's privacy and enforce the norms which are applicable to the context.

5.2 Deontic Ontology

The PSL ontology and our extended deontic ontology are a modular set of theories in the language of first order logic. In the PSL ontology, processes are described as a certain structure of multiple activities. However, this structure might admit of many instantiations which depending on how constrained the structure is might be considerably different from one another [8]. For example in the scenario in Fig. 1, DMO performs four activities, (i) Read BP data from PHR, (ii) analyze the data, (iii) prepare the referral, (iv) and communicate the referral with the Health club. If there were not any constraints, these activities could have occurred in any order. However, this is not the case since for the workflow to deliver the functionality the only acceptable instantiation of these four activities is occurrence of the activities in a specific order as mentioned above. Therefore the PSL ontology introduces the concepts of *activity tree* and *occurrence tree* to differentiate between a structure and its instantiations.

PSL-Core [16] introduces the basic constructs to reason about activities, activity occurrences, timepoints, and objects that participate in activities. Other core theories of PSL capture the intuition for how simpler activities form a new complex activity and occurrences of its subactivities [16]. The relationship between activity and activity occurrences is represented by the $occurrence\_of(o, a)$ relation. The $subactivity(a_1, a_2)$ relation captures the fact that a_1 is a subactivity of a_2 allowing complex activities to form. Consequently, $subactivity\_occurrence(o_1, o_2)$ (o_1 is a subactivity occurrence of o_2) represents the composition relation over activity occurrences. Complex activities are composed of sets of atomic activities which in turn are either primitive (i.e. they have no proper subactivities) or they are concurrent combinations of primitive activities. To capture ordering constraints over the subactivity occurrences, PSL uses the $min\_precedes(s_1, s_2, a)$ relation denoting that subactivity occurrence s_1 precedes the subactivity occurrence s_2 in occurrence of the complex activity a. The relation $root(s, a)$ denotes that the subactivity occurrence s is the root of an activity tree for a.

Occurrences of atomic activities form the occurrence tree whose branches are equivalent to all discrete sequences of occurrences of atomic activities in the domain [16]. Although occurrence trees characterize all sequences of activity occurrences, not all of these sequences will intuitively be physically possible within a given domain. Therefore the subtree of the occurrence tree that consists only of possible sequences of activity occurrences is referred to as the legal occurrence tree. The $legal(o)$ relation specifies that the atomic activity occurrence o is an element of the legal occurrence tree. The activity tree is a subtree of the legal occurrence tree characterizing the occurrences of complex activities.

In PSL, properties of the domain that change due to activity-occurrences are modeled as *fluents*. Therefore, if there is a fluent in our domain (if there is a property that changes) there must also be an activity that introduces that change. In other words, nothing changes unless there is an activity as a root cause for that change. The PSL ontology formalizes the notion of change for a domain properties in terms of occurrence of some activities. We extend this notion and show that we can use the PSL formalism to also reason about the compliance or violation of privacy in terms of changes in the properties of a *context* and its corresponding *norms* as articulated in the theory of CI [31].

5.3   Contextual Integrity as Constraints on Activity Occurrences

We formalize the concepts in CI using deontic ontology. Core to our model are activities and their occurrences. Activities are used to capture the static structure of a personal workflow. Participants (e.g. DMO and the Health club) communicate with each other by performing some activities (e.g. send PHR data). Associated with activities are the subject of privacy (i.e. Mary in our scenario) and resources (i.e. BP data in our scenario). The dynamic behaviour of a workflow is expressed by describing occurrences of activities. As activities occur and the world unfolds, elements of a context (canonical activities of a context, roles that actors play, purpose of the context) may or may not change. By precise representation of activity occurrences we are able to reason whether a context has changed or not.

The semantics of activity occurrences are also used to constrain the possible occurrences with respect to the norms of a context. The occurrence of an activity is legal (privacy is respected), if it does not violate the norms of the context that the activity belongs to. In other words, we relate the concepts of privacy compliance to the logical concept of satisfiability and entailment of legal occurrences of activities in PSL.

In addition to PSL theories, we need two sets of axioms to reason about privacy in the personal web, *context change* and *norm description*. The first set guarantees that any change in the contexts is associated with occurrences of some activities. The second set explicitly describes constraints over occurrences of such activities.

Context Change. As defined in CI, a *context* is a collective notion described by following properties: actors, roles of actors, purposes, canonical activities, and norms [31]. Expressing contexts in the Smart Privacy Model is equivalent to capturing all circumstances that may change the context properties listed above. Context's change, denoted as $\Sigma_{context}$, is a set of axioms that guarantees any change in a context's properties is associated with occurrences of some atomic activities and a context cannot change during an atomic activity occurrence. For example if over the course of the personal workflow execution, the Health club starts participating in an activity. According to CI, this is a change in the context, since the actor of the context has changed. Therefore, there should exist an occurrence of an activity associated with this incident. The following class of sentences formalizes the fact that when the participation of an actor in a context changes, there always exists the occurrence of an atomic activity:

$$participates\_in(x, o_1, t_1) \land \neg participates\_in(x, o_1, t_2) \land before(t_1, t_2) \implies$$
$$\exists t_3, t_4, o_2, o_3(sub\_occ(o_2, o_1) \land sub\_occ(o_3, o_1) \land participates\_in(x, o_2, t_3) \land$$
$$\neg participates\_in(x, o_3, t_4) \land next\_subocc(o_2, o_3, a))$$

In order to capture the changes in a context due to the changes in the *purpose* of a context or the *role* that an actor plays, we define two *fluents* named $for\_purpose(a, p)$ and $in\_role(g, r, a)$. The former represents the property that the purpose for the activity a is p. The latter represents that agent g is playing the role r in the activity a. In the PSL ontology, fluents are changed by the occurrence of activities, and a fluent can only be changed by the occurrence of some activities. The following axiom denotes that after occurrence o of an activity a the purpose cannot change from p_1 to p_2. The axioms capturing change for the actors' roles can be written similarly.

$$(\forall o, a, p_1, p_2)occurance\_of(o, a) \wedge prior(for\_purpose(a, p_1), o)$$
$$\wedge hold(for\_purpose(a, p_2), o) \implies$$
$$(p_1 = p_2)$$

Norms. The second class of axioms in our deontic ontology represents the transmission norms that govern the privacy constraints on information flow and denoted as Σ_{norms}. There are two main classes of context norms. Norms that prohibits actions to occur if certain conditions are not satisfied, which is also sometimes called *provisions* and norms that allow actions to occur only if the agent commits to perform a set of other actions in the future, which is also called obligations [38]. PSL offers a general formula that with incorporating different temporal literals can be used to map provisions and obligations. PSL uses the process description for atomic activity to constrain the legal occurrence tree with the following general form:

$$(\forall o)occurrence\_of(o, a) \wedge legal(o) \implies \varphi(o)$$

Where $\varphi(o)$ is a formula that specifies the constraints on the legal activity occurrence. In the process description this general form can be used to bind occurrence of an activity to the state that holds prior to the activity occurrence. It can be used also for other kinds of temporal preconditions that are independent to the state or when the norm implies necessity of occurrence of another activity. For example the known to me privacy feature in our motivating example expresses a precondition for access and can be represented as follows:

$$(\forall o_1)occurance\_of(o_1, PHR\_data\_access) \wedge legal(o_1) \implies$$
$$(\exists o_2)occurence\_of(o_2, previous\_encounter) \wedge (earlier(o_2, o_1) \wedge legal(o_2)$$

This axiom denotes that prior to occurrence of access to PHR data, previous encounter of Mary and DMO should have occurred.

The general form can also be used to capture obligations by incorporating the *begin_of* literal. For example, the privacy setting constraints audit log expresses an obligation for DMO and can be represented as the following deontic constraint. This axiom denotes that any occurrence of PHR data access activity requires occurrence of audit log activity sometimes in the future but prior to the occurrence of the access activity.

$$(\forall o_1)occurance\_of(o_1, PHR\_data\_access) \wedge legal(o_1) \implies$$
$$\exists(o2)occurance\_of(o_2, audit\_log) \wedge (begine\_of(o_2) > (begine\_of(o_1)) \wedge legal(o_2)$$

As these examples demonstrate, we use the same semantics for expressing the *context change* and its applicable *norms*. When privacy settings are transcoded as the constraints over the occurrences of particular activities, regardless of which service is responsible for the occurrence of an activity, the constraint implied by the set of axioms capturing the context change and its norms will be enforced, thus, supporting the interoperability of privacy settings across multiple services.

5.4 Static Ontology

The deontic ontology as described above works in the spirit of a static ontology. The static ontology, denoted by T_{static} in our model characterizes classes of entities used in the deontic ontology, their properties and their relationships. In PSL, resources that are required for an activity to occur can be specified as *objects*. For example, for the the the *send_data* activity to occur, two objects are required to exist at the same time prior to occurrence of this activity, a data sender as a participant and a data item as a resource. In the preceding subsection we used the concept of activity occurrence in PSL to capture the concepts of *context change* and *norms* in CI. We use the static ontology to map all classes of objects in CI that participate in the occurrence of activities. The top class in our static ontology is the PSL object class. We describe some of the subclasses of the object class below.

For a PSL activity to occur all characteristics of Participants of a context (actors in CI) need to be defined unambiguously. We have three classes of participants, DateReceiver (the one who receives the personal information), DataSender (the one who sends the personal information), and DataSubject (the one whose personal information is at stake). A DateReceiver or a DataSendercan be further specialized to UncoveredEntity (entities that do not consider themselves as covered organizations under the specify privacy Act) and CoverdEntity. Data items, purposes, roles are also subclass of PSL object. Roles are described by a lattice. The superclass role is used to describe all possible participants' roles. Other subclasses can be used for specialized roles such as patients, researchers, and physicians. The researcher role can be further specialized to academic researcher, and so on.

The static ontology contributes to the smart privacy model by providing support for interoperability and more effective use of knowledge about contexts and their information transmission norms. This static ontology will be formulated in description logic

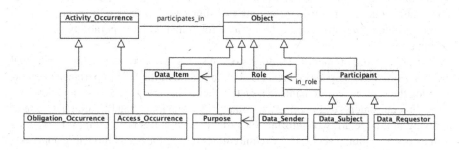

Fig. 10. Static ontology (partial)

(DL), supported by the web ontology language OWL DL [39]. Fig. 10 shows a partial representation of classes and properties in our static ontology.

5.5   Antecedents for the Reasoning Problems

We can now, relate the issues of compliance to the logical concepts of satisfiability and entailment. Entailment is key to understand whether a context complies with the information flow constraints associated with that context. Every reasoning problem in the smart privacy model has the following sets of sentences in the antecedent:

$$T_{psl} \cup T_{static} \cup \Sigma_{norms} \cup \Sigma_{context}$$

When these sets of sentences are consistent, the privacy constraints are complied with and enforced in the workflow. If this is inconsistent, then either a precondition is not satisfied or an obligation is violated. In the former case the activity has not occurred and the workflow is terminated, but in the latter the activity occurred and the query returns where and when a responsible agent failed to comply with the norms of the context.

6   Related Work

Privacy has been included in the PHR research agenda in recent years through a number of scientific surveys on privacy impacts of using PHR systems [40], [39]. The authors in [41] and [42] identified the privacy risks associated with PHR usage. They showed how privacy boundaries change when PHRs are used instead of classical medical records. Gellman et al. [41] and Wynia et al. [42] provided a set of recommendations including changes in the privacy legislations and educating PHR users in order to reduce PHRs privacy risks.

While the studies mentioned above discuss important aspects of privacy challenges in PHRs, their proposed solutions are limited to a set of recommendations. Therefore, there is a lack of tool to support users to manage their privacy in the personal web contexts in general and in PHR context in particular. In PHR systems, it is mainly a contractual agreement that guides to collection, use and disclosure of an individuals health information. In other words, in the PHR context, the freedom of individuals to have full access to their own health data, comes with the toll to take on the responsibility of self-managing their privacy when dealing with multiple services and applications. The goals of our research were providing tool support for privacy settings comprehensibility problem and proposing a framework for semantic interoperability of privacy settings.

The privacy requirements of information systems are analyzed, using conceptual models, from different perspectives. He et al. in [43] identified the importance of incorporating the privacy requirements in a system design in early stages of system development. In requirements engineering community, i* social modeling [8], after a decade of applying in a large array of information systems design, has been seen as a modeling framework to capture users privacy requirements. Using the social modeling approach, Liu et al. in [33] and Yu et al. in [34] modeled stakeholders of an information system as actors with different privacy goals along with other quality goals such as security, accessibility and usability. All these goals are modeled as soft-goals in the i* terminology. Then the authors analyzed, through a network of intentional dependency between actors, how achievement of these goals might be affected or how the privacy risks, threats, and vulnerabilities can be identified. Along this direction, the Secure Tropos [36], an agent-oriented security requirements engineering modeling technique, has been developed by extending i* social modeling to address privacy requirements by including notions of ownership, permission, and delegation [37].

In the body of research introduced above, conceptual modeling is mainly used to elicit privacy requirements that need to be satisfied in the system development level. In the direction of using conceptual modelling for end-users Liaskos et al. in [32] proposed using goal-models as the overlaying reasoning structure that can be utilized by end-users in order to manage the personalization capabilities of the common personal software systems. The methodology proposed in [32] has examined on a particular email-client software to show that, using goal models, the users high level goals and preferences can be translated to configurations that satisfy those goals. While this study considered using conceptual modeling at the user level, the exploited conceptualization approach is limited to the individual goal models thus preventing the reasoning about the effects of picking one or another feature on goals of other stakeholders (social modeling) in a privacy-sensitive process to be investigated.

Compared to the privacy policy language frameworks (e.g. P3P[13], XACML [14]) and their logical counterparts (e.g. LPU[18], Privacy API[19], our work on PGSM addresses different needs. These frameworks and the preference languages built upon P3P (e.g., APPEL[44], XPref [45]) are mainly designed to express the compliance of privacy rules and regulations by an institution or a website. Besides being cumbersome to be used by an end-user, these frameworks also suffer from semantic incompatibility with the user's perspective of privacy, such as the intrinsic flexibility in a user's privacy goals. Proposals such as S4P preference language [46] addresses the flexibility of the user's privacy preferences. However, it does not offer a solution for expressing the high-level user goals. In this sense our work complements the language offered in [46].The run-time model of our framework, the Smart Privacy ontology, compared to [14] is more expressive since it allows more complex obligations, such as users' obligation (as opposed to systems' obligations), repeating pre- and post-obligations as well as multiple responsible agents for an obligation [47] to be expressed. Our solution also uses less complex logical machinery (first order logic versus temporal logic) compared to [18]. The PSL ontology used in our ontology is highly expressive, while the PSL constructs also can be easily and systematically extended to capture more complex privacy processes.

The novelty of our research lies in alleviating the toll on the users by incorporating the knowledge of privacy experts in the decision process and reusing the privacy settings for enforcement purposes across multiple services, hence facilitating the substitution of PHR services without affecting the PHR users' privacy preferences. We also provide tool support, offering a systematic way in which a user can proactively understand the consequences of sharing as the configuration of the privacy settings change.

7 Conclusions and Future Work

This paper proposes a privacy model for the personal web applications from the user's perspective, instead of the system's perspective. We recognize that users of PHR systems are given privacy options at the system level without a clear connection to their own individual privacy goals. We identify this gap, and develop the PGSM model and methodology. PGSM provides users with a mapping between the high level user goals and low-level system privacy features.

The proposed a framework that addresses two important challenges of the personal web privacy, comprehensibility problem when privacy settings are configured by a user and interoperability of privacy settings when multiple participants are collaborating in a personal workflow. The proposed PGSM model supports the users' privacy configuration tasks, captures the experts' privacy knowledge in a particular PHR information-sharing context. Thus, the model allows the privacy knowledge to be encoded, transferred and reused. The reasoning guide that the PGSM model offers during the usage life-cycle of an application can help PHR users to make informed privacy decisions. In this sense, the model contributes to the comprehensibility of the privacy configuration task performed by the PHR users. The initial survey results presented in [12] suggest that the PGSM model is useful to privacy experts. Furthermore, the privacy experts see value if PGSM model is used by the PHR end-users.

The second model proposed in our framework, the smart privacy model, allows the privacy settings that finally has been selected by a user to be enforced by the participants in a personal workflow. The model supports interoperability and reusability of privacy settings among multiple services. This semantic interoperability allows a user substitutes one service with another in her personal workflow without requiring to express her privacy preferences repeatedly. In the future, we plan to generate privacy patterns based on the generic PHR usage scenarios using features of the PGSM and smart privacy models.

Acknowledgments. Special thanks go to Prof. Eric Yu, Prof. Michael Grüninger, and Office of the Information and Privacy Commissionaire (IPC Ontario) for their valuable help on modeling the privacy problem and evaluation of the PGSM model. Financial support from the Natural Sciences and Engineering Research Council of Canada, and from the IBM Canada Center of Advanced Studies on Collaborative Research (CAS) Privacy Award, are greatly acknowledged.

References

1. Chignell, M., Cordy, J., Ng, J., Yesha, Y. (eds.): The Smart Internet. LNCS, vol. 6400. Springer, Heidelberg (2010)
2. Mandl, K.D., Kohane, I.S.: No Small Change for the Health Information Economy. N. Engl. J. Med. 360(13), 1278–1281 (2009)
3. Chechik, M., Simmonds, J., Ben-David, S., Nejati, S., Sabetzadeh, M., Salay, R.: Modeling and analysis of personal web applications: A vision. In: Proc. of CASCON, vol. 10 (2010)
4. Eytan, T.: Coming to Social Media in Care Deliver Tech Demo Day: Lininkg Social Networks and PHRs (2011), http://www.tedeytan.com/2011/07/28/8708

5. Mandl, K., Simons, W., Crawford, W., Abbett, J.: Indivo: a personally controlled health record for health information exchange and communication. BMC Medical Informatics and Decision Making 7(1), 25 (2007)
6. Markle Foundation: Knowledge network: Survey on public opinions on the potential and privacy considerations of individually controlled electronic personal health records. Knowledge Network, Connection for Health (2008)
7. Pollach, I.: What's wrong with online privacy policies? Commun. ACM 50(9), 103–108 (2007)
8. Yu, E., Giorgini, P., Maiden, N., Mylopoulos, J.: Social Modeling for Requirements Engineering. MIT Press (2011)
9. Greenspan, S., Borgida, A., Mylopoulos, J.: A requirements modeling language and its logic. Information Systems 11(1), 9–23 (1986)
10. Nuseibeh, B., Easterbrook, S.: Requirements engineering: a roadmap. In: The Future of Software Engineering, pp. 35–46. ACM (2000)
11. OpenOME: An open-source Organization Modeling Environement (OME) (2010), https://se.cs.toronto.edu/trac/ome/wiki
12. Samavi, R., Consens, M.P., Topaloglou, T.: Privacy goals and settings mediator model for PHRs. In: SocialCom/PASSAT, pp. 1141–1146 (2011)
13. Cranor, L., Langheinrich, M., Marchiori, M., Reagle, J.: The platform for privacy preferences (P3P)1.0 specification. W3C Recommendation (2002), http://www.w3.org/TR/P3P/
14. OASIS: OASIS eXtensible Access Control Markup Language v2.0 (XACML) (February 2005)
15. Backes, M., Pfitzmann, B., Schunter, M.: A toolkit for managing enterprise privacy policies. In: Proc. ESORICS, pp. 162–180 (2003)
16. Gruninger, M.: Ontology of the process specification language. In: Handbook on Ontologies, pp. 575–592 (2004)
17. Cavoukian, A.: Privacy By Design, Take The Challeneg. Office of Information and Privacy Commissioner of Ontario (2009)
18. Barth, A., Datta, A., Mitchell, J.C., Nissenbaum, H.: Privacy and contextual integrity: Framework and applications. In: Proc. SP, pp. 184–198 (2006)
19. May, M.J., Gunter, C.A., Lee, I.: Privacy APIs: Access Control Techniques to Analyze and Verify Legal Privacy Policies. In: CSFW, pp. 85–97. IEEE Computer Society (2006)
20. Pollach, I.: Online privacy as a corporate social responsibility: an empirical study. Business Ethics: A European Review 20(1), 88–102 (2011)
21. HL7 International: Consent directive use cases. online by Community-Based Collaborative Care (2008), http://wiki.hl7.org/index.php?title= Consent_Directive_Use_Cases
22. Van Lamsweerde, A.: Goal-oriented requirements engineering: A guided tour. In: RE, pp. 249–262. IEEE (2001)
23. Giorgini, P., Mylopoulos, J., Nicchiarelli, E., Sebastiani, R.: Reasoning with goal models. In: Conceptual Modeling-ER 2002, pp. 167–181 (2003)
24. Sebastiani, R., Giorgini, P., Mylopoulos, J.: Simple and minimum-cost satisfiability for goal models. In: Persson, A., Stirna, J. (eds.) CAiSE 2004. LNCS, vol. 3084, pp. 20–35. Springer, Heidelberg (2004)
25. Kvale, S., Brinkmann, S.: Interviews: Learning the craft of qualitative research interviewing. Sage Publications (2008)
26. Horkoff, J., Yu, E.: Finding solutions in goal models: an interactive backward reasoning approach. In: Parsons, J., Saeki, M., Shoval, P., Woo, C., Wand, Y. (eds.) ER 2010. LNCS, vol. 6412, pp. 59–75. Springer, Heidelberg (2010)

27. Grau, G., Horkoff, J., Yu, E., Abdulhadi, S.: I star guide (2010),
    `http://istar.rwth-aachen.de/tiki-view_articles.php`
28. Horkoff, J.: Iterative, Interactive Analysis of Agent-goal Models for Early Requirements
    Engineering. PhD thesis, University of Toronto (2012)
29. Grau, G., Franch, X., Maiden, N.A.M.: Prim: An i*-based process reengineering method
    for information systems specification. Information & Software Technology 50(1-2), 76–100
    (2008)
30. Strohmaier, M., Horkoff, J., Yu, E., Aranda, J., Easterbrook, S.: Can patterns improve i* mod-
    eling? two exploratory studies. Requirements Engineering: Foundation for Software Quality,
    153–167 (2008)
31. Nissenbaum, H.: Privacy in Context: Technology, Policy, and the Integrity of Social Life.
    Stanford Law Books (2009)
32. Liaskos, S., Lapouchnian, A., Wang, Y., Yu, Y., Easterbrook, S.: Configuring common per-
    sonal software: a requirements-driven approach. In: RE, pp. 9–18. IEEE (2005)
33. Liu, L., Yu, E., Mylopoulos, J.: Security and privacy requirements analysis within a social
    setting. In: RE, pp. 151–161. IEEE (2003)
34. Yu, E., Cysneiros, L.: Designing for privacy in a multi-agent world. Trust, Reputation, and
    Security: Theories and Practice (2003) 259–269
35. Samavi, R., Topaloglou, T.: Designing privacy-aware personal health record systems. In:
    Song, I.-Y., et al (eds.) ER Workshops 2008. LNCS, vol. 5232, pp. 12–21. Springer, Heidel-
    berg (2008)
36. Mouratidis, H., Giorgini, P., Manson, G.: When security meets software engineering: a case
    of modelling secure information systems. Information Systems 30(8), 609–629 (2005)
37. Giorgini, P., Massacci, F., Mylopoulos, J., Zannone, N.: Modeling security requirements
    through ownership, permission and delegation. In: RE, pp. 167–176. IEEE (2005)
38. Hilty, M., Basin, D., Pretschner, A.: On obligations. In: di Vimercati, S.d.C., Syverson, P.,
    Gollmann, D. (eds.) ESORICS 2005. LNCS, vol. 3679, pp. 98–117. Springer, Heidelberg
    (2005)
39. Halamka, J., Mandl, K., Tang, P.: Early experiences with personal health records. Journal of
    the American Medical Informatics Association 15(1), 1–7 (2008)
40. Kaelber, D., Jha, A., Johnston, D., Middleton, B., Bates, D.: A research agenda for per-
    sonal health records (phrs). Journal of the American Medical Informatics Association 15(6),
    729–736 (2008)
41. Gellman, R.: Personal health records: Why many phrs threaten privacy. Technical report,
    World Privacy Forum (2008)
42. Wynia, M., Dunn, K.: Dreams and nightmares: practical and ethical issues for patients and
    physicians using personal health records. The Journal of Law, Medicine & Ethics 38(1),
    64–73 (2010)
43. He, Q., Antón, A., et al.: A framework for modeling privacy requirements in role engineering.
    In: Proc. of REFSQ, vol. 3, pp. 137–146 (2003)
44. Cranor, L., Langheinrich, M., Marchiori, M.: A P3P preference exchange language 1.0 (AP-
    PEL1.0). W3C Working Draft (2002)
45. Agrawal, R., Kiernan, J., Srikant, R., Xu, Y.: An xpath-based preference language for P3P.
    In: WWW, pp. 629–639 (2003)
46. Becker, M., Malkis, A., Bussard, L.: S4p: A generic language for specifying privacy pref-
    erences and policies. Technical report, Technical Report MSR-TR-2010-32, Microsoft Re-
    search (2010)
47. Ni, Q., Bertino, E., Lobo, J.: An obligation model bridging access control policies and privacy
    policies. In: Proc. SACMAT, pp. 133–142 (2008)

Intelligence for the Personal Web[*]

Marie Matheson[1], Patrick Martin[1], Jimmy Lo[2], Joanna Ng[2],
Daisy Tan[2], and Brian Thomson[2]

[1] School of Computing, Queen's University
Kingston, ON, Canada K7L 3N6
{martin,matheson}@cs.queensu.ca
[2] IBM Canada Toronto Laboratory
Markham, ON L6G 1C7
{jimmylo,jwng,tand,thomson}@ca.ibm.com

Abstract. The traditional paradigm for Web interactions, where the interactions are server-driven rather than user-driven, has limitations that are becoming increasingly apparent. The *Personal Web* proposes to provide intelligent services that support a more user-centric interaction paradigm in order to allow the user to more easily assemble and aggregate web elements to accomplish specific tasks.

In this paper we examine the role predictive analytics can play in intelligent services supporting decision-making tasks and describe the *Predictive Analytics in Smart Interactions Framework* (*PASIF*), which is a framework for incorporating predictive analytics into intelligent services. PASIF achieves effective levels of support in the dynamic real-time environment of the Personal Web by incorporating ensemble models and techniques to detect and adapt to concept drift in the data sources.

Keywords: Personal Web, predictive analytics, real-time analytics.

1   Introduction

The concept of the *Personal Web* turns the focus of the Web onto the user by proposing a people-centric integration of information, services and web content. The goal of the Personal Web is to allow the user to more easily assemble and aggregate web elements to accomplish specific tasks [1].

In order to achieve this vision web services need to support *smart interactions* by becoming more responsive to the needs of the specific user and situation, or in other words more intelligent. As an example, consider an e-commerce website where users can shop for clothing. Suppose that Alice shopped at this online store a few months ago, browsed the collections that were available then, and bought a few items she liked. She returns to browse the site again today, hoping to find a product she wants to buy. New items have been added, but Alice still needs to browse through many items

---

[*] This research is supported by the Centre for Advanced Studies, IBM Canada Ltd. and MITACS.

M. Chignell et al. (Eds.): The Personal Web, LNCS 7855, pp. 113–130, 2013.

she has already seen and dismissed the last time she visited the online store. Some of the clothes she looks at are not available in her size, and some cannot ship to her address. Further, Alice likes to keep to a budget and does not typically look at clothes beyond a certain price level. An intelligent shopping service would consider Alice's profile and past behavior and general sales trends in presenting products to Alice as she browses the store.

Consider a hospital emergency room as a second example. When patients first enter the hospital emergency room they are interviewed by a nurse who makes an initial assessment of their conditions and their priorities for further evaluation. An intelligent assessment support service would provide decision support for the nurse by analyzing the information provided by a patient along with the patient's medical history and demographics to provide recommendations concerning the assessment. The service would also analyze the current state of the emergency room relative to the patient in order to recommend a priority for further evaluation.

In both of these examples, the smart interactions with the web service are driven by the needs of the user and are intended to provide support for the user in accomplishing the task at hand. They follow the principle that the less a person needs to know about a task they need to accomplish the better. In other words, the more knowledge the system can provide about a task, the less the user needs to know in order to successfully accomplish it.

We observe that intelligent services intended for the Personal Web should therefore be following:

- *Context-aware* – the service should exploit data about the user and the current situation to provide personalized support.
- *Socially-aware* – the service should exploit available historical data that is relevant to the user and the task, for example demographics, existing relationships and transaction histories.
- *Real-time* – the service should provide the support when it is needed during the interaction.
- *Predictive* – the service should anticipate the user's needs and have the support ready.

In this paper we specifically focus using predictive analytics to provide intelligent services for decision-making tasks.

Predictive analytics are used to analyze large amounts of data with a large number of variables to predict or recommend future actions. They can use a variety of techniques including clustering, classification, decision trees, neural nets, regression modeling and hypothesis testing. Expanding from business intelligence, predictive analytics attempts to form predictions about some future behaviour using data that has been gathered and stored about previous interactions of the system or other data relating to it [2].

Intelligent services must also provide their support online while interacting with the user. Real-time data analytics, also known as real-time data integration and real-time intelligence, use data as it becomes available, along with other available data resources as they are needed, in order to form dynamic predictions and analysis on data as it is being collected [3]. By employing real-time analytics, information can be collected about a user and incorporated efficiently into the current predictive analytics system used by a web service.

Furthermore, effective real-time analytic systems must be able to adapt to changes in the underlying distribution of data as the system runs. This underlying change is known as *concept drift* [1]. For example, in e-commerce systems this might describe a shift in the products people are interested in buying. In an emergency room scenario, it could describe the recognition of a new epidemic or a change in the set of available treatments. Intelligent services that are intended for long-term use are prone to concept drift. Thus, effective prediction services need to adapt to these changes in distribution by incorporating concept drift detection techniques.

In this paper we consider the role predictive analytics can play in intelligent services supporting decision-making tasks and describe the *Predictive Analytics in Smart Interactions Framework* (*PASIF*), which is a framework for incorporating predictive analytics into these services. We adapt a data warehousing framework proposed for Customer Relations Management [4] to provide the foundation for the data-extraction, transformation and loading of data collected online into an efficient and organized mining database. Predictive models are then built offline using a subset of data from the mining database for training, and are used in conjunction with data collected about current interactions to provide real-time support. As the data is collected, concept drift detection techniques are used to determine if changes have occurred in the way users are interacting with the system. User feedback is used to determine which models and data types best represent the needs of users, using a weighted ensemble modeling technique.

The remainder of this paper is organized as follows. Section 2 surveys work on predictive analytics and real-time data analytics. Section 3 presents the PASIF framework for incorporating predictive analytics into intelligent services. It also describes the design and proof-of-concept implementation of the predictive service subsystem, which is the key component of the framework, and the specific techniques that are used to accomplish real-time interaction and adaptation to concept drift. Section 4 presents experimental results for the implementation, and discusses the performance of the framework and its feasibility for being deployed on real systems. Section 5 summarizes the paper and suggests directions for future work.

2   Background and Related Work

In this section we first provide brief overviews of key background areas for our work, namely predictive analytics, recommendation systems and real-time analytics. We then examine related work in the area of real-time analytic frameworks.

2.1   Predictive Analytics

Predictive analytics use data-mining techniques in order to make predictions about future events, and make recommendations based on these predictions. This should not be confused with business analytics. Similar to predictive analytics, business analytics use data mining techniques, but rather than modeling or predicting future behaviors, trends in past data are found and used to anticipate what might happen in the future [2]. The focus is on finding patterns and tendencies that have occurred in the past and linearly projecting them into the future. The trends are simply extended in order to make a prediction, with the assumption that the system will continue to behave exactly as it has in the past.

Predictive analytics perform many of the same tasks as business analytics, and are often built upon business analytic systems. It can be said that predictive analytics are prescriptive, rather than descriptive [4]. For example, if a model is able to predict errors based on a correlation of variables then it should be able to do an analysis and recommend a solution. Additionally, predictive analytics is able to not only deal with continuous changes, but discontinuous changes as well. Surveys of predictive analytic techniques are given elsewhere [5,6].

2.2   Recommendation Systems

A growing issue for computational systems is the problem of information overload [7]. This is when there is an overwhelming amount of data that is made available to users, making it difficult for them to identify and locate the particular information that is relevant to them. Recommendation systems provide a form of information filtering that removes extraneous data and presents to the user only the small subset of available information that is considered to be most applicable to the current user task.

Recommendation systems use a form of predictive analytics. By predicting what information is most valuable to a user, recommendation systems help decide which data to display and how to present it is a useful way. Recommendation or information filtering will be essential in many Personal Web services.

In order to make recommendations, the system can make use of available statistical data about the user and other users with similar preferences, their profile and demographic information, and the current context of the application environment in order to decide which data is most relevant to the specific user and situation.

Recommendation systems are particularly prominent in applications involving electronic commerce. Electronic commerce, or E-commerce, consists of the buying and selling of products or services over a computer network, most commonly, the Internet. Personalized recommendations are utilized in these applications to enhance responsiveness of customers and relationship marketing [8]. Principally, statistical and knowledge discovery techniques are used to make product recommendations in real-time customer interactions in online shopping environments [9].

Personalized recommendations system approaches can be classified as either content-based or preference-based [8]. In the content-based approach, techniques such as associative rule mining are applied to a customer's purchase history in order to offer product recommendations to them. In the preference-based approach, product recommendations are made based on other customers who have similar interests and historical data, using techniques such as collaborative filtering.

2.3   Real-Time Data Analytics

Real-time data analytics, also known as real-time data integration and real-time intelligence, use data as it is available, along with all other available resources as they are needed, in order to form dynamic predictions and analysis on data [10]. By using real-time analytics, information is kept current in order to form better models of the system, and quick decisions can be made.

For example, the current interactions of an e-commerce customer, such as what they are looking at and the way they are browsing, can be used in real-time to make decisions about what information should be shown to them. Further, the data collected about this interaction can be incorporated quickly into the larger scale models of the site's prediction systems. Real-time data analytics should also be able to adapt quickly to changes in the data.

``Real-time" refers to systems in which the computer responds fast enough so that the user believes it is either immediate, or nearly so. It might also mean that the system reacts in some acceptable amount of time, where this amount of time depends on the specific application. Consider, for example, the work of Zhang et al [10] on streaming data analytics for health-care scenarios. The framework is intended to be used to help users to monitor and query trends in physiological signals data, with real-time detection and response to adverse trends.

Concept drift in data-streams occurs when the underlying trends in the data change over time [3]. Two types of concept changes might be detected in a data set. A sudden short-term change is called a stream burst. Stream bursts are of interest in many applications such as automated stock trading algorithms. A long-term change in the underlying distribution of the process generating the data is called a distribution change. This might prompt a change in the way the system works or how we model the data.

There are two common approaches to concept drift detection [11]. The first is the sliding window method. The system uses two windows of data: one that represents the current data trends, and a second which represents the most recent underlying distribution. A concept drift is indicated if the conceptual difference between the two windows is greater than some threshold. When such a drift is detected, the reference window is reset to the current one. In the second approach, the system uses the reference data distribution to predict what the distribution of incoming data should be, and uses the difference between the projected and actual distributions as the prediction error.

In both methods, the window size determines what type of concept change is detected. Small windows detect stream bursts, but may not detect slow distribution changes. A larger window detects the distribution changes, but may overlook stream bursts. Our framework described here makes use of these concept drift detection techniques in order to adapt to changes in user behaviour.

2.4   Real-Time Analytic Frameworks

In this section, we examine frameworks that address real-time data mining in web-service environments and that share a similar goal with the predictive analytic framework proposed in this paper.

Bigus et al [4] present a *CRM Analytics Framework* that provides an end-to-end solution for developing and deploying pre-packaged predictive modeling business solutions, recognizing the fact that useful data may be spread out across multiple data sources. The framework consists of a system that integrates the data based on meta-data, and allows data mining analysis to be executed without manual tuning while utilizing multiple data mining resources. This is done by assessing the relevance of available data for the problem at hand, identifying a set of data fields for use in the mining schema and building ETL scripts for transforming the data to the mining schema.

It is often the case that a data mining engine is specialized with one or more specific purposes in mind, and is strong at one type of task but inadequate at another. By creating a standardized data warehouse, Bigus et al create a framework that allows communication with multiple data mining engines, and therefore benefits from each engine's expertise.

In this paper we propose an end-to-end predictive analytic framework (PASIF) for extracting and aggregating data from heterogeneous sources that is similar to the CRM framework. We alter the data mining subsystem in order to provide real-time responses to user interactions, concept drift detection and adaptive modeling in order to fit the intelligent service paradigm.

The *5-Essentials (5E) Framework* proposed by Wong et al [12] is suggested to perform real-time data mining tasks over the Internet. This framework focuses on integrating the following ``essential'' properties:

- Object-based parallelism.
- Selection of a suitable inter-object interaction pattern.
- Reduction of communication overhead by applying a correct programming model (sequential, logically non-distributed, and logically distributed).
- Mobility of program objects.
- Determination of hardware architecture (physically distributed or non-distributed) best suited for timeliness.

The 5E project focuses on two main objectives. The first is to find the correct pattern for inter-object communications among collaborating mobile data-mining objects. The second, since many parallelization methods exist, is to identify those methods that work best for both passive and active object-based mining. The primary goal of the framework is distributed data-mining over the Internet.

Similar to the 5E framework, we are looking to create a framework which performs real-time data-mining. Many tools exist for data-mining with efficient, reliable and well-studied algorithms. We choose to make use of these mining engines and attempt to fit them into a real-time system, rather than the less-studied distributed algorithms. Thus, while the 5E framework shares a common goal as the PASIF framework, the approaches used are not useful for our system.

Deng et al [13] propose a framework based on environmental modeling. The goals of their framework are similar to our own, namely to enable real-time modeling, support real-time data collection, support continuous feedback and detect concept drift. They break modeling into two levels: global and local. The local environment is used for modeling centralized environment elements and the global environment is used to support distributed data mining. We use similar approaches to the local environmental modeling of Deng et al, such as the sliding window approach for concept drift detection, periodic and aperiodic dynamic data mining, and redundant synchronous model selection and updating.

3   The PASIF Framework

Predictive Analytics in Smart Interactions Framework (PASIF) is intended to provide real-time predictive analytics for intelligent services that support decision-making tasks in the Personal Web. PASIF's key components, as shown in Figure 1, are a data warehouse service to collect and integrate data from heterogeneous data sources relevant to the decision-making task and a prediction service to build and maintain predictive models to support the decision-making task.

3.1   Overview

The steps involved in using PASIF, which are illustrated in Figure 1, are the following:

1. **Define data warehouse schema.** The heterogeneous data sources which are relevant to the decision-making task are selected and from each source, the attributes that may be useful in building prediction models are identified. An appropriate database schema is defined to store the necessary data.
2. **Develop data warehouse Extract-Transform-Load (ETL) routines.** Relevant data from the data sources are retrieved, transformed and loaded into the data warehouse. These routines can be run periodically to keep the warehouse relatively consistent with data sources.
3. **Define mining database schema.** One or more predictive modeling approaches can be tied to each table in the data warehouse. An appropriate mining schema contains both extracted and predicted attributes, so reporting can be performed on the results of the prediction models. The mining database differs from the data warehouse in the way that it organizes the data. It is made with the intention of having information pre-arranged in a manner that is easy to access for a given model.

4. **Design mining database ETL routines.** Relevant data is retrieved from the data warehouse, transformed and loaded into the mining database. Similar to the data warehouse ETL routines, these can be run periodically for data consistency.

5. **Build prediction models.** One or more prediction models are developed from the data in the mining database in order to form the support required by the system interaction. For a given task, input data is collected and fed into the models to produce output that helps in decision-making.

6. **Validate and update prediction models.** A closed loop analysis is performed to validate the predictive models by measuring the success of the output they produce. If the degree of success is not sufficient, then the models are updated.

3.2   Support for Real-Time Predictive Analytics

PASIF's main objective is to provide support for real-time predictive analytics within intelligent services. Classical data mining is designed to address offline data analytics. While the currently available techniques are reliable and produce accurate analysis of data sets, they typically do not support all the requirements for real-time analytics, such as meeting specific time constraints or adapting to continuous non-stationary data [13]. PASIF provides an adaptive framework for classical data mining techniques so that the requirements of real-time analytics are met while still benefitting from the reliability of the algorithms and existing data mining engines. It employs a number of techniques to ensure the necessary adaptability.

Mining Database

The data used by the predictive models is extracted from the data warehouse and stored in a mining database. The mining database is organized into tables that are relevant to specific predictive models and data types, so building and updating predictive models is fast and simple.

As new data arrives and is added to the system, the prediction service analyses trends in the data to determine if any data records have become outdated. Such data records can be removed from the mining database in order to make room for new data, and to keep models current.

Prediction Service

As new information about the user is gathered, it is immediately processed by the prediction service. Prediction models are built offline using information stored in the mining database and, once built, they are deployed to be used online. The prediction service parses the important information from data collected during an online interaction and inputs this data into the prediction models in order to obtain predictions and decisions relevant to the specific user. The prediction service makes decisions and returns almost immediate responses in order to provide real-time interactions with the user.

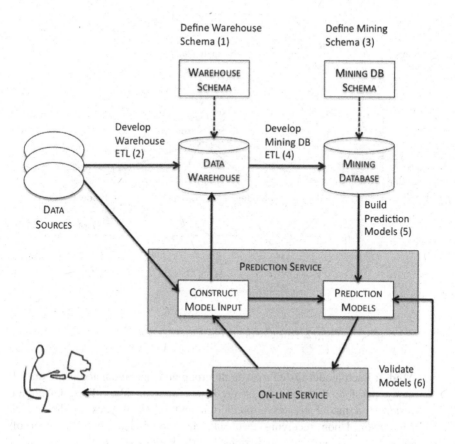

Fig. 1. PASIF Structure

Based on feedback from the user or online service, the model's response is validated. Here, a model might be determined to be outdated, or it may be determined that concept drift has occurred. In this case the predictive service adapts by rebuilding or altering the models, or a subset of them, in the background in order to produce better predictions in the future.

The structure of the Prediction Service is shown in Figure 2. Details of its design and implementation are available elsewhere [6]. The components of the service are the following:

- **Instance:** An instance is a set of attributes describing a specific interaction. For example, in an e-commerce scenario, an instance might describe a specific customer visiting the website, and the set of items they have in their shopping cart.

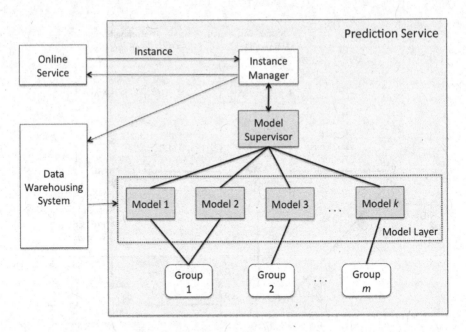

Fig. 2. Structure of the Prediction Service

- **Model:** Each model is tied to a single group and can be created using one of many possible data mining or predictive analytic algorithms. Given an instance, a model creates a prediction and relays it back to the model supervisor. Upon receiving feedback, the model can alter the level of influence it has on future predictions, by adjusting its weight.
- **Model Supervisor:** The model supervisor deploys models and builds new models when concept drift is detected. The model supervisor combines the individual model predictions, as well as relaying feedback to the models. It also controls the deletion of models if either a model is determined to be too poorly fitted to the data, or if inferior models need to be removed in order to make room for new models that might fit better.
- **Instance Manager:** The instance manager handles all instances that have been collected by the system. When a new model is initialized, the model supervisor sends a request to this manager for a specific set of instances from which the model will be built. In the full end-to-end system, the instance manager communicates with the mining database.
- **Group:** A group is a family of models of the same type. Possible groups for the e-commerce example might include models built using customer, transactional, or interactive and click-stream data.

Models are built offline and then made available in the online service. All models are created in the background, using classical data-mining strategies, rather than using streaming or evolutionary data mining strategies, which update models rather than rebuilding them. With this approach, we are able to frequently prune data which saves disk space and keeps models current.

We use Weka [14,15], an open source implementation of common machine learning algorithms, in our prototype implementation of the prediction service. For our testing purposes, we create models of the following Weka model types: bayes network, averaged one-dependence estimator (AODE), k-nearest neighbours, and multi-channel classification. Given a set of unlabelled attributes, a Weka model can produce a label or prediction for that record. For example, given a set of demographic data about a customer who is not yet associated with group of similar customers, the Weka models can assign that customer to a group.

We use a weighted ensemble-based modeling method [3,6] that builds multiple models and produces a decision by combining their predictions. The models can be built using different data sets and different methods. To produce the combined result each model is given a weight that is updated based on the model's performance, in order to give better performing models more influence.

Ensemble-based modeling also provides a good platform for asynchronous model updates. When a new model is added, it is included in the model set with a weight initially set to the average of all current weights in the system. A simple weight adjustment routine is executed which redistributes the weights such that their sum is one. When a model is deleted, it is removed from the set, and the remaining weights are adjusted.

We collect feedback on the performance of the models to determine when it is necessary to rebuild them either because of concept drift in the source data for the model or simply because a sufficient amount of new data has been received and it should be reflected in the models. A sliding window approach is used to detect concept drift but rather than looking for drift in the distributions of the source data we look for drift in the performance of models and groups of models.

We use the performance of the model as a drift detection parameter rather than the distributions in the source data for two reasons. First, the calculation to detect drift is efficient when using model performance. Second, the prediction service can build models for multiple data sources and using performance as the drift detection parameter can be used for any data source without needing to know what attributes are available and their expected distributions.

Concept drift in the data used by a model detected if the difference in the average number of successful results for the model in the current and reference windows exceeds a predefined threshold. If the performance of a model begins degrading, then it indicates that a change has occurred in the underlying system, and new models should be built using data that reflects the new distribution.

Considering an example intelligent service such as a personalized shopping site, the Prediction Service would operate as follows. When a user enters the site or performs an operation, a new *instance*, that is a new set of data attributes, is sent to the Instance Manager. The data is relayed to the data warehousing system, which uses extract-transform-load routines to retain the important information, and update the mining database.

Simultaneously, the Instance Manager parses the instance and creates Weka objects that can be input to models of the available groups in order to create a prediction. For example, given a set of items in a customer's shopping cart, the input object for an item set modeler might be a list of integers representing the number of each possible item in the shopping cart along with their quantity. A second input object could be a set of demographic attributes derived from the user ID using the mining database.

The input objects are sent to the Model Supervisor, which then relays the appropriate object to each model in the set of active models and waits for a response. Each model creates a prediction for the data it has received and responds to the Model Supervisor with its independent decision. The Model Supervisor aggregates the model predictions and responds to the online service with a final prediction of how to best react to the user. In the shopping site scenario this could be a product recommendation for the user, or layout changes to the website to make browsing more personalized to the user's tendencies.

Feedback can be returned to the Model Supervisor during an interaction with a user. The Model Supervisor can then adapt the models, if needed, according to the feedback. For example, in the shopping site scenario, a customer may be presented with a product determined to be a good match for them by the system. If the user looks further into this product, the system will receive positive feedback, or if the customer ignores the suggestion, the system receives negative feedback.

When positive feedback is received, the Model Supervisor analyzes which models contributed to the successful interaction, and rewards them by increasing their weight. Those models that did not contribute, or negatively influenced the decision, are penalized with a decrease in weight. After the model weights have been adjusted, they are scaled in order to again have all model weights sum to one. When the Model Supervisor receives negative feedback it penalizes those models that contributed to the failed interaction. When a model's weight decreases past a lower threshold, it is deleted from the model set. New models are created to replace deleted or out-of-date models either periodically when enough new data has been accumulated or when concept drift is detected. Further details of how the Prediction Service adapts are given by Matheson [6].

4   Empirical Study of Prediction Service

We now present an empirical study of a proof-of-concept implementation of the Prediction Service component of PASIF. The goal of the study is to examine the performance of the component, which is measured in terms of the percentage of instances of a dataset that are correctly labeled by our prediction models. We compare the performance of several versions of the Prediction Service component in order to evaluate the impact of ensemble and adaptive modeling on the performance.

4.1   Test Data Set

We were not able to obtain suitable test data sets for an e-commerce scenario like the one used in this paper for our study of the performance of the Prediction Service so we instead use the Agaricus-Lepiota (Mushroom) data set from the UCI Machine Learning repository [16]. This data set includes descriptions of hypothetical samples corresponding to 23 species of gilled mushrooms in the Agaricus and Lepiota Family. Each species is identified as edible, poisonous, or of unknown edibility. The latter class was combined with the poisonous one. It is known that no simple rules exist for determining the edibility of a given mushroom. The data consists of 22 categorical attributes, 8124 instances, and contains missing values.

The Agaricus-Lepiota data set provides a reasonable substitute for e-commerce data in our experiments. It contains a relatively large number of categorical attributes and has missing values, which would be the case for say customer profile and transaction data sets. It also allows us to conduct experiments to evaluate the three key aspects of the Prediction Service, namely multiple data sources, adapting to changes in the data streams and the ability use incoming data to produce real-time adaptations of the prediction models. Multiple data sets are simulated by breaking the attributes of the data set into three subsets, and treating them as distinct data sources, and thus model groups. Changes in the data streams, that is concept drift, are simulated by reversing the labels of part of the data set.

4.2   Experimental Design

In our experiments we consider the following four cases:

- **Base Case:** The base case involves a single set of the three predictive models, with no drift detection. The models use only one data set for each model group, weighted equally, consisting of all data collected so far in the system at any given point. Models are rebuilt at constant intervals of 400 instances, which was determined through experimental runs to provide low overhead, while providing noticeable improvement in forming accurate predictions.
- **Online Adaptive Models:** The adaptive modeling case keeps a single model for each model group and the models are equally weighted. A model is rebuilt, at minimum, every 400 instances, or sooner if concept drift is detected. A sliding window of size 20 is used, with a constant distance reference window kept at a distance of 200. We choose the window size of 20 because it is large enough to hide outlying or atypical results, such as instances that are significantly more difficult to classify than others, while keeping the window small enough that it does not smooth over drifted areas or create a significant detection lag.
- **Ensemble Models:** Ensemble model testing is done using an upper bound of 20 models in the system, and no concept drift detection. Consistent with the experiments for the base case, models are rebuilt once for every 400 instances introduced to the database.

- **Online Adaptive and Ensemble Models:** The modeling approaches used in the second and third test cases are combined. An upper bound of 20 models is used. Data models are rebuilt and replaced at least once for every 400 added instances, as well as when concept drift is detected, using a sliding window of size 20, and a constant reference window distance of 200.

In all experiments we start with an initial data set of the first 800 data points to build the three initial models (one for each data group), and use the remaining 7324 data points to simulate data that is collected online. These numbers are based on experimental runs used to determine how many data points are needed to build a reasonable model, while leaving as much testing data as possible.

Each result is the average of five runs. For each of the runs, the data has been pre-shuffled at random to produce a unique arrangement. The set of runs are identical for the four cases. For the concept drift scenario, the first 4000 instances are identical to those of the non-drifted data set. The remaining 4125 instances have opposite labels, to simulate a complete conceptual change in the underlying data.

4.3   Results

We examine the performance of each case for the two scenarios in which the source data sets have consistent data distributions and have concept drift. We are interested in the relative accuracy of the modeling approaches, which we define as the percentage of correctly labeled instances, their ability to handle concept drift and their suitability for a real-time analytics requirement.

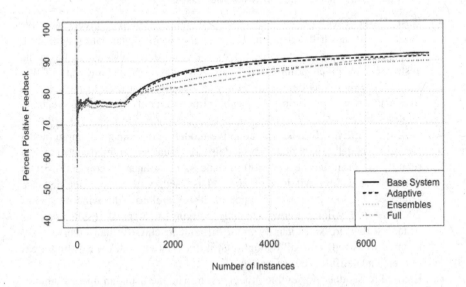

Fig. 3. Accuracy for data without concept drift

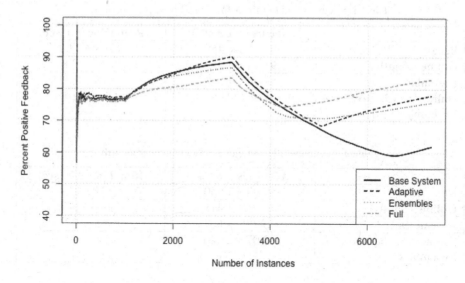

Fig. 4. Accuracy for data with concept drift

For the Base Case, as shown in Figure 3, the accuracy of the system continues to improve as more data is collected when there is no concept drift. However, Figure 4 shows that, when concept drift is introduced, accuracy begins to decline and the system is unable to recover until the amount of data supporting the new underlying distribution outnumbers that which supports the initial distribution.

The Online Adaptive Models, as shown in Figure 3, perform comparably to the Base Case when there is no concept drift. Since no drift is detected, the adaptive method, like the base case, uses the full data set to create predictive models. Minimal overhead is added by checking for drift, since no rebuild is triggered. Figure 4 illustrates that when concept drift does take place, the Online Adaptive Models, which only use data since drift has occurred, are more accurate than the Base Case and Ensemble Models.

In Figure 3, the Ensemble Models lose some accuracy due to incorporating some models built without the complete set of all data collected. However, in Figure 4, the Ensemble Models quickly adapt to changes in distribution by granting more weight to models with better performance. Since models which use more data from the new distribution have significantly better performance, they quickly rise in weight. However, without concept drift detection the data set selection is not optimized, and the Adaptive Models eventually outperform it.

In Figure 3, the combined Adaptive and Ensemble Models perform comparable to the other cases. Some loss of accuracy occurs for similar reasons as seen in the Ensemble Models. However, as more instances are collected, the prediction service converges to the better models and has an overall performance comparable to the other cases. In Figure 4, this modeling approach benefits from the quick reaction speed of ensemble models, as well as the overall performance of the adaptive model, producing results with significantly improved accuracy.

Table 1. Accuracy and run-times for data without concept drift

	Accuracy ± σ (%)	Run-Time ± σ (sec)
Base	92.36 ± 1.455	8.265 ± 1.04
Online Adaptive	91.45 ± 1.389	10.157 ± 0.84
Ensembles	89.90 ± 1.400	9.776 ± 0.82
Online Adaptive + Ensembles	91.96 ± 2.057	11.574 ± 1.18

Table 2. Accuracy and run-times for data with concept drift

	Accuracy ± σ (%)	Run-Time ± σ (sec)
Base	61.99 ± 1.550	8.331 ± 0.94
Online Adaptive	78.06 ± 1.416	12.060 ± 1.09
Ensembles	75.75 ± 1.608	9.965 ± 1.21
Online Adaptive + Ensembles	83.07 ± 2.220	13.115 ± 1.12

Tables 1 and 2 summarize the accuracy and total average run-times for each experimental case for data without concept drift and with concept drift, respectively. The Base Case and the Ensemble Models behave the same regardless of whether or not concept drift exists so their times do not differ significantly in the two scenarios. The Adaptive Models have additional overhead to check for concept drift and to rebuild models. The Ensemble Models have additional overhead associated with rebuilding and making use of a larger number of models. The combined Adaptive and Ensemble Models incur the overhead associated with both methods.

We see in Figures 3 and 4, however, that the combined Adaptive and Ensemble Models perform, on drifted data, an average of 21.08% better than the Base Case, 5.01% better than the Adaptive Models alone, and 7.31% better than Ensemble Models alone. The combined modeling approach requires almost 60% more execution time for the whole test workload than the basic unsophisticated system but amortized over more than 8,000 instances the additional delay per interaction is not significant. Therefore the combined Adaptive and Ensemble Models produce results with significant improvement in accuracy while still interacting with the user in real-time.

5   Summary

The traditional paradigm for Web interactions, where the interactions are server-driven rather than user-driven, has limitations that are becoming increasingly apparent. The *Personal Web* proposes to provide a more user-centric interaction paradigm in order allow the user to more easily assemble and aggregate web elements to accomplish specific tasks. In order to progress towards this paradigm of smart interactions we need to develop intelligent services that are context-aware, socially-aware, react in real-time and are able to predict the user's needs.

In this paper we examine the role predictive analytics can play in intelligent services supporting decision-making tasks and describe the *Predictive Analytics in Smart Interactions Framework* (*PASIF*), which is a framework for incorporating predictive analytics into intelligent services. PASIF achieves effective levels of support in the dynamic real-time environment of the Personal Web by incorporating ensemble models and techniques to detect and adapt to concept drift in the data sources.

PASIF helps to satisfy the above requirements for intelligent services as follows:

- PASIF supports context-awareness in that a predictive model used by PASIF can be built from context information such as shopping cart contents or click-stream data.
- PASIF supports social-awareness in that a predictive model used by PASIF can be built from information such as demographics, existing relationships and transaction histories.
- PASIF provides decision-making results in real-time. We show experimental results to verify that PASIF can improve the accuracy of predictions without adding significantly to the delay experienced by the user.
- PASIF supports the creation and maintenance of predictive models that attempt to anticipate the user's needs.

Directions for future work on this topic include the following. First, we plan to improve the run-time performance of the prediction service by using threads to allow for concurrent model building, rather than the sequential system currently implemented. Second, we plan to implement and analyze a proof-of-concept prototype of a complete PASIF and examine issues that may arise in the connection between the prediction service and the data warehousing portions of the framework. Third, we want to study how to provide increased user control such as a method for users to select a desired outcome of the analysis and a way for users to provide input in terms of the type of model to be used.

References

1. Ng, J.: The Personal Web: Smart Internet for Me. In: Proceedings of First Symposium on the Personal Web (2010)
2. Agosta, L.: The Future of Data Mining – Predictive Analytics. DM Review (2004)
3. Abdulsalam, H., Skillicorn, D., Martin, P.: Classification Using Streaming Random Forests. IEEE Transactions on Knowledge and Data Engineering 23(1), 22–36 (2011)
4. Bigus, J., Chitnis, U., Deshpande, P., Kannan, R., Mohania, M., Negi, S., Deepak, P., Pednault, E., Soni, S., Telkar, B., White, B.: CRM Analytics Framework. In: Proc. of 15th Int. Conf. on Management of Data (COMAD 2009), Mysore, India (2009)
5. Martin, P., Matheson, M., Lo, J., Ng, J., Tan, D., Thomson, B.: Supporting Smart Interactions with Predictive Analytics. In: Chignell, M., Cordy, J., Ng, J., Yesha, Y. (eds.) The Smart Internet. LNCS, vol. 6400, pp. 103–114. Springer, Heidelberg (2010)
6. Matheson, M.: PASIF: A Framework for Supporting Smart Interactions with Predictive Analytics. MSc thesis, School of Computing, Queen's University (2011)

7. Tung, L., Xu, Y., Li, Y.: A framework for e-commerce oriented recommendation systems. In: Proceedings of the 2005 International Conference on Active Media Technology (AMT 2005), May 19-21, pp. 309–314 (2005)
8. Chuang, H., Wang, L., Pan, C.: A Study on the Comparison between Content-Based and Preference-Based Recommendation Systems. In: Fourth International Conference on Semantics, Knowledge and Grid, SKG 2008, December 3-5, pp. 477–480 (2008)
9. Sarwar, B., Karypis, G., Konstan, J., Riedl, J.: Analysis of recommendation algorithms for e-commerce. In: Proceedings of the 2nd ACM Conference on Electronic Commerce, EC 2000, Minneapolis, Minnesota, United States, October 17-20, pp. 158–167. ACM, New York (2000)
10. Zhang, Q., Pang, C., McBride, S., Hansen, D., Cheung, C., Steyn, M.: Towards Health Data Stream Analytics. In: Proceedings of 2010 IEEE/ICME International Conference on Complex Medical Engineering (CME), pp. 282–287 (2010)
11. Tsai, C., Lee, C., Yang, W.: An Efficient and Sensitive Decision Tree Approach to Mining Concept-Drifting Data Streams. Informatica 19(1), 135–156 (2008)
12. Wong, A., Wu, R.: 5E: A framework to yield high performance in real-time data mining over the Internet. In: Proceedings of the Fourth International Conference/Exhibition on High Performance Computing in the Asia-Pacific Region, pp. 708–713 (2000)
13. Deng, X., Ghanem, M., Guo, Y.: Real-Time Data Mining Methodology and a Supporting Framework. In: Proceedings of Third International Conference on Network and System Security (NSS 2009), pp. 522–527 (2009)
14. Hall, M., Frank, E., Holmes, G., Pfahringer, B., Reutemann, P., Witten, I.: The WEKA Data Mining Software: An Update. SIGKDD Explorations 11(1) (2009)
15. Holmes, G., Donkin, A., Witten, I.: WEKA: A machine learning workbench. In: Proceedings of 1994 Second Australian and New Zealand Conference on Intelligent Information Systems, pp. 357–361 (1994)
16. Frank, A., Asuncion, A.: UCI Machine Learning Repository. University of California, Irvine, School of Information and Computer Sciences (2010),
http://archive.ics.uci.edu/ml

Communities, Artifacts, Interaction and Contribution on the Web

Eleni Stroulia

Computing Science Department, University of Alberta, Edmonton, Canada
stroulia@ualberta.ca

Abstract. Today, most of us are members of multiple online communities, in the context of which we engage in a multitude of personal and professional activities. These communities are supported by different web-based platforms and enable different types of collaborative interactions. Through our experience with the development of and experimentation with three different such platforms in support of collaborative communities, we recognized a few core research problems relevant across all such tools, and we developed SociQL, a language, and a corresponding software framework, to study them.

Keywords: social networks, computer-supported collaboration, wikis, virtual worlds, web-based collaborative platforms.

1 Introduction and Background

The World Wide Web was conceived and born out of the desire to support information exchange, communication and collaboration. In its 30-year history (and it is flabbergasting to think about how short this history is in terms of time, and how dense it is in terms of events and innovations) it has more than fulfilled its promise and vision while at the same time undergoing three interesting transformations.

Originally, the objective of the web community was to enable document publishing and to advance large-scale information communication. The first beneficiaries of this platform were members of the academic and research community who had the knowledge and skills (a) to develop "web portals" even without any development tools, and (b) to access the published information through the original crude client applications. Through this activity, the first broadly usable clients and web-development toolkits were developed and gave rise to portals supported by traditional and new content owners, such as mainstream print publishers (MIT's Tech newspaper in 1991, BBC's TV program in 1994, and the Clinton White House in 1994) and new content providers (Yahoo in 1994). In this stage, the web was *a web of information* broadcasted by few to many.

The second phase in the Web's history was brought about by the advent of e-commerce sites (Amazon and eBay in 1995), which gave rise to *the web of applications.* In this new phase, the web became a ubiquitous platform, through which to deliver innovative services. The number of providers increased dramatically as the

M. Chignell et al. (Eds.): The Personal Web, LNCS 7855, pp. 131–150, 2013.

community became ever more creative about the types of services that could migrate to the web. The number of consumers also exploded with the increased availability of user-friendly browsers, search engines (Alta Vista, the first multilingual engine, was launched in 1995), and email-service providers for individuals (Hotmail was launched in 1996). Still, the communication model was that of broadcasting by relatively few to many.

This model changed with the advent of bulletin boards, originally associated with ecommerce web sites, and wikis and blogs, easy-to-use publication tools for individuals. These tools brought about *the personal web*, a continuously available whiteboard, hosting everyman's opinions and personal expressions, across the world.

And as an increasing variety of tools has become available – for searching, tagging, visualizing and connecting personal posts, published through any of the multitude of available platforms – *the social web* has now emerged. Today each one of us is linked to a multitude of others through our on-line presence: to the authors of the blogs to which we comment, to the other consumers of the products and services we have bought or are considering buying, to the members of our professional communities (LinkedIn and ResearchGate), to the people whose micro-blog postings we follow (twitter), to our on-line friends (Facebook, Google+), to the members of our virtual-world communities (Second Life), and to the users of the on-line tools we use.

Clearly, the original web vision, of supporting collaboration, has been evolving throughout these phase transitions, and today, it appears that the potential for innovative modes of web-enabled collaboration has reached new heights. It is in fact at the core of the "smart planet"[1] *interconnectedness* vision, which includes (a) data, (b) system, and (c) people interconnectedness.

In our work, motivated primarily by the need to support collaborative software development, we have developed a family of web-based systems for supporting, managing and analyzing different types of collaborative activities. These tools have been motivated by different specific requirements, although they all belong in the general area of tools in support of web-based collaboration. In this paper, we aim to reflect upon this work as a whole and to place each activity within a common conceptual framework that could potentially drive further work in the field.

In the rest of this paper, we discuss the background of this work and we place it in the context of a two-dimensional design space, defined in terms of types of platforms on which collaborative tools are built and in terms of the collaborative interactions they may support (Section 2). Next, we review three tools developed by our group, all designed to support collaborative teams on the web (Section 3) and we discuss some interesting research questions pertinent to all these types of systems (Section 4). Next, we review our work on SociQL, a social query language designed to support different types of analyses across different social systems, such as the ones described in Section 3 (Section 4). Finally, we conclude with some thoughts on what we expect to be the next important innovations to come (Section 5).

---

[1] http://www.ibm.com/smarterplanet/ca/en/overview/
ideas/index.html?re=sph

2   Collaboration in the Social Web

In the past several years, our team has developed three different web-based systems to support, manage and analyze a corresponding number of types of collaborative work. Looking back through this work, we have attempted to place it within a coherent conceptual framework by categorizing each tool in terms of two dimensions: (a) the types (and flexibility) of collaborative practices they support, and (b) the types of technology/platform on which they have been developed. Figure 1 illustrates this two-dimensional space and highlights a few interesting collaborative systems including our own.

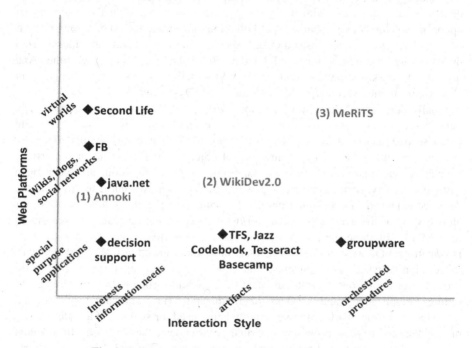

Fig. 1. Collaboration Tools in the Platform-Interaction Space

As shown in the vertical axis of Figure 1, the ***adopted platforms*** represent a spectrum of technologies. On one end of the spectrum, we have special-purpose applications, which are designed to support a specific task and make strong assumptions about the roles and capabilities of the collaborating individuals. This class of web-based applications exhibits a large variation in terms of the actual tasks they support, in terms of how strictly they regiment the roles and interactions of their members and the workflows of their activities, and in terms of their underlying architecture: they range from client-server systems with thick clients, to web-accessible applications with thin browser-based clients, to highly dynamic responsive Ajax-based clients. In this class, we generally understand the applications labeled as "groupware". In a still interesting – although not recent any more – overview of the domain, Grudin [1,2] organizes the early groupware applications under the *workflow-support* and *decision-support* categories. The former category includes tools that aim to systematize the organization's tasks usually through form-based interfaces. The latter includes meeting-room and issue-tracking systems mediating decision-making activities among the members of an organization. The former tend to support well-defined activities whereas the latter are envisioned as supports for persons' decision making.

More recently, we have witnessed the emergence of a large family of traditional browser-based web applications that support the publication of content by individuals and the sharing of this content by more or less "formal" groups.[2] The overall intent in this category is not to directly support a purposeful collaborative activity of a well-defined group of people with distinct roles, but rather to enable the discovery of opportunities for content sharing and collaboration across the web, through *wikis*, *blogs* and *social networks*. Instead of task-specific roles, individuals are characterized by their own self-descriptions and by the reputations they build over time. And instead of workflow-orchestrated task-specific activities, individuals engage in general information seeking/publishing/sharing/editing behaviors.

Finally, the recent advent of *virtual worlds,* i.e., general-purpose massively multiplayer 3D environments, best exemplified by Second Life (www.secondife.com), has enabled a new breed of interactions mediated not by information but by virtual environments and objects, often – but not necessarily – simulating real spaces and real objects. Some of these environments focus on a particular activity, such as playing games or listening to music, but many of them are designed to provide a virtual environment, in many ways parallel to the real world; for an overview of the available virtual worlds circa 2009, the interested reader should refer to [3]. In these environments, the general objective is not simply to share information but to express oneself and meet other like-minded virtual-world denizens. In addition, in these environments, one can engage in simulations of real-world activities for the purpose of entertainment (i.e., dancing), commerce (i.e., buying and selling virtual goods and services) and education (i.e., simulating professional procedures). Virtual worlds are increasingly being used for supporting a wider variety of applications; beyond providing a virtual environment, they are used to augment with an alternate layer applications and services in the real world. In our own work, we have explored three different types of virtual-world uses as mirrors or the real world, or as alternative places in which to conduct realistic simulations relying on real-world systems, or as trans-reality places [4,5].

In the horizontal axis of Figure 1, we have identified three interesting points in the spectrum of collaborative practices, identified in terms of the "contract" that the collaborators assume about "what is being shared". At the very **informal** end of collaboration practices, we have fluid communities of individuals with common interests and/or expertise. Participation in these communities requires only that

---

[2] For a comprehensive list of social applications today, the interested reader should visit http://www.theconversationprism.com/ for an interesting infographic of the social media universe today.

individuals share a common natural language, in terms of which to express themselves and contribute to the community conversations. For example, regular blog readers interact through their blog entries and Second-Life users interact with each other through voice and text messaging.

As the degree of the community formality increases, participation requires a shared common understanding of what artifacts are shared within the community. For example, participants of a retailer's loyalty program may share product reviews, structured in terms of particular questions of interest, or buyers/sellers of pre-owned goods may describe their products in terms of standard conventions, including pictures, description, original cost, and level of use. At this level, the objective is still information sharing, although this information may directly support an activity; for instance, information about an object on a web-based marketplace is intended to support an economic transaction, which, however, may not be mediated by the marketplace web application (the two parties may simply contact each other through email).

As the community matures further, a shared understanding emerges about the activities that can effectively be supported based on the information shared by the community members. As an example, consider software teams using web-based software-productivity tools, such as version-control and project-management tools. These tools imply a specific set of activities, i.e., adding, committing, updating files; editing tasks and timelines; and keeping track of one's own working hours. These activities are supported directly by the collaborative web application, although they are not necessarily strictly orchestrated. Similarly, when visiting a virtual-world clothes' retail space, users may try clothes on their avatars, decide to buy them and pay for them with virtual currency. The virtual-world does not orchestrate these activities, but the owners and visitors participate in these transactions guided by their shared understanding of how retail works.

The tools described in the next Section are examples of these three types of collaborative practices, developed on two of the most recent commodity social platforms, namely wikis and virtual worlds. Our experience with these systems led to the formulation of the research questions in Section 4, and has motivated the design of SociQL (described in Section 5) as a language and an implementation framework to study these questions. Section 6 concludes with a summary of our experience to date and outlines some promising avenues for future work.

3   A Suite of Collaborative Platforms

Our team has been exploring this space of collaborative web-based tools and has designed and developed a suite of systems across this space, which we describe in some detail in the remainder of this Section. For each of these tools, we first discuss the requirements motivating its design, next we review its major functionalities, and finally, we point out the most interesting findings through our experience with it. Our experience building and evaluating these tools eventually led us to recognize some common themes in the nature of the data collected in these tools, the interactions of the tools' users, and the analyses that might be of interest to the members of the collaborative teams and their managers. We explore these themes in Section 4. More recently, we started exploring these common themes in the design and development of SociQL, a language for querying and analyzing systems supporting the activities of teams, and, more generally, social networks. SociQL is described at a high level in Section 5, and in more detail in [6].

3.1   Annoki

Annoki [7] is a wiki-based collaborative platform, designed to support communities of interest, sharing information based on their members' common interests. The original envisioned usage scenario for Annoki was to support the collaboration activities of our research team, such as keeping track of the lab software and hardware resources, maintaining a list of the publications relevant to our research and our discussions about them, and maintaining a research log including research problems, methodological decisions, development plans and timelines and ideas explored, rejected, modified or under consideration. Having such a shared resource recording our research activities was intended to support the authoring of theses and publications and to enable the faster on-boarding of new team members.

We chose to develop Annoki on top of MediaWiki primarily because of the general popularity of the MediaWiki platform, which implies an easy learning curve, as most users are somehow familiar with it, if only based on Wikipedia, the most popular MediaWiki tool. Second, and more importantly, MediaWiki provides a natural metaphor for understanding the general class of communities-of-practice applications, where information resources (corresponding to wiki *pages*) are shared and collaboratively manipulated by *users*. Users can informally and collaboratively edit the shared resources, and can reflect upon them and discuss about them on special-purpose *discussion pages* attached to each page. The evolution of the resources, the users, and their communications is automatically tracked and reported through the *recent-changes* and *history* MediaWiki tools, which can also be configured to push email notifications to the users interested in *watching* particular pages of interest. MediaWiki, as is the case with wikis in general, does not yet afford rich data views, but its software architecture is extendible enough to allow us to alleviate this shortcoming. The Annoki toolkit adds the following set of extensions to the MediaWiki features.

Namespace-Based Access Control: Wikis are designed for open sharing and collaborative editing of resources, providing only very coarse-grained access-control mechanisms: a page can either be editable by community members or the general public, or not. However, in the context of organized groups, individuals usually assume different roles, with different privileges, which could (and frequently should) be recognized and/or enforced by their collaboration tools.

In Annoki, we piggybacked a flexible access-control system on the MediaWiki concept of *namespaces*. A namespace is a cluster of related pages, the title of which start with the same prefix, i.e., the namespace title. Each Annoki user has his own namespace and, by default, all pages he creates belong in this namespace. Additional namespaces can also be defined to organize wiki pages that belong to a group of users. A namespace can be "public", in which case everyone can read its pages, and if they are not protected, edit its pages. If a namespace is not public only the users associated with it can read/edit its pages. Users can be flexibly assigned to multiple namespaces and pages can move from one namespace to another to increase/restrict their visibility. In this manner, layers of access rights can be supported for personal, project-specific, organization-related, and publicly accessible content.

Interactive Visualizations: Wikis were originally conceived as hypertext platform, where users share textual content, structure its presentation through a limited set of formatting metadata, and link it to existing content through hyperlinks. Although each page editor may have an understanding of how his pages connect to the rest of the wiki content, find one's way through the links presents a challenge to new visitors. The wealth of information that is accrued in a wiki comes at a cost: the more pages a Wiki has, the more difficult it becomes to navigate through it. It is common for a Wiki page to contain a sizable number of links in its body text. Users have to read through the text to locate these links and to guess where to navigate next. It is also easy for users to feel "lost" after having gone through a number of links, since the standard wiki interface does not provide any navigation context. In our earlier work [8] we studied how a graph-based representation of a wiki content, where individual pages are represented as nodes and URLs between them are represented as edges, impacts the ability of users to search through the wiki content and answer pertinent questions. In this study, we found that searching through such a graph indeed decreases the number of pages that a user has to visit to complete the task.

Inspired from this study, Annoki is equipped with a rich, interactive, Ajax-based visualization, WikiMap, a visualization of the whole wiki structure (users, pages, links among pages and authorship relations between users and pages). WikiMaps enable Annoki users to obtain a global view of its content and its evolution history. In addition, wiEGOs (wiki-integrated Electronic Graphic Organizers [9]) are visualizations of the semantic structures implicit in a set of special template-based pages (i.e., tree, topic, persuasion, brainstorm, story, and decision maps, as well as flowcharts). wiEGOs extend the template concept of MediaWiki, by associating a visual structure with the standard organization structure of pages that are instances of templates, enabling the creation and editing of template instances through a visual interface.

Contribution Analysis: Wikis are designed to support collaborative content development, without focusing on individual contribution: looking at a wiki page, one cannot distinguish the individual contributions of its editors. As wikis are adopted for institutional purposes, where contributors are likely driven by career goals, it becomes interesting to support the ability to recognize each editor's contributions. In [10] we studied the question of how to assess the editors' contributions by developing a suite of sentence-based metrics and comparing them against users' perception of contribution. Through this study we found that users' perception of contribution was strongly correlated with significant content addition and deletion, as well as hyperlink addition.

Driven by our original hypothesis, that in institutional contexts wiki users are (at least partially) driven by their desire to distinguish themselves among their peers through their contributions, we developed a special purpose pie-chart visualization to communicate the type and percentage of each individual editor's contribution on a page. This visualization can clearly convey the various contribution metrics to the wiki users. Through interviews with potential users, we concluded that such tools are likely to change wiki editors' behavior, motivating editors to contribute in ways that would result in increasing their "slice" of the pie chart, thus making their contribution obvious to the wiki community. Through our experience with Annoki after this visualization was actually deployed, we collected anecdotal evidence that this is indeed true, namely explicit communication of contribution motivates further contribution, at least to some editors; however, we have not conducted a formal experiment to precisely investigate this phenomenon.

Experience with Annoki: Through our experience using Annoki, we discovered that the biggest challenge in the adoption of the tool was the lack of a well-defined process guiding its use. The most satisfied users were those who adopted (or developed on their own) a consistent style for editing, structuring and linking their pages, such as daily task records, for example. Without such a consistent usage style, searching and finding information becomes more difficult, thus substantially undermining the usefulness of the tool. Support mechanisms such as visual exploration of the wiki content (through the WikiMap) and additional page meta-data (such as keywords) can help users to more easily find information [8], but they are effective when they reflect a conceptual organization structure underlying the wiki content.

3.2   WikiDev2.0

Having used Annoki for over three years in our lab, we recognized an opportunity to adopt it as a lightweight tool for supporting the collaboration among software developers working on team projects. Traditional software-collaboration tools, such as version-control repositories and bug trackers, have focused primarily on supporting the sharing and management of technical software artifacts, such as software source code, other assets like configuration files and scripts and images, formal documentation and tasks. However rich information can be extracted by understanding the relations between activities across tools and by analyzing the informal communication among developers, in terms of emails and text messages. Recognition of this fact has given rise to the software-engineering field of "mining software repositories" and was the motivating factor behind our WikiDev2.0 [11,12,13,14] project.

WikiDev2.0 was conceived as a lightweight platform through which (a) to integrate information about the software artifacts produced in the variety of tools used by the software team (code, documentation, communication messages etc), (b) to analyze this information in order to infer interesting relations among these artifacts, the team members and their activities, and (c) to present views on this information and its analyses that cut across the individual tool boundaries. In WikiDev2.0, a software team is assigned a namespace and information from the different tools the team is ingested in different types of template-based wiki pages. To date we have integrated SVN, Bugzilla, e-mail, and IRC with WikiDev2.0. Each file in SVN is represented as a wiki page and its history can be explored through wiki differencing. Bugzilla tickets are also represented as wiki pages. Each team is associated with a mailing list, whose archive is ingested as yet another wiki page, and an IRC channel, monitored by a chat-bot that records the exchanges through this channel in another wiki page. In addition to these automatically constructed pages, team members can create wiki pages for whatever purpose they choose. Throughout our experience over about four years using this tool to support undergraduate software-engineering courses, we noticed that teams created pages to keep track of their internal timelines, their weekly progress and their own information documentation of different aspects of the software project. Finally, each project namespace has a page that includes visualizations of several straight-forward productivity and communication analyses, including how frequently team members commit in SVN, how frequently changes to the project files are committed, and how frequently each team member communicates with the others.

WikiDev2.0 caters to the needs of small communities – i.e., software teams – engaged in a purposeful activity – i.e., the development of software – producing structured artifacts – i.e., source code, test suites, and documentation. This is different from the usage scenario envisioned for Annoki, which was conceived to enable a researcher community to share information of common interest, where the interests were loosely and implicitly defined by virtue of membership in the community. In WikiDev2.0 we revisited and reformulated the question of contribution analysis: instead of developing metrics to evaluate the contribution of individuals to different (types of) pages, we focused instead on recognizing the dependencies between contributions of different types.

The *code and communication clustering* analysis of WikiDev2.0 [11] was conceived as a means of correlating technical software artifacts and their contributors with contributions to informal communications (i.e., email messages and IRC chats). The analysis consists of the following steps. The first step involves parsing of all the textual information associated with the input information feeds, to recognize mentions of team members (their names, nicknames, or IDs) and software artifacts (classes, methods and interfaces). The recognized references reflect the *explicit relations* between people, code, and communication artifacts. A subsequent step calculates further *implicit relations* and provides further insights about hidden dependencies among these artifacts. This analysis is performed within non-overlapping, sliding, week-long windows, and the result is the correlation of developers' contributions to software artifacts with communications among the developers. Examination of the resulting clusters led us to recognize discussions among the team members about specific artifacts and who is (should be) currently working on what artifact. Such discussions can be potentially relevant in identifying people who should be consulted when a particular artifact is being maintained, thus actually informing the team members' work.

In the above process, relations among the various data elements contained in the wiki are inferred on the basis of shared keywords, i.e., shared team-members' names and class/method identifiers. Aiming to better analyze the WikiDev2.0 textual content, we developed a *syntactic-semantic text-analysis* method [14]. The method consists of three steps. First, all sentences from WikiDev2.0 wiki pages, email messages and IRC chats are extracted and parsed. The resulting parse trees are annotated with semantic tags, based on a (partially project specific) vocabulary of known terms. For example, all references to programming languages, tools and activities (such as developing, testing etc) are recognized and correspondingly annotated, as are all mentions of team-members' names and code-artifact identifiers. Finally, a set of rules, such as "*S:<team-member name> V:develop O:<class-identifier>*", are matched against the annotated syntax trees to extract subject-predicate-object triples, corresponding to relations such as "*who worked on what*", "*who has experience in what*" etc.

Both the above analyses were conceived as a means to understand the software team process. To help the team members themselves improve their awareness of their project artifacts and activities, we developed two alternative visualizations [12] of the WikiDev2.0 content. The first was a traditional graph-based visualization accessible through WikiDev2.0 itself; the second was developed based on a city metaphor in the OpenWonderland virtual world. We experimentally evaluated the relative MERiTS of the two visualizations by having subjects access them to answer questions about the underlying software project. We found that the two views were rather complementary: in most questions where the subjects had trouble finding the answer in one system, it was easier for them in the other system. However, overall the more traditional WikiDev2.0 graph-based visualizations seemed to be a slightly easier platform. This can be attributed to the fact that WikiDev2.0 has a more intuitive and familiar interface (hyperlinks and web pages) compared to navigating in a virtual world. However, neither platform showed a clear advantage over the other since half of our small set of subjects (4) preferred WikiDev2.0 while the other half chose WikiDev3D.

Experience with WikiDev2.0: Through our experience using WikiDev2.0 we found that the feature most appreciated by the developers was the feedback they received by the instructor and TAs on their deliverables. Using the team's WikiDev2.0 area as the repository of all team deliverables and feedback enabled the tighter interaction and gave the teams more confidence about their progress. We found that the clustering analyses we developed on the WikiDev2.0 content, whether through simple information-retrieval mechanisms [11] or through natural-language analyses [13], did provide useful insights to the instructor about the team interactions and progress, which could potentially enhance the instructor's ability to provide useful feedback. With respect to supporting the developers' awareness of their project, there is a lot of work in the area exploring various styles of information visualizations and dashboards. Many of these mechanisms are promising although no conclusive overarching theory has emerged yet on the developers' information-access patterns of their software repositories.

3.3   MERiTS

The MERiTS system [15,3,16,17,18,19] is the third of our collaborative-work support tools and it focuses on collaborative activities that are more complex and involve complex orchestrated interactions among individuals, in addition to the exchange of textual information (as in Annoki) and sharing of information about well-defined work products (as in WikiDev2.0). Most professional roles require knowledge and procedural skills in performing role-specific tasks as well as communication skills for interacting with other professionals, and it is increasingly recognized that the role of education is to enable students to competently perform in their eventual professional roles, as opposed to just acquiring facts and learning to perform procedures. In this light, traditional textbook-and-lecture teaching methods are gradually giving way to simulation-based case scenarios, where students have the opportunity to experience situations in which they have to apply their knowledge and skills as would be expected of them in their future professional roles. However, conducting simulations is a challenging proposition, given the costs associated with acquiring the necessary equipment and hiring instructors and facilitators to conduct the simulations, and the limited number of students that can participate in any given simulation session. Virtual worlds are online platforms that combine the accessibility and collaboration possibilities of the web with the immersive, realistic qualities of virtual reality, offering an appealing and cost-effective alternative for conducting simulations in the context of competency-based training programs. Our MERiTS tool [19] was conceived to enable (a) instructors to specify educational scenarios, and (b) students to experience those scenarios in a realistic, interactive manner.

The MERITS framework offers two important features. The first involves a method and tool support for *specifying complex collaborative processes,* in terms of BPEL workflows, including tools for specifying the behavioral capabilities of the various roles in the process in terms of web services invoked by avatar actions in the virtual world, as well as developing behavioral scripts for real-object simulacra in the virtual world. The second important feature is a *comprehensive action-recording* tool [18] that produces a compact synchronized trace of all in-world actions of all simulation participants, which can then be parsed to identify action patterns of pedagogical interest.

The MERITS architecture mimics the three-tiered structure of traditional web-based applications, with a virtual world as the user interface, a BPEL orchestrated set of software services as the application logic (that is, the software implementing the automated activities of the service-delivery process), and a resource repository maintaining a record of the archival data of the organization and the transient data of each service-delivery simulation scenario. Instructors can specify relevant educational entities by updating the resource repository through web-based forms, accessing REST APIs of the repository. The BPEL workflows that specify the behaviors of people and objects in the scenario may, in principle, be created using graphical, web-based tools. However, there are conceptual challenges involved in the specification of a BPEL workflow that make merely providing a graphical interface insufficient for removing implementation barriers for non-technical users.

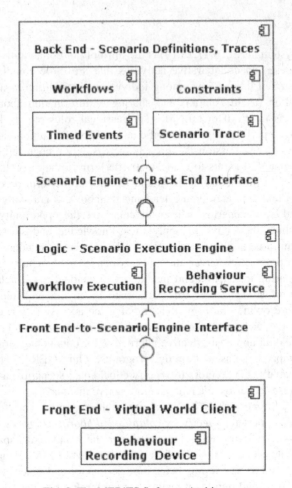

Fig. 2. The MERiTS Software Architecture

At run time, the BPEL workflows are enacted through the interactions of people and objects in the virtual world and through the behaviors of underlying automated software systems. When a student performs an action through his or her avatar, a behavior script is executed in the virtual world. The execution of this script may (a) change the state of the virtual world and (b) change the state of the corresponding workflow, shown in the second tier in the diagram in Figure 2. In our implementation, the server interprets the action in the context of the overall process workflow to determine how the scenario should proceed in response to the action. The BPEL workflow can also be connected to external devices, thus allowing the simulation to extend beyond the boundaries of a particular educational institution. For example, in a healthcare education context, where we have primarily evaluated MERiTS, the system may be connected to a web service that provides simulated patient data.

The MERiTS system enables the scalability of simulation-based teaching and learning. On one hand, virtual-world simulations can be cost-effectively accessible by many more students, across geographical and institutional boundaries, than their more realistic counterparts. On the other, the trace-recording and analysis functionality is essential for "scaling up" the capacity of instructors to evaluate the competence of their students as they go through simulations; by inspecting the recorded trace and its analyses, instructors can obtain a good understanding of the their students' competence.

The question of relative contribution analysis for each of the participants is still relevant but takes a different form in MERiTS: a person's contribution to the accomplishment of the simulated activity is measured by analyzing the recorded simulation trace to calculate the distinct activity steps taken by this individual, the correctness of the timing of these steps, and the lack of violations of the activity constraints.

Experience with MERiTS: We have deployed MERiTS in several different scenarios, which can be classified in one of two categories. In the first case [4], the scenario simulates a classroom setting, replacing a more traditional web-based teleconferencing tool. In a study where students in an interprofessional health-sciences course met and planned the discharge of standardized patient in the virtual world, we faced interesting usability challenges since many participants found it difficult to learn how to interact in the virtual world. Moreover, some facilitators "lost control" of their classrooms as inattentive students starting experimenting with the tool distracting everyone from the educational activity. In this deployment style, we found that the fairly large number of students in the classroom made it difficult for the students and the instructor to migrate their normal class-interaction patterns (being attentive, taking turns, etc) to the virtual world.

In a later case study of individual nursing students simulating an asthma-emergency scenario latter type of scenarios [19] we found that the students had much less difficulty interacting with the virtual world, even though the environment was more complex. In this study, students were more prepared (they went through a tutorial before class) and found the experience "low pressure", "less threatening than their clinical hours" and "valuable for nursing programs". In spite of the students' overall positive experience with the simulation, our analysis of their competence through pre- and post-simulation questionnaires did not show improvement that could be attributed to learning through the simulation; this finding is in agreement with much current education literature.

4   Common Themes in Social Applications

Developing and reflecting upon the three systems we described in the last section, we have come up with a set of research questions (and associated technical challenges) that cut across most, if not all, web-based social systems today. We review these questions in this section, organized in two different groupings of "analysis questions" around social systems and possible "services supported" by social systems.

Today, there exists a plethora of social-networking sites, each one supporting different types of "connections" among members and catering to different demographics. Some sites enable bi-directional connections, like Facebook; others enable the organization of connections in conceptual clusters, like Google+ circles; yet others only support directed connections, like Twitter. MySpace caters to a younger demographic than Facebook, which in turn is surpassed in popularity by Orkut in Brazil. In addition to these "superficial" differences, each of these social networks encourages different types of communications. Facebook appeals to people who want to keep in touch with family and friends, where Twitter seems to be the medium of choice for people who want to share and access information from a wide variety of channels. Facebook favors deeper connections and enables the organization of these connections in groups so that different personas can be projected to each of them. Google+ takes this idea even further enforcing people to register their true identity with the system but supporting the differentiation of the spheres of socialization through circles. Twitter, on the other hand, encourages maximization of connections (followers) and enforces a single persona on its users, who cannot distinguish their followers in groups.

Clearly these differences deserve deeper analysis; in the mean time, all of these networks share three important concepts, i.e., they define and support *communities*, that enable *contribution* through sharing of different types of content over different types of channels, and as a result they enable individuals to *influence* each other.

4.1   Recognizing Communities

Groups of collaborating people are not uniformly cohesive. Some members are more highly connected to each other than to the rest of the group. This is a corollary to the "homophily" [20] phenomenon. Homophily is the tendency of individuals to associate and bond with similar others. Individuals in homophilic relationships share common characteristics (beliefs, values, behaviors, etc.) that make communication and relationship formation easier. If homophily is indeed a pervasive phenomenon in groups, the question becomes (a) how one might recognize the relations that underlie it in each particular collaborative/social system, and (b) how one would go about supporting the emerging homophilic groups (i.e., sub-communities).

Let us review the issue of "recognizing and supporting sub-communities". It is a problem relevant to all the three systems we discussed above, but its various instances differ from each other and, therefore, the three systems address it in slightly different ways. Annoki members are associated with individual- and project-related namespaces that contain pages; the implication is that sub-communities are either person- or project-centric. In Annoki, there is a single relationship among users, namely page co-editing, therefore the namespaces completely capture the relations among users: users co-edit the pages in their namespaces. As a result, there is no need to recognize implicit sub-communities. Individuals are explicitly assigned to projects, or, alternatively, based on their evolving interests, they may search and find interesting content and decide to join (and leave) the projects in which this content belongs.

WikiDev2.0 also supports the organization of individuals in projects. Individuals do not flexibly choose their groups; they are assigned to them and the user-project relationship does not change. However, within a project team, there are many possible relations among the team members, such as working on the same artifacts, working on the same tasks (i.e., tickets), communicating with each other through one channel (email) or another (wiki pages). We have analyzed these relationships of team members, both direct (through common artifacts) and indirect (through communications), to recognize subgroups of individuals who have frequently communicated with each other. Furthermore, through further inspection of the resulting clusters, we can examine how frequently two team members belong in the same cluster. Such co-occurrence of members in clusters would implicitly indicate an increased degree of collaboration of the corresponding team members, which may or may not be reflected in the explicit communications of these team members in email.

In the workflow-defined simulations of MERITS, the activities and the relations of the participants are explicitly represented in terms of the workflows they enact. However, in cases of more open-ended activities within a virtual classroom, special-purpose relations (like communication) can be used as the basis for recognizing sub-communities of people who interact more closely with each other.

4.2   Recognizing Contribution

As the collaborating community increases, the nature of what is being shared becomes less well defined, and the nature and amount of an individual's contribution becomes more difficult to discern. MERiTS workflows usually involve small teams of about 3-4 professionals that collaborate in well-defined ways, interacting with task-specific (virtual) artifacts and orchestrating their interactions in terms of BPEL-specified workflows. In WikiDev2.0, most teams consist of four to six developers (plus TAs and instructors) and the team members share software artifacts (which, however, are produced using tools external to WikiDev2.0). In contrast, the Annoki installation in our group has about 200 members (some of whom are not active any more) who communicate through natural-language text.

MediaWiki, as well as most wikis, offers a differencing capability, which summarizes the contribution of an individual to a specific version. Annoki provides a more sophisticated contribution analysis and visualization tool, which summarizes the contribution of an individual to a wiki page over its lifecycle [10]. WikiDev2.0 implicitly recognizes contribution through its visualizations of the frequency of SVN commits, wiki-page edits, and email communications. Furthermore, analysis of the clusters in WikiDev2.0 can shed further insight on the contributions of an individual, although this is not an automated inference. MERITS measures contribution in terms of actions taken in the context of accomplishing a collaborative workflow. Through its recorded activity logs one can define further metrics of interest based on the participants' in-world activities and measure contribution in different ways. For example, one can imagine that it would be interesting to identify the persons who talked the most during a session or the person who made the most interactive gestures (like shaking hands for example) with others.

This discussion is motivated by the assumption that a person's "importance" within a community is related to the person's "contribution" to the community's activities and assets. Many domain-specific importance metrics can be based on different person attributes, but contribution appears to be a cross-domain metric of an individual's importance within the community.

Related to the concept of contribution is the concept of influence. Within a collaborating community, people influence their collaborators through their contributions. Not all contributions however are equally likely to be "consumed" by other team members and to influence other people's contributions. In WikiDev2.0, the clustering process implicitly attempts to recognize the members' influence to code artifacts by collecting references of other materials, associated with team members, to these artifacts. In MERiTS, influence can be perceived directly through analysis of the workflows, where data/artifact production/consumption relationships as well as ordering relations between steps, can be assumed to define influence of the producer to the consumer and of the preceding to the subsequent actor.

Recognizing densely connected clusters of individuals, based on their shared properties, their relations and the strength of these relations, and understanding the interactions among individuals and the flow of influence that these interactions imply are two important recurring themes in social/collaborative systems. These phenomena are of interest to sociologists and, at the same time, understanding how they manifest themselves in a particular community is key to more effectively supporting the community and its objectives. SociQL was designed to support the representation of questions relevant to these themes and the access of social systems to answer these questions.

5   SociQL

Through the above discussion on the collaborative tools developed by our group (Section 3) and the two interesting (and recurring) problems in the general area of social platforms (Section 4), we have explored some of the variety in the area of social/collaborative applications. Nevertheless, research, aiming to understand how these communities work and how they can most effectively be supported, is fundamentally interested in answering a common set of core questions. These questions include, but are not limited to, the following: What types of individuals belong in the community? How are they related to each other? How do these relations become evident? What are the interesting substructures through which subgroups of community members are related? Who are the most influential individuals in the community? How does the community evolve over time and space?

The above questions are fundamentally sociological in nature, and, in order to be able to systematically explore them across a variety of applications, a *social query language* is needed. The syntax of this language should express the concepts of individuals, relations, communities, structure and influence with first-order primitives and should support the intuitive expression of the above questions. Furthermore, this language should be associated with a systematic methodology for how it should be mapped to the concepts of each particular social-collaborative application.

SociQL [6,21] is a language developed by our group to meet exactly the above requirements. Unlike generic web-query languages, SociQL is designed to support the examination of sociological questions, relying on the *object-centered sociality* theory [22]. While recognizing the social interaction between *individuals*, this theory exalts the role of *specific objects* as the reasons why social actors affiliate with each other; essentially the theory assumes that objects constitute the reasons why (and the evidence of) people relating to each other in communities.

For this reason, we define the SociQL data model around the concept of an **object**. For instance, in the context of WikiDEv2.0, a class (an object) connects the team members who have contributed to its development. Similarly, a mail message (an object) connects the parties (sender and recipients) who have access to it. In the MediaWiki-based Annoki, the wiki pages are the objects that connect the pages authors. In MERiTS, the avatars are connected through the simulacra of the real-world objects they manipulate as well as through their communication objects, i.e., their text and voice utterances. Each SociQL object is represented in terms of a pair, associating a unique identifier with the object type. **Relations** among objects are assumed to be binary and are represented as tuples, consisting of the identifiers of two related objects and the type of the relation.

In SociQL, both objects and relationships are described by **properties** (actual data), such as the login ID of a team member (object property) or the timestamp when a developer last committed a class (relation property). The properties of an object are represented as tuples associating the object identifier with a property and its value. The properties of a relation are represented as tuples associating the participating object identifiers, the relation type, the relevant property and its value.

SociQL also distinguishes the **context** in which properties are defined to describe the objects and relationships. For instance, the same query might return different email addresses for the same individual depending on the context in which the query is asked[3]: in Annoki, the email address of the individual as a researcher will be returned, while in WikiDev2.0, his address as a student participating in a course will be returned. In practice, each context corresponds to a different social/collaborative system. It is the notion of context that enables us to use SociQL to interlink different community platforms and integrate the knowledge about individuals and their relations that is currently hoarded in a variety of silos.

Once the objects, relations and properties of a social application have been mapped in SociQL, i.e., SQL queries or REST APIs have been implemented to retrieve them from the subject system and expose them in the simple SociQL representation described above, one can examine several interesting sociological questions relying on the algorithms implemented the SociQL engine.

First, one can express basic questions in terms of basic SociQL queries as follows:

SELECT $relation\text{-}label_1(o_1, o_2)$
FROM object-type o_1, object-type o_2, $relation\text{-}label_2(o_1, o_2)$
WHERE $o_1.property\text{-}label=property\text{-}value.$

---

[3] Note that SociQL has not been integrated with Annoki, WikiDev2.0 or MERiTS; it has been integrated with two different systems (see [20]). Our examples in this section on its use with Annoki, WikiDev2.0 and MERiTS are envisioning its application in these systems.

The above query will first identify all object pairs (o_1, o_2), where the value of the property *property-label* of o_1 is *property-value*, and o_1 and o_2 are related through the relation *relation-label$_2$*. Next, it will select the subset of these pairs that are also related through the relation *relation-label$_1$*.

More interestingly, building on the above basic query, one can retrieve dependency *paths* between objects. A path expression implies a sequence of objects o_0, r_1, ... o_i, r_{i+1}, ..., r_n, o_n, where r_1, ..., r_n represent relations, o_0, ..., o_n denote objects, and for each i, there is a relation r_i between o_{i-1} and o_i. Starting from the object o_0 and ending in the object o_n there may be several paths that match this expression. Path expressions are helpful to find all connections and possible influence zones in social networks. For instance, when querying for all paths connecting two developers in WikiDev2.0, we might discover that they are related through their co-editing of the same class, or through their exchange of an email message, or through the fact that one developed a class depending on a second class developed by the other.

In addition, the SociQL toolkit includes the implementation of several centrality measures that can be used to filter the results returned by any SociQL query. In this manner, after having discovered all the developers with whom a particular developer is connected through paths of up to n steps, we may filter (and or sort) them according to their importance in terms of their centrality according the email-sharing relation, in order to find who of these retrieved connections is the most prolific email correspondent.

6   Summary and Conclusions

In this paper, we have attempted to review, in broad strokes and through the perspective of our own experience, the general area of social collaborative platforms. We believe that this area of research activity and real-world-driven innovation has revolutionized once more our idea of the role of the web. From a repository of authoritative information, to a distributed application platform, to a forum of personal expression, to a community, the web has now become fundamentally entrenched in our every-day activities. And, given the variety of activities currently taking place "on the web" in some form or another, and the variety of web-based platforms that one can adopt to develop tools to support these activities, developing, managing and analyzing these collaborative web-based systems is a unique challenge.

Our group has been investigating several aspects of this general problem, through the process of designing, developing, deploying and evolving three different web-based collaborative tools. Reflecting upon the process of developing these tools, and the lessons we learned through our experimentation with them, we have recognized the need for a systematic methodology for studying these systems. This methodology must (a) enable users to express interesting sociological questions, (b) provide computational support for systematic analysis of interesting community phenomena, and (c) enable the integrated analysis of information captured in different communities. These are the requirements driving the design of SociQL, which, to date, has been used to study four different communities.

This is clearly an active and fascinating area with a huge number of open questions and substantial opportunities for the development of innovative intelligent services. In the future, we plan to integrate SociQL to all three tools and to further expand its syntax and its analyses.

Acknowledgments. This work was generously supported by NSERC, iCORE, IBM, and was conducted in collaboration with B. Tansey, K. Bauer, M. Fokaefs, D. Chodos, D. Serrano and D. Barbosa.

References

1. Grudin, J.: Computer-Supported Cooperative Work: History and Focus. IEEE Computer 27(5), 19–26 (1994)
2. Grudin, J.: Groupware and Social Dynamics: Eight Challenges for Developers. Commun. ACM 37(1), 92–105 (1994)
3. Chodos, D., Naeimi, P., Stroulia, E.: A simulation-based training framework for health-science education on video and in a virtual world. Journal of Virtual Worlds Research 2(1) (April 2009)
4. Gutierrez, L., Stroulia, E., Nikolaidis, I.: fAARS: A Platform for Location-Aware Trans-reality Games. In: Herrlich, M., Malaka, R., Masuch, M. (eds.) ICEC 2012. LNCS, vol. 7522, pp. 185–192. Springer, Heidelberg (2012)
5. Stroulia, E.: Smart Services Across the Real and Virtual Worlds. In: Chignell, M., Cordy, J., Ng, J., Yesha, Y. (eds.) The Smart Internet. LNCS, vol. 6400, pp. 178–196. Springer, Heidelberg (2010)
6. Serrano, D., Stroulia, E., Barbosa, D., Guana, V.: SociQL: A Query Language for the SocialWeb. In: Kranakis, E. (ed.) Mathematics in Industry. Advances in Network Analysis and its Applications, vol. 18, pp. 381–406. Springer, Heidelberg (2013), http://dx.doi.org/10.1007/978-3-642-30904-5_17
7. Tansey, B., Stroulia, E.: Annoki: A MediaWiki-based Collaboration Platform. In: Web2SE: First Workshop on Web 2.0 for Software Engineering, ICSE 2010 (2010)
8. Espiritu, C., Stroulia, E., Tirapat, T.: ENWiC: Visualizing WIKI semantics as Topic Maps: An automated topic discovery and visualization tool. In: Proceedings of the 8th International Conference on Enterprise Information Systems, Paphos, Cyprus, May 23-27, pp. 35–42 (2006)
9. Hall, T., Strangman, N.: Graphic organizers, Wakefield, MA. National Center on Accessing the General Curriculum (2002), http://aim.cast.org/learn/historyarchive/backgroundpapers/graphic_organizers (retrieved October 2012)
10. Arazy, O., Stroulia, E., Ruecker, S., Arias, C., Fiorentino, C., Ganev, V., Yau, T.: Recognizing Contributions in Wikis: Authorship Categories, Algorithms, and Visualizations. Journal of the American Society for Information Science and Technology (JASIST) 61(6), 1166–1179 (2010)
11. Bauer, K., Fokaefs, M., Tansey, B., Stroulia, E.: WikiDev 2.0: Discovering Clusters of Related Team Artifacts. In: CASCON 2009, Toronto, Canada, November 2-6 (2009)
12. Fokaefs, M., Serrano, D., Tansey, B., Stroulia, E.: 2D and 3D Visualizations in WikiDev2.0. In: ERA track, 26th IEEE International Conference on Software Maintenance ICSM 2010, Timisoara, Romania, September 12-18 (2010)

13. Fokaefs, M., Tansey, B., Ganev, V., Bauer, K., Stroulia, E.: WikiDev 2.0: Facilitating Software Development Teams. In: 14th European Conference on Software Maintenance and Reengineering (CSMR 2010), Madrid, Spain, March 15-18 (2010)
14. Hasan, M., Stroulia, E., Barbosa, D., Alalfi, M.: Analyzing Natural-Language Artifacts of the Software Process. In: ERA track, 26th IEEE International Conference on Software Maintenance, ICSM 2010, Timisoara, Romania, September 12-18 (2010)
15. Boechler, P., Carbonaro, M., Stroulia, E., King, S., de Jong, E., Chodos, D.: Technical Challenges And Solutions For Creating Virtual Environments For A Health Science Interprofessional Course. The Internet Journal of Allied Health Sciences and Practice 9(4) (October 2011)
16. Chodos, D., Stroulia, E., Kuras, P., Carbonaro, M., King, S.: MERITS Training System - Using Virtual Worlds for Simulation-based Training. In: The International Conference on Computer Supported Education, CSEDU 2010, Valencia Spain, April 6-9,
17. Chodos, D., Stroulia, E., King, S.: Developing a Virtual-World Simulation. In: Third International Workshop on Software Engineering in Healthcare (SEHC 2011), ICSE 2011, pp. 71–78 (2011)
18. Chodos, D., Stroulia, E., King, S., Carbonaro, M.: A framework for monitoring instructional environments in a virtual world. British Journal of Educational Technology (accepted September 2012)
19. Chodos, D.: Using Virtual Worlds for Scenario-based Training. Ph.D. University of Alberta (Fall 2012)
20. Anagnostopoulos, A., Kumar, R., Mahdian, M.: Influence and correlation in social networks. In: Proceeding of the 14th ACM SIGKDD International Conference on Knowledge Discovery and Data Mining, KDD 2008, New York, NY, USA, pp. 7–15 (2008)
21. Ganev, V., Guo, Z., Serrano, D., Barbosa, D., Stroulia, E.: Exploring and Visualizing Academic Social Networks. In: The 19th the ACM Conference on Information and Knowledge Management, CIKM 2010 Demo (2010)
22. Knorr-Cetina, K.: Sociality with objects: social relations in postsocial knowledge societies. Theory, Culture & Society 14(4), 1–30 (1997)

The SMARTERCONTEXT Ontology and Its Application to the Smart Internet: A Smarter Commerce Case Study

Norha M. Villegas[1,2,3] and Hausi A. Müller[1]

[1] University of Victoria, Victoria, Canada
hausi@cs.uvic.ca
[2] Icesi University, Cali, Colombia
nvillega@cs.uvic.ca
[3] IBM Canada CAS Research, Toronto, Canada

Abstract. In the *smart internet* interactions must be situation-aware and smart. That is, they must be realized with awareness of, and adaptation to users' individual and collective context situations. Therefore, context management is crucial to deliver contents and services that are relevant to the user's matters of concern. This paper presents the SMARTERCONTEXT ontology, our semantic web approach to context representation and reasoning applicable to user-centric domains of the smart internet. We illustrate the application of the SMARTERCONTEXT ontology using a *personal web* case study based on IBM's *smarter commerce* initiative. This case study demonstrates how our ontology supports context representation and reasoning to improve the relevance of retailer offers with respect to shopper situations. Our ontology is the core of the SMARTERCONTEXT infrastructure, our context management solution that exploits user web interactions as sources of meaningful personal context information, and empowers users to control context gathering and provisioning.

Keywords: dynamic context, smart internet, personal web, context representation, semantic web, ontologies, context reasoning, smarter commerce.

1 Introduction

In the smart internet, contents and services are discovered, aggregated and delivered dynamically, interactively, fully or semi-automatically in response to evolving user concerns, and under heterogeneous system infrastructures [1]. Therefore, the realization of the smart internet is highly dependent on its capabilities to understand the situation of users, individually and collectively, and the situation of services with respect to the matters of concern (mocs) of the users for which they are intended. Moreover, as mocs continuously evolve (e.g., the user's location, agenda, or shopping list change over time), context representation and reasoning mechanisms must be flexible enough to support, at runtime, the modeling of new context types and changes in inference rules.

The smart internet's three main principles are defined as follows: (i) a user-centric model for instinctive interactions, (ii) sessions for users and their mocs, and (iii) collective and collaborative web interactions [1]. These principles pose many different

M. Chignell et al. (Eds.): The Personal Web, LNCS 7855, pp. 151–184, 2013.

technological challenges. Among these challenges, context management (i.e., context representation, reasoning, gathering, provisioning, and the adaptation of context models and reasoners at runtime) constitute a major research problem [2,3]. First, user-centric models for instinctive interactions must include the relevant characteristics of context entities that describe the situation of users and services. Second, personal mocs must be explicitly modeled and managed as evolving context facts across sessions. Finally, collective and collaborative web interactions require the identification of not only individual but also social and activity context [2], to manage the satisfaction of individual mocs taking into account the social context sphere within which users interact.

To tackle the context awareness challenges posed by the smart internet, we developed the SMARTERCONTEXT context manager. Our solution provides an effective mechanism to model user mocs in the form of context facts. Most importantly, it tracks changes in their states to support smart internet applications in the delivery of personalized services and contents to users. This paper presents the SMARTERCONTEXT ontology which is the core of context representation and reasoning in our solution. Our ontology supports the specification of personal context information using context models that are in the form of *linked data* [4]. We designed the SMARTERCONTEXT ontology in such a way that it can be extended by either creating further layers in its hierarchical structure, or integrating existing domain-specific semantic web vocabularies into its layers. To the best of our knowledge, our ontology is the only existing context representation and reasoning mechanism, intended for user-centric web applications, that defines a common framework to integrate domain-specific vocabularies and reasoning rules. Thus, the goal of our ontology is not to provide exhaustive context vocabularies. The motivation of this paper is to illustrate how to extend the SMARTERCONTEXT ontology according to the context awareness requirements of particular domains. For this, we use a *personal web* case study based on the IBM's *smarter commerce* initiative,[1] where the management of context information optimizes the shopper's web experience [5]. For example, by providing retailers with meaningful information about the intents and situations of online shoppers to deliver the proper offer, to the right customer, at the most convenient time.

The remaining sections of this paper are organized as follows. Section 2 introduces the smarter commerce case study and explains, in general terms, the application of our SMARTERCONTEXT solution to this case study. Section 3 presents the semantic web foundations of the SMARTERCONTEXT ontology. Section 4 presents methodological aspects of the definition of the ontology. Section 5 illustrates the application of the SMARTERCONTEXT ontology to context representation in the smarter commerce case study. Section 6 explains the foundational module of the SMARTERCONTEXT ontology. Section 7 presents the modules that extend the ontology for realizing context representation and reasoning in the personal web and the smarter commerce case study. Section 8 explains the context reasoning capabilities supported by the ontology. Section 9 discusses related work. Section 10 posits research challenges and summarizes ongoing work. Finally, Section 11 concludes the paper.

---

[1] http://www.ibm.com/smarterplanet/us/en/
smarter_commerce/overview

2   Context Management with SMARTERCONTEXT

2.1   The Smarter Commerce Case Study

Suppose that Norha is a frequent mobile shopping user. To optimize her shopping experience, she registered herself into the SMARTERCONTEXT infrastructure to create her context sphere (the repository of personal context managed by SMARTERCONTEXT). SMARTERCONTEXT gathers relevant context about Norha's situations from different sources such as her mobile devices, and her web interactions. This information is represented using the SMARTERCONTEXT ontology and processed to provide Norha's favorite applications with relevant context about her shopping preferences and situations. Suppose Norha registered the shopping mobile applications of Target,[2] Sears,[3] and Walmart[4] (assuming that these are applications compliant with SMARTERCONTEXT) into her personal context sphere. An application compliant with SMARTERCONTEXT tracks user web interactions and processes Resource Description Framework (RDF) [6] models based on the SMARTERCONTEXT ontology. As a result, the SMARTERCONTEXT infrastructure is now able to gather and provide Norha's relevant context information from and to these retailers. Norha also integrated into her context sphere her shopping list (an application compliant with SMARTERCONTEXT deployed in her mobile device), and her preferred location (e.g., Victoria, BC).

From the very first time Norha browses any of the integrated retailer applications, these applications can take advantage of Norha's personal context to improve her shopping experience. Suppose Norha is browsing the Target's product catalog. Since the application knows Norha's situation and preferences, it suggests relevant products accordingly. Norha can interact with these products through web interactions such as likes, tags, wish lists, and rankings. Product categories involved in these interactions constitute relevant context information that is then integrated into the user's personal context sphere. The SMARTERCONTEXT reasoning engine uses gathered context to infer implicit context facts. In this way SMARTERCONTEXT provides more accurate information about Norha's preferences to authorized applications.

Suppose now Norha is visiting Edmonton and has just arrived at West Edmonton Mall.[5] As soon as she gets into the mall, the smarter commerce application in her mobile device suggests deals available at the stores located in the mall, according to her preferences and shopping list. These stores correspond to those that provide the shopping applications integrated into her context sphere. Moreover, shopping preferences of people in her social network can be taken into account by SMARTERCONTEXT to suggest relevant products available at the mall.

2.2   SMARTERCONTEXT Overview

To manage context information with the goal of improving user shopping experiences as described in the case study, we implemented the SMARTERCONTEXT infrastructure [5]. Our context management solution (i) gathers context from the interactions of

---

[2] http://www.target.ca
[3] http://www.sears.ca
[4] http://www.walmart.ca/en
[5] http://www.wem.ca

users with web entities (e.g., the interactions of Norha with the products offered in Target's catalog); (ii) integrates this context into the user's personal repository of context information called the *personal context sphere (PCS)*; (iii) reasons why the information is stored in a PCS (e.g., to suggest products related to the products from Sears catalog that the user just added into her wish list); (iv) provides meaningful context to any web application compliant with SMARTERCONTEXT, authorized by the user, and related to the user's current web experience—we call these applications personal web enabled (PWE) applications; and (vi) enables users to delete and modify personal context, as well as to grant and deny context sharing privileges when desired.

The SMARTERCONTEXT infrastructure is composed of a context reasoning engine that relies on the SMARTERCONTEXT ontology and uses semantic web technologies to infer implicit context facts, and a cloud-based service component architecture (SCA) infrastructure that exploits web services to implement context gathering and provisioning. For the smarter commerce case study, SMARTERCONTEXT includes a browser extension for the identification of context providers and consumers such as PWE sites with which the user interacts. These web sites must deploy an interoperability component that enables them to exchange context information with the SMARTERCONTEXT engine. This interoperability component implements two services. The first service is to obtain the context provided by the SMARTERCONTEXT infrastructure. The second is to send context gathered from the interactions of users with web entities to the SMARTERCONTEXT infrastructure. This component includes also two internal methods. The first one keeps track of user interactions (e.g., likes and wishes), and the other one processes RDF/XML context messages.

Figure 1 below provides an overview of our SMARTERCONTEXT solution applied to a smarter commerce case study. The big circle represents the user in her online shopping experience. PWE-Site 1 and 2 are two web sites that are able to communicate with the SMARTERCONTEXT engine. The user authorized SMARTERCONTEXT to gather personal context from her interactions with these web sites, and to provide them with relevant context about her. Suppose user Norha uses a PWE-browser (a browser enabled with the SMARTERCONTEXT extension) to load an online shopping catalog provided by PWE-Site 1 (i.e., Label 1). Suppose the user adds into her wish list a pair of earrings available in this catalog. Since PWE-Site 1 is a context provider authorized by the user, SMARTERCONTEXT gathers meaningful context about Norha's preferences from this interaction (i.e., Label 2 and 3). The SMARTERCONTEXT component deployed at PWE-Site 1 sends this context information in the form of an RDF/XML message to the SMARTERCONTEXT infrastructure, which integrates the gathered context into the user's PCS. The SMARTERCONTEXT engine infers new context facts about Norha's preferences based on the information stored in her context repository. For example, the engine can infer that Norha may be interested in the product category "necklaces" since she added the "earrings" category into her wish list. Suppose now the user interacts with PWE-Site 2 (i.e., Label 4). Since it is an authorized context consumer, SMARTERCONTEXT provides PWE-Site 2 with relevant context about Norha's preferences. This web site can now exploit this information to deliver more relevant shopping offers to the user (i.e., Label 5).

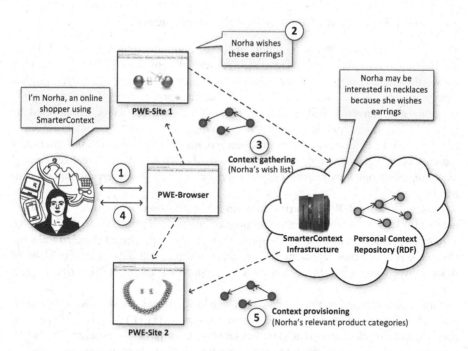

Fig. 1. Our SMARTERCONTEXT solution applied to the smarter commerce case study

Further details on our SMARTERCONTEXT infrastructure and its user-controlled privacy and security mechanisms are available in [5] and [7], respectively.

3   Semantic Web Foundations

The semantic web can be defined as an extension of the web that enables systems to smartly search, combine, and process web data based on the meaning that this data has to humans [8]. This extension exploits the potential of the web since it allows data sharing effectively across the internet [9].

Semantic web technologies provide the means to build models that allow the description of anything in the web, to reason about the knowledge encoded by these models, and to transmit this knowledge among web resources [8]. Our solution exploits semantic web technologies to manage context information as required by the smart internet. First, RDF provides the framework to represent context entities and describe relevant information about them. Thus the SMARTERCONTEXT ontology is based on RDF. Second, RDF, RDF Schema (RDFS) [10], and OWL [11] provide the semantic mechanisms to reason about context entities. Reasoning rules in SMARTERCONTEXT can be defined hierarchically such that more general rules are useful across the corresponding sub-domains. Finally, XML, RDF and OWL provide the data integration and interoperability mechanisms for context gathering and provisioning.

3.1   Linked Data and the Resource Description Framework

The vision of the semantic web relies on linked data, a common framework based on RDF for sharing data and integrating a variety of applications [9,8]. Linked data allows the creation of typed links between data from different sources. This implies data published on the web such that it is machine-processable, it has an explicit meaning, and can be linked to other data sets. SMARTERCONTEXT, supported by linked data, realizes context gathering and provisioning by making context information available to be discovered, and machine-processable since context information is represented in a standardized way. Furthermore, SMARTERCONTEXT realizes context reasoning as its ontology provides explicit semantics that allow inferring implicit context facts.

Linked data uses RDF to describe things in any application domain using typed statements also known as labeled links. Building on top of RDF, the SMARTERCONTEXT ontology provides the entity types (context things), object properties (labeled links between entity types that represent context relationships), and data properties (labeled links between entity attributes and their corresponding values) to describe context entities.

Linked data is based on two fundamental web technologies, Uniform Resource Identifiers (URIs) [12], and the HyperText Transfer Protocol (HTTP) [13]. A URI is a compact sequence of characters that identifies an abstract or physical resource. The HTTP protocol provides a mechanism for retrieving information about entities identified by URIs. RDF is based on the principle that things can be described by making statements about their properties and corresponding values. For this, RDF encodes data in the form of statements defined as *subject, predicate, object* triples [6]. The subject is the entity the statement is about, the predicate is the property being described about this entity, and the object corresponds to the value of the described property.

Figure 2 depicts a simple RDF statement with corresponding subject, predicate, and object. This statement provides context information about our user's preferred location: "Norha" (the subject) has "preferred location" (the predicate) "Victoria" (the object). Subject, predicate, and object are identified by a URI. For convenience, RDF specifications use a shorthand for referring to URI references (QName). In this way, the full URI is defined by appending the local identifier to the abbreviation (QName prefix). For example, the statement presented in Fig. 2 involves two QName prefixes: `pwc:` to abbreviate the namespace of one of the modules of the SMARTERCONTEXT ontology: `http://smartercontext.org/vocabularies/pwc/v5.0/pwc.owl#`, and `geo:` to abbreviate the namespace of the vocabulary for geographical locations: `http://smartercontext.org/vocabularies/rdf/geo.rdf#`.

Table 1 provides the list of namespaces and corresponding prefixes for the schemas and ontologies used throughout this paper. Protégé [14], the tool used to create and edit ontologies in the SMARTERCONTEXT project, can easily be used to visualize the ontologies described in this paper.

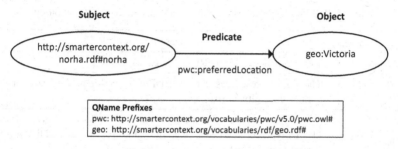

Fig. 2. A simple RDF statement

Table 1. RDF and OWL schemas, and ontologies used throughout the paper

Prefix	Namespace
gc:	smartercontext.org/vocabularies/gc/v5.0/gc.owl#
pwc:	smartercontext.org/vocabularies/pwc/v5.0/pwc.owl#
shopping:	smartercontext.org/vocabularies/shopping/v5.0/shopping.owl#
geo:	smartercontext.org/vocabularies/rdf/geo.rdf#
google:	smartercontext.org/vocabularies/rdf/googleproducts.rdf#
deals:	smartercontext.org/vocabularies/rdf/dealcategories.owl#
rdf:	www.w3.org/1999/02/22-rdf-syntax-ns#
rdfs:	www.w3.org/2000/01/rdf-schema#
owl:	www.w3.org/2002/07/owl#

3.2 Vocabularies

Semantic web vocabularies are collections of classes and properties expressed in RDF using types from the RDF Vocabulary Definition Language (RDFS) [10] and the Web Ontology Language (OWL) [11].

RDF Vocabulary Definition Language (RDFS). RDF Schema is a semantic extension of RDF that defines classes and properties used to describe classes, properties, and other RDF resources. Tables 2 and 3 summarize the classes and properties from the RDFS specification [10] used in the SMARTERCONTEXT ontology.

The Web Ontology Language (OWL). RDFS is suitable for modeling simple ontologies and has limited knowledge inference capabilities [8]. To model more complex knowledge, the semantic web provides OWL, an expressive representation language based on formal logic. OWL is used to model ontologies. An OWL ontology is a set of classes, properties, and individuals useful to describe entities and the relationships among them in a particular application domain. Classes are instances of `owl:Class`, which is a subclass of `rdfs:Class`. Therefore, as described in Table 2, OWL classes

Table 2. RDF Schema classes used in our SMARTERCONTEXT ontology

Class	Description
rdfs:Resource	Any entity described by RDF — e.g., user Norha.
rdfs:Class	The class of resources that are RDF classes — e.g., a class User that defines the entity Norha.
rdfs:Literal	The class of resources that are values such as strings or integers. Literals may be typed or untyped — e.g., the values for the age and the address of user Norha.
rdfs:Datatype	Any datatype defined in the XML Schema [15].

Table 3. RDF Schema [10] properties used in our SMARTERCONTEXT ontology

Property	Description
rdfs:range	Defines the universe of possible values of a property — e.g., the possible values of the property `pwc:preferredLocation` correspond to entities of type *Location* context.
rdfs:domain	States that any resource with a given property is an instance of one or more classes — e.g., any resource that has a preferred location is an instance of class *User*.
rdf:type	States that a resource is an instance of a class — e.g. Norha is an instance of type *User*.
rdfs:subClassOf	States that all the instances of a class are instances of another one — e.g., every instance of class User is an instance of class *HumanEntity*.
rdfs:sub PropertyOf	States that all the resources related by a property are also related by another one — e.g., if *Norha* is related to *Peter* by the property *daughterOf*, and *daughter of* is a subproperty of *relative of*, *Norha* is related to *Peter* by the property *relative of*.

are RDF resources of type class. Individuals correspond to instances of classes. OWL defines two types of properties, abstract properties and concrete properties. Abstract properties relate individuals with individuals, whereas concrete properties link individuals with data values. Both are subtypes of *rdf:Property*.

The SMARTERCONTEXT ontology is based on RDF and a subset of the OWL-Lite [16] specification. Taking into account that pure RDFS is not sufficient for context reasoning as envisioned in SMARTERCONTEXT, we decided to use the simpler version of OWL called OWL-lite which provides enough support for context representation and reasoning. Table 4 describes the OWL-Lite properties used in our SMARTERCONTEXT ontology.

Table 4. OWL-Lite [16] properties used in our SMARTERCONTEXT ontology

Feature	Description
owl:inverseOf	If properties P_1 and P_2 are inverse, then if X is related to Y by P_2, then Y is related to X by P_1 — e.g., properties *hosts* and *hosted by* are inverse. Thus, if CASCON 2012 is *hosted by* Hilton Markham, then Hilton Markham *hosts* CASCON 2012.
owl:Transitive Property	If a property P is transitive, then if X is related to Y by P, and Y is related to Z by P, then X is related to Z by P — e.g., *located in* is a transitive property. If Norha is *located in* Victoria, and Victoria is *located in* British Columbia, then Norha is *located in* British Columbia.
owl:Functional Property	A property that has at most one value — e.g., the year a human entity was born.
owl:Symmetric Property	If a property P is symmetric and X is related to Y by P, then Y is related to X by P — e.g., the property *near to* is symmetric. If Victoria is *near to* Vancouver, then Vancouver is *near to* Victoria.

4 Introduction to the SMARTERCONTEXT Ontology

The SMARTERCONTEXT ontology is an RDF-based vocabulary defined to represent explicit context information, and to reason about these context representations to derive implicit context facts at runtime. The version of the SMARTERCONTEXT ontology presented in this paper relies on OWL-Lite to reason about context information using formal logic [16]. That is, context reasoning capabilities are based on the RDFS classes presented in Table 2, the RDFS properties presented in Table 3, and the subset of OWL-Lite properties presented in Table 4.

4.1 Methodological Aspects

The genesis of our context manager and the SMARTERCONTEXT ontology is an extensive survey on context modeling and context management approaches in different problem domains of context-aware computing [2]. The motivation of this systematic literature review, from the perspective of the smart internet, was the identification of context modeling and context management requirements to support context-awareness as required by smart interactions and services. As a result, we proposed a general classification of context information. This general classification, known as the *General Context (GC)* taxonomy, constitutes the fundamental module of the SMARTERCONTEXT ontology.

4.2 Requirements Analysis

We define the requirements for context representation in user-centric smart internet applications as follows:

RQ-i. Context information must be gathered and provided in an interoperable way.

RQ-ii. It must be possible to represent context entities, the relationships among them, the properties that characterize their situation, and the relationships between these entities and the user.

RQ-iii. Timeliness modeling must be supported (i.e., the representation of past, present and future situations).

RQ-iv. Context representations must be able to adapt at runtime according to changes in the situation of users and systems. That is, context entities may appear, disappear or be modified dynamically without affecting the relevance of the context management infrastructure.

Regarding RQ-i, the knowledge represented in a semantic format is better suited for interoperation from the perspective of systems and knowledge sources [8]. Concerning requirement RQ-ii, RDFS and OWL-Lite provide sufficient expressiveness to characterize context types with corresponding properties, and to represent context relationships, constraints and granularity levels. Concerning RQ-iii and RQ-iv, context models based on RDF graphs support the representation of context data over time, and can easily be modified at runtime to add or delete context facts according to changes in context situations [5,17].

4.3   Extensibility and Modularity

Modularization, as in many other domains, is a best practice in ontology design [8]. The increasing size and complexity of context models require collaborative design. Moreover, the design of loosely coupled ontologies facilitates their processing, maintenance and evolution. Modular ontologies also guarantee privacy and security requirements since it is easier to control the level of exposure of sensible data [7].

We designed SMARTERCONTEXT as a modular and extensible ontology. Its foundational module, *general context (GC)*, enables context representation and reasoning for any problem domain of the smart internet. Because of its modular structure, the SMARTERCONTEXT ontology supports vertical and horizontal extensibility. *Vertical extensibility* makes the SMARTERCONTEXT ontology applicable to different problem domains. It is realized by defining more specialized modules that inherit from the GC module or other modules derived from GC. The application of the SMARTERCONTEXT ontology to a particular domain may imply the definition of several hierarchical levels. For example, to support context-awareness in the personal web (PW) we derived from GC the *personal web context (PWC)* module. The PWC module supports context representation and reasoning in any problem domain of the PW. To apply SMARTERCONTEXT to a particular application of the PW, the recommended practice is to extend the PWC module further by defining more particular context types and context reasoning rules according to the specific domain. For example, we derived from PWC the *shopping* module to support context representation and reasoning in our smarter commerce case study [5]. *Horizontal extensibility* is realized by importing existing vocabularies into any of the ontology's modules.

Table 5. RDF triples that illustrate the personal context sphere for user Norha

#	Subject	Predicate	Object
1	google:XBox_360_Consoles	rdf:type	shopping:ProductService Category
2	gabriel.rdf#gabriel	rdf:type	gc:HumanEntity
3	google:Earrings	rdf:type	shopping:ProductService Category
4	geo:Victoria	rdf:type	gc:GeoLocation
5	deals:Gyms_&_ Fitness_Centers	rdf:type	shopping:ProductService Category
6	google:Electric_Grills	rdf:type	shopping:ProductService Category
7	google:Tennis_Shoes	rdf:type	shopping:ProductService Category
8	http://www.wem.ca	gc:geoLocation Classification	"Place"^^xsd:string
9	http://www.wem.ca	rdf:type	gc:PhysicalLocation
10	http://www.wem.ca	rdf:type	gc:PhysicalLocation
11	norha.rdf#norha	pwc:isInterestedIn	deals:Gyms_&_ Fitness_Centers
12	norha.rdf#norha	pwc:hasIntegrated	http://www.sears.ca
13	norha.rdf#norha	shopping:toBuy	google:Electric_Grills
14	norha.rdf#norha	gc:locatedIn	http://www.wem.ca
15	norha.rdf#norha	pwc:marriedTo	gabriel.rdf#gabriel
16	norha.rdf#norha	rdf:type	pwc:User
17	norha.rdf#norha	pwc:likes	google:XBox_360_Consoles
18	norha.rdf#norha	pwc:preferredLocation	geo:Victoria
19	norha.rdf#norha	shopping:wishes	google:Earrings
20	norha.rdf#norha	pwc:hasIntegrated	http://www.target.ca
21	norha.rdf#norha	pwc:hasIntegrated	http://www.walmart.ca.en
22	norha.rdf#norha	shopping:toBuy	google:Tennis_Shoes
23	norha.rdf#norha	pwc:colleagueOf	tatiana.rdf#tatiana
24	http://www.walmart.ca/en	rdf:type	pwc:PWESite
25	http://www.sears.ca	rdf:type	pwc:PWESite
26	http://www.target.ca	rdf:type	pwc:PWESite

5   Context Representation in the Personal Web

Context information in our context management solution is represented in the form of RDF graphs where resources and predicates (nodes and arcs) are compliant with the types defined in the SMARTERCONTEXT ontology. In the case study presented in this paper these types correspond to the classes, object properties, and data properties defined in the ontology's modules: GC, PWC, and Shopping, including their horizontal extensions.

A partial version of a context sphere for user Norha in the scenario described in Sect. 2.1 is available in `http://smartercontext.org/examples/norha.rdf`. This context model is composed of 26 SMARTERCONTEXT triples detailed in Table 5. As explained in Section 3.1, each triple represents an RDF statement, context facts in SMARTERCONTEXT, defined by a subject, a predicate, and an object.

The World Wide Web Consortium[6] (W3C) provides an RDF validation service[7] useful to visualize small RDF graphs. It is possible to visualize the exemplar of user Norha's context repository used in this paper by copying the RDF/XML contents to the "Check by Direct Input" field of the validator, or by entering the URL of the model (`http://smartercontext.org/examples/norha.rdf`) in the field "Check by URI" of the validator.

6   The General Context (GC) Module

The GC module defines context types (classes), abstract properties (relationships between classes), and concrete properties (links between attributes of individuals and their corresponding values) applicable to any problem domain, for instance the smart internet.

6.1   Context Entities in the GC Module

Table 6 details the entities defined in the GC module. For each class, it presents the corresponding context entity type (column *Entity*), the class the entity is derived from (column *Superclass*), and a description of the role that the entity plays in the SMARTERCONTEXT ontology (column *Description*). This column schema is used to describe the class types of the ontologies presented in the subsequent sections of this paper.

6.2   Object Properties in the GC Module

Table 7 presents the object properties (abstract properties) defined in the GC module. GC's object properties constitute context relationships between context entities defined in the GC module or in any of its extensions. For each object property, this table presents in column *Domain* the values of the domain, in column *Range* the values of the range, in column *Features* whether the property is transitive (T), functional (F), or symmetric

---

[6] `http://www.w3.org/`
[7] `http://www.w3.org/RDF/Validator`

Table 6. Context entities defined in the GC module of the SMARTERCONTEXT ontology

Entity (Class)	Superclass	Description
ContextEntity	owl:Thing	The superclass of any context type.
ActivityContext	ContextEntity	Actions and tasks performed by an object - e.g., attending a meeting.
IndividualContext	ContextEntity	Anything that can be observed about an isolated object - e.g., the object location.
ArtificialEntity	IndividualContext	Entities resulting from human actions or technical processes - e.g., buildings, hardware and software configurations.
GroupEntity	IndividualContext	Groups of subjects that share common characteristics but not necessarily interact with each other - e.g., Canadian women.
HumanEntity	IndividualContext	Any information about a person's behavior, preferences, characteristics and way of interacting with a system - e.g., an online shopper.
NaturalEntity	IndividualContext	Living and non-living entities which are not the direct result of any human activity - e.g., weather conditions.
LocationContext	ContextEntity	The place of settlement or activity of an object.
PhysicalLocation	LocationContext	A physical place of settlement or activity of an object - e.g., University of Victoria.
GeoLocation	PhysicalLocation	The latitude and altitude that describe a physical location.
VirtualLocation	LocationContext	Location describable by a URI - e.g., namespace of the SMARTERCONTEXT ontology.
Endpoint	VirtualLocation	A URI that identifies the location of a computational resource - e.g., the SOAP address of a context sensor exposed as a service.
TimeContext	ContextEntity	Provides context about a specific date and time, but also categorical information such as holidays, working days, and meeting schedules - e.g., Boxing Day.
DefiniteTime	TimeContext	Represents time frames with specific begin and end points (i.e., the duration of a conference).
IndefiniteTime	TimeContext	Expresses a recurrent event which is happening while another situation is taking place. It is not possible to know its duration in advance -e.g., the time a service is online.

(S), and in column *Inverse Of* the properties that are inverse of the described property. This column schema is used to describe object properties in the PWC and Shopping modules of the SMARTERCONTEXT ontology.

The `associationRelationship` object property represents aggregation and association context relationships (different than functional and social relations). Both its domain and range correspond to entities of the type `contextEntity`. `locationRelationship` includes any object property with range equal to the `LocationContext` type. GC defines no domain for the `LocationContext` property as it may depend on the specific application domain. `hostedBy` and `locatedIn` are sub-properties of `locationRelationship`. The value of `hostedBy` in a triple represents a `LocationContext` entity that hosts the `ActivityContext` entity represented by the subject. The value of `locatedIn` represents the location where the subject (an `IndividualContext` or `LocationContext` entity) is located in. The `functionalRelationship` object property refers to information about the usage that an object can make of another. As indicated by its domain and range, functional relationships can exist between any pair of context entities. The value of the `hosts` property, which inherits from `functionalRelationship`, corresponds to a scheduled event that has place in the `LocationContext` entity represented by the subject. Finally, the `socialRelationship` object property emerges from the interrelation between individuals of type `HumanEntity` and `GroupEntity`. Samples of this relational context are affiliations, colleagues, and customers.

Table 7. Object properties defined in the GC module of the SMARTERCONTEXT ontology. The *T* in column *Features* stands for owl:TransitiveProperty.

Property	Domain	Range	Features	Inverse Of
association Relationship	ContextEntity	ContextEntity	-	-
location Relationship	-	LocationContext	-	-
hostedBy	ActivityContext	LocationContext	-	hosts
locatedIn	IndividualContext LocationContext	LocationContext	T	-
functional Relationship	ContextEntity	ContextEntity	-	-
hosts	LocationContext	ActivityContext	-	hostedBy
social Relationship	GroupEntity HumanEntity	GroupEntity HumanEntity	-	-

6.3   Data Properties in the GC Module

Table 8 details the data properties (concrete properties) defined in the GC module. Data properties allow the description of context attributes (i.e., characteristics of context entities). All of these properties correspond to functional properties, that is, properties that have at most one value. The domain corresponds to the context entity type for which the data property is defined. The range details the valid data types for the values of the properties. In many cases, the range of a data property is restricted to a set of specific values. Such is the case of the `geoLocationClassification` data property.

6.4 Horizontal Extension in the GC Module

Foundational elements defined in the GC module can be extended horizontally by importing concrete vocabularies. In this case study we extended the GC module by defining a vocabulary to characterize `GeoLocation` entities and the relationships among them. Any other semantic web geographical vocabulary can be used for this extension.

Table 8. Data properties defined in the GC module of the SMARTERCONTEXT ontology. All of the properties in this table correspond to functional properties.

Property	Domain	Range	Value Description
address	GeoLocation	xsd:string	Corresponds to a String literal that denotes the exact location of a GeoLocation context entity.
endDateTime	DefiniteTime	xsd:dateTime	A dateTime value that denotes the end time of DefiniteTime context entity (the last value of the time interval).
geoLocation Classification	GeoLocation	"City", "Country", "Neighborhood", "Place", "Region"	Classifies GeoLocation context types.
latitude	GeoLocation	xsd:string	The angular distance north or south of the Equator, in degrees, minutes, and seconds of a GeoLocation context entity.
longitude	GeoLocation	xsd:string	The angular distance, in degrees, minutes, and seconds, of GeoLocation context entity east or west of the Prime (Greenwich) Meridian.
startDateTime	DefiniteTime	xsd:dateTime	A dateTime value that denotes the beginning of a DefiniteTime context entity (the initial value of the time interval).
zipCode	GeoLocation	xsd:string	A string value that corresponds to the postal code of the GeoLocation entity represented by the subject.

7 SMARTERCONTEXT in the Personal Web

7.1 The Personal Web Context (PWC) Module

The PWC module extends the GC module vertically to define context types, object properties and data properties required to represent and reason about context information in context-aware applications within the personal web domain.

Context Entities in the PWC Module. Table 9 details the entities defined in the PWC module. PWConcern allows smart interactions and services to understand the nature of users mocs at a specific time (e.g., whether the user is surfing the web for shopping or social activities). The PWConcern entity defines seven categories of personal web concerns: *Academic, Business, Entertainment, Healthcare, Shopping, Social,* and *Travel.*

Table 9. Context entities defined in the PWC module of the SMARTERCONTEXT ontology

Entity (Class)	Superclass	Description
PWConcern	gc:ActivityContext	Classifies web resources and activities a user performs in the web - e.g., shopping, academic, healthcare.
ScheduledEvent	gc:ActivityContext	A calendar event defined in a personal agenda - e.g., a business trip.
PhysicalEntity	gc:ArtificialEntity	A context entity that is not available as a web entity. E.g., the user's preferred currency.
WebResource	gc:ArtificialEntity	Web elements the user interacts with such as web sites, and web services - e.g., Walmart's shopping site.
PWESite	WebResource	Represents a web site compliant with the SMARTERCONTEXT framework [5].
WebEntity	WebResource	Any entity available on the web different than PWE sites and web services - E.g., products or services offered online, a personal health record.
WebService	WebResource	Any web service relevant to the user - e.g., a service for payments with credit cards.
User	gc:HumanEntity	Refers to any information about the user's behavior and preferences -e.g., security profiles, language preferences, and personal information.

Object Properties in the PWC Module. Table 10 details the object properties (abstract properties) defined in the PWC module. Column *Features* indicates whether the property is transitive (T), functional (F), or symmetric (S). PWC object properties,

which extend from the object properties defined in the GC module, allow the definition of context relationships between context entities defined in the PWC module or in
any of its extensions.

The concerns property associates context entities of type ScheduledEvent,
gc:NaturalEntity, gc:ArtificialEntity, gc:LocationContext,
and gc:GroupEntity with relevant categories defined as entities of type
PWConcern (e.g., a personal calendar event associated with a shopping
concern). hasIntegrated allows the integration of any instance of type
IndividualContext to the user's context sphere (e.g., a personal agenda
application integrated through a web service). isNearTo associates two entities of type gc:GeoLocation as close to each other (within a short distance).
Since property isNearTo is symmetric, it applies to both entities. Property
preferredLocation defines a gc:GeoLocation entity as the user's favorite
place of settlement. As it is a functional property, each user can have one preferred location at most. concerns, and hasIntegrated are sub-properties of
gc:associationRelationship. isNearTo, and preferredLocation
are sub-properties of gc:locationRelationship, which is sub-property of
gc:associationRelationship.

Property identifiedBy is useful for identifying context entities of type
WebResource. The value of this property is an entity of type gc:Endpoint. For
example a shopping web site identified by its URL http://www.amazon.ca/.
scheduledFor is used to define the schedule of calendar events. Both
identifiedBy and scheduledFor are functional properties and inherit from
gc:functionalRelationship. Another PWC object property that extends from
gc:functionalRelationship is userInteraction. This property is abso-
lutely crucial for context integration in the personal web since the user is the one who
knows about web entities and their relationship with her own situation. User interactions
provide the means to identify context entities relevant to the user's situation throughout
her web experience. For example, through a simple interaction such as *liking* a product, the user provides the SMARTERCONTEXT infrastructure with relevant information
about her preferences. The current version of the SMARTERCONTEXT ontology subdi-
vides user interactions defined in the PWC module in the following object properties:
dislikes, isInterestedIn, likes, ranked, and tagged.

Social context relationships (gc:socialRelationship) emerge from the
interrelation between entities of type GroupEntity and HumanEntity. The PWC
module defines the following object properties to represent social relationships in any
application domain of the personal web: affiliatedWith, associates,
colleagueOf, engagedTo, friendOf, and relativeOf, which
is subdivided in childOf, marriedTo, parentOf, and siblingOf.
affiliatedWith and associates are inverse. colleagueOf, engagedTo,
and friendOf are symmetric properties and apply between two entities of type
gc:HumanEntity. childOf and parentOf are inverse properties.

Data Properties in the PWC Module.   Table 11 details the data
properties (concrete properties) defined in the PWC module. The data

Table 10. Object properties defined in the PWC module of the SMARTERCONTEXT ontology. The *S* and the *F* in column *Features* stand for owl:SymmetricProperty and owl:FunctionalProperty, respectively.

Property	Domain	Range	Features	Inverse Of
concerns	ScheduledEvent gc:NaturalEntity gc:ArtificialEntity gc:LocationContext gc:GroupEntity	PWConcern	-	-
hasIntegrated	User	gc:IndividualContext	-	-
isNearTo	gc:GeoLocation	gc:GeoLocation	S	-
preferredLocation	User	gc:GeoLocation	F	-
identifiedBy	WebResource	Endpoint	F	-
scheduledFor	ScheduledEvent	gc:DefiniteTime	F	-
userInteraction	gc:HumanEntity	gc:IndividualContext	-	-
dislikes	User	gc:IndividualContext	-	-
isInterestedIn	User	gc:IndividualContext	-	-
likes	User	gc:IndividualContext	-	-
ranked	User	gc:IndividualContext	-	-
tagged	User	gc:IndividualContext	-	-
affiliatedWith	gc:HumanEntity	gc:GroupEntity	-	associates
associates	gc:GroupEntity	gc:HumanEntity	-	affiliatedWith
colleagueOf	gc:HumanEntity	gc:HumanEntity	S	-
engagedTo	gc:HumanEntity	gc:HumanEntity	S	-
friendOf	gc:HumanEntity	gc:HumanEntity	S	-
relativeOf	gc:HumanEntity	gc:HumanEntity	S	-
childOf	gc:HumanEntity	gc:HumanEntity	-	parentOf
marriedTo	gc:HumanEntity	gc:HumanEntity	S	-
parentOf	gc:HumanEntity	gc:HumanEntity	-	childOf
siblingOf	gc:HumanEntity	gc:HumanEntity	S	-

properties birthYear, emailAccount, givenName, hasGender, lastName, and preferredLanguage define attributes of context entities of type gc:HumanEntity. rankingValue rates any entity of type gc:IndividualContext. It is used together with the ranked object property. scheduledEventDescription and scheduledEventTittle describe attributes of calendar events (i.e., instances of type ScheduledEvent).

Table 11. Data properties defined in the PWC module of the SMARTERCONTEXT ontology

Property	Domain	Range	Value Description
birthYear	gc:HumanEntity	xsd:int	Functional. The year a human entity was born.
emailAccount	gc:HumanEntity	xsd:string	An email account associated with the human entity represented by the subject.
givenName	gc:HumanEntity	xsd:string	Functional. The given name of the human entity represented by the subject.
hasGender	gc:HumanEntity	"Female", "Male", "NotSpecified"	Functional. The gender of the human entity represented by the subject.
lastName	gc:HumanEntity	xsd:string	Functional. The last name of the human entity represented by the subject.
preferred Language	gc:HumanEntity	xsd:string	The preferred language of the human entity represented by the subject.
rankingValue	gc:Individual Context	xsd:int	Functional. The ranking value assigned by the user to the entity represented by the subject.
scheduledEvent Description	ScheduledEvent	xsd:string	Functional. The description of the scheduled event represented by the subject.
scheduledEvent Title	ScheduledEvent	xsd:string	Functional. The title of the scheduled event represented by the subject.

7.2 The Shopping Module

The SMARTERCONTEXT Shopping module is an extension of the PWC module that supports context representation and reasoning in smarter commerce applications based on the PW. This section presents how we extended the PWC module, horizontally and vertically, to realize user-centric shopping interactions in our smarter commerce case study [5].

Context Entities in the Shopping Module. Table 12 details the classes defined as context entity types in the shopping module.

Object Properties in the Shopping Module. Table 13 details the types required to represent context relationships in the Shopping module. The relatedProductOrService object property, which extends from gc:associationRelationship, denotes that two product or service categories are related to each other (e.g., complementary products such as necklaces and earrings). preferredCurrency, preferredDeliveryMethod, and

Table 12. Context entities defined in the Shopping module of the SMARTERCONTEXT ontology

Entity (Class)	Superclass	Description
Currency	pwc:PhysicalEntity	Represents one of the user's preferred currencies - e.g., CAD, USD.
Delivery Method	pwc:PhysicalEntity	Represents one of the user's preferred delivery methods - e.g., Fedex.
Payment Method	pwc:PhysicalEntity	Represents one of the user's preferred payment methods - e.g., credit card, PayPal.
ProductService Category	pwc:WebEntity	Denotes a product or a service category offered online - e.g., Clothing, Electronics.

preferredPaymentMethod extend from gc:functionalRelationship and associate currencies, delivery methods and payment methods to the user. Four new types of user interactions extend pwc:userInteraction in the Shopping module. The first one, doesNotWish, indicates that the product or service category represented by the object cannot be part of the user's wish list. The second one, purchased, allows the SMARTERCONTEXT infrastructure to identify products the user purchased during her interactions with a particular shopping site. The third one, toBuy, indicates that the product or service category represented by the object is in the user's shopping list. Finally, the wishes object property represents that the corresponding product or service category was added by the user into her wish list.

Table 13. Object properties defined in the Shopping module of the SMARTERCONTEXT ontology. The *S* in column *Features* stands for owl:SymmetricProperty.

Property	Domain	Range	Features	Inverse Of
relatedProduct orService	ProductService Category	ProductService Category	S	-
preferred Currency	pwc:User	Currency	-	-
preferred DeliveryMethod	pwc:User	DeliveryMethod	-	-
preferred PaymentMethod	pwc:User	PaymentMethod	-	-
doesNotWish	pwc:User	ProductService Category	-	-
purchased	pwc:User	ProductService Category	-	-
toBuy	pwc:User	ProductService Category	-	-
wishes	pwc:User	ProductService Category	-	-

Table 14. Data properties defined in the Shopping module of the SMARTERCONTEXT ontology

Property	Domain	Range	Value Description
billingAddress	PaymentMethod	xsd:string	Functional. A string that represents the billing address of a PaymentMethod context entity.
cardNumber	PaymentMethod	xsd:string	Functional. A string that represents the card number of a PaymentMethod context entity.
expiration Month	PaymentMethod	xsd:int	Functional. An int that represents the expiration month of a PaymentMethod context entity.
expirationYear	PaymentMethod	xsd:int	Functional. An int that represents the billing address of a PaymentMethod context entity.
nameOnCard	PaymentMethod	xsd:string	Functional. A string that represents the name on card of a PaymentMethod context entity.
payment MethodType	PaymentMethod	xsd:string	Functional. A string that represents the type of a payment method - e.g., Visa, Mastercard, PayPal.
targetedFor Gender	Product ServiceCategory	Female, Male, None	Functional. A string that indicates whether the product or service category is intended for a particular gender.
verification Number	PaymentMethod	xsd:string	Functional. A string that represents the security number of a PaymentMethod context entity.

Data Properties in the Shopping Module. Table 14 details the data properties (concrete properties) that allow the definition of context attributes for context entities in the Shopping module.

Horizontal Extension in the Shopping Module. The Shopping module of the SMARTERCONTEXT ontology is extended horizontally by importing two RDF vocabularies that characterize products and services. Both vocabularies extend from the ProductServiceCategory context type. The first vocabulary corresponds to the *Google Product Taxonomy* [18]. This taxonomy categorizes products in Google's search results. Google provides this taxonomy in two formats, as a plain text file and as a spreadsheet. We converted this hierarchical set of product categories into an RDF vocabulary. The second vocabulary corresponds to the *Groupon Deal Categories* [19]. This taxonomy, available in JSON, XML and spreadsheet formats, provides the complete set of categories used by Groupon to characterize deals offered to users via email. To integrate this taxonomy into the Shopping module of the SMARTERCONTEXT ontology, we generated it as an RDF vocabulary [20].

8   Context Reasoning with the SMARTERCONTEXT Ontology

Context reasoning in the SMARTERCONTEXT framework relies on *deduction rules* supported by the RDFS specification and a subset of the axioms defined in OWL-Lite. Besides standard RDFS and OWL-Lite rules, SMARTERCONTEXT allows the definition of particular reasoning rules according to the problem domain. The definition of domain-dependent reasoning rules is part of the vertical extension capabilities of SMARTERCONTEXT.

The following two sub-sections present selected rules used in our smarter commerce case study to infer context facts about the preferences and situations of user Norha in the shopping scenario described in Section 2.1. Using RDF graph representations of context facts, we illustrate how each rule is applied by the SMARTERCONTEXT engine to infer implicit context facts which are represented by dashed arcs. Explicit context facts about user Norha are borrowed from the partial view of her context sphere[8] detailed in Table 5.

8.1   RDFS and OWL-Lite Deduction Rules

Jena[9] is the semantic web platform that supports context reasoning in SMARTERCONTEXT. Context reasoning rules in Jena are defined as a set of premises, a list of conclusions, and an optional name and optional direction. Each term of a Jena rule corresponds to either a triple pattern, an extended triple pattern, or a call to a built-in function [21]. This sub-section illustrates the application of standard RDFS and OWL-Lite axioms to context reasoning with the SMARTERCONTEXT ontology.

Reasoning from Subclasses. The following deduction rules exploit the semantic characteristics of the `rdfs:subClassOf` object property.

Rule 1 $(?A\ rdfs : subClassOf\ ?B), (?v\ rdf : type\ ?A) \rightarrow (?v\ rdf : type\ ?B)$

Example:

Fig. 3. Inferring implicit context facts with Rule 1

Rule 1 enables the inheritance of a resource's membership in a class A to the superclasses of A. In the example, since the product category `google:Earrings` is a subclass of the product category `google:Jewelry`, and the concrete product `sears.rdf#18KGoldEarrings` is an instance of `google:Earrings`, then this product is also an instance of `google:Jewelry`. An application of this rule to

---

[8] http://smartercontext.org/examples/norha.rdf
[9] http://jena.sourceforge.net/inference

smarter commerce is the inference of product and service preferences from the interactions of a user with particular products. For example, knowing that the user has earrings in her wish list (cf. triple 19 in Table 5), it is possible to infer that she would be interested in other jewelry categories.

Rule 2 $(?A\ rdfs : subClassOf\ ?B), (?B\ rdfs : subClassOf\ ?C) \rightarrow$ $(?A\ rdfs : subClassOf\ ?C)$

Example:

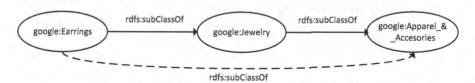

Fig. 4. Inferring implicit context facts with Rule 2

Rule 2 implements the transitivity of the rdfs:subClassOf object property. The example of this rule states that since google:Earrings is a subclass of google:Jewelry, and google:Jewelry is a subclass of google:Apparel_&_Accessories, then google:Earrings is a subclass also of google:Apparel_&_Accessories. In our shopping scenario, rules 1 and 2 can be combined to infer that the user may be interested in products of the category apparel & accessories, given that earrings is in her wish list.

Reasoning from Subproperties. The following deduction rules exploit the semantic characteristics of the rdfs:subPropertyOf object property.

Rule 3 $(?A\ rdfs : subPropertyOf\ ?B), (?v\ ?A\ ?y) \rightarrow (?v\ ?B\ ?y)$

Example:

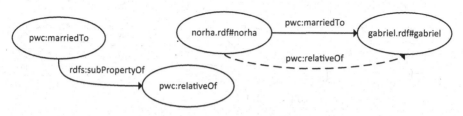

Fig. 5. Inferring implicit context facts with Rule 3

Rule 3 states that any triple with a predicate defined by a property A is also valid for the predicates defined by the superproperties of A. The example illustrates this rule using properties that correspond to family relationships between human entities. Shopping preferences are undeniable affected by the preferences and needs of the shopper's close family. The SMARTERCONTEXT ontology defines `pwc:marriedTo` as a sub-property of `pwc:relativeOf`. In the example, since Norha is married to Gabriel, SMARTERCONTEXT will infer that Norha is a relative of Gabriel.

Rule 4 $(?A\ rdfs\ :\ subPropertyOf\ ?B), (?B\ rdfs\ :\ subPropertyOf\ ?C)\ \rightarrow$ $(?A\ rdfs : subPropertyOf\ ?C)$

Example:

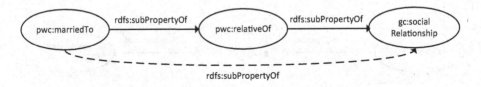

Fig. 6. Inferring implicit context facts with Rule 4

Rule 4 implements the transitivity of the `rdfs:subPropertyOf` object prop-erty. The example of this rule states that since `pwc:marriedTo` is a sub-property of `pwc:relativeOf`, and `pwc:relativeOf` is a subproperty of `gc:socialRelationship`, it is possible to infer that any pair of human entities that are married to each other, are not only relatives of each other, but also are socially related to each other. By the combination of rules 3 and 4 for Norha's context sphere, it is possible to infer that a social relationship holds between her and the human entity `gabriel.rdf#gabriel`.

Reasoning from Property Restrictions. The following deduction rules exploit the semantic characteristics of `rdfs:domain` and `rdfs:range`.

Rule 5 $(?A\ rdfs : domain\ ?B), (?u\ ?A\ ?y) \rightarrow (?u\ rdf : type\ ?A)$

Example:

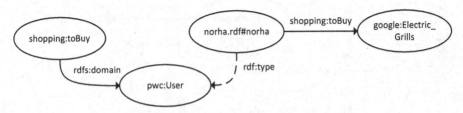

Fig. 7. Inferring implicit context facts with Rule 5

As explained in Section 3.2, the domain of a property in SMARTERCONTEXT defines the valid context types for the subjects of the triples where this prop-erty acts as the predicate. Therefore, Rule 5 is useful to infer from a triple, the type of the subject context entity by looking at the domain of the predicate. For example, the SMARTERCONTEXT ontology defines the context type `pwc:User` as the domain of the property `shopping:toBuy`. Therefore, from the context fact `(norha.rdf#norha shopping:toBuy google:Electric_Grills)`, SMARTERCONTEXT infers that `norha.rdf#norha` is an entity of type `pwc:User`.

Rule 6 $(?A\ rdfs : range\ ?B), (?u\ ?A\ ?y) \rightarrow (?y\ rdf : type\ ?B)$

Example:

Fig. 8. Inferring implicit context facts with Rule 6

Rule 6 allows the inference of class memberships for objects of triples. The range of a property in a particular triple defines the valid types for the objects of the triple. In the example of this rule it is possible to infer that `google:Electric_Grills` is an entity of type `shopping:ProductServiceCategory`, given that the latter is the range of the `shopping:toBuy` property in SMARTERCONTEXT. Rules 5 and 6 are useful in smarter commerce scenarios for instance to recommend product or service categories by inferring the types of particular products the user has interacted with, and applying complementary rules such as rules 1 and 2.

Reasoning from Transitive Properties. The following deduction rules exploit the semantic characteristics of transitive properties in OWL-Lite.

Rule 7 $(?A\ rdf : Type\ owl : TransitiveProperty), (?u\ ?A\ ?v), (?v\ ?A\ ?x) \rightarrow (?u\ ?A\ ?x)$

Example:

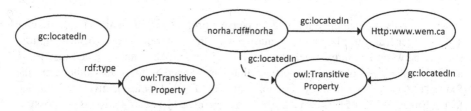

Fig. 9. Inferring implicit context facts with Rule 7

Rule 7 enables transitivity for any property that is defined as a transitive property in SMARTERCONTEXT. In the example, since `gc:locatedIn` is a transitive property,

Norha is located in West Edmonton Mall (`http://www.wem.ca`), and this mall is located in Edmonton, SMARTERCONTEXT infers from Norha's context sphere that she is located in Edmonton. Location-based context facts are crucial to suggest user-centric deals, products, and services effectively.

Reasoning from Symmetric Properties. The following deduction rules exploit the semantic characteristics of symmetric properties in OWL-Lite.

Rule 8 $(?A\,rdf : Type\,owl : SymmetricProperty), (?u\,?A\,?v) \rightarrow (?v\,?A\,?u)$

Example:

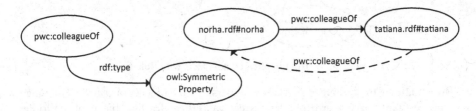

Fig. 10. Inferring implicit context facts with Rule 8

Symmetric properties state that if the context relationship represented by the property is valid for subject u and object v, it is valid also for v acting as the subject and u as the object of the relationship. `pwc:colleagueOf` is a symmetric property in SMARTERCONTEXT. Therefore, given that from Norha's context sphere the human entity `tatiana.rdf#tatiana` is a colleague of Norha, Norha is a colleague of Tatiana.

Reasoning from Inverse Properties. The following deduction rules exploit the semantic characteristics of the `owl:inverseOf` object property.

Rule 9 $(?A\,owl : inverseOf\,?B), (?u\,?A\,?v) \rightarrow (?v\,?B\,?u)$

An interesting application of inverse properties in smarter commerce and in general in the smart internet is the inference of social relationships between context entities. `pwc:parentOf` and `pwc:childOf` are examples of object properties that are inverse to each other in the SMARTERCONTEXT ontology. For example (cf. Fig. 11 below), given the context fact (`gabriel.rdf#gabriel pwc:parentOf jg.rdf#jg`), it is possible to infer the fact (`jg.rdf#jg pwc:childOf gabriel.rdf#gabriel`). Particularly in shopping scenarios, the shopping list of a parent could be affected by the shopping list of his kid and vice versa (although the second case is generally less probable than the first one).

Example:

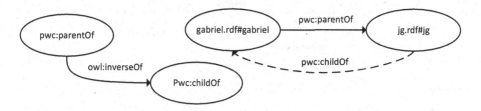

Fig. 11. Inferring implicit context facts with Rule 9

8.2   SMARTERCONTEXT Deduction Rules

This section presents selected rules that we defined in the SMARTERCONTEXT ontology to extend the standard reasoning capabilities provided by RDFS and OWL-Lite (cf. Section 8.1).

Rule 10 (pwc:NearTo) $(?a\,gc:locationRelationship\,?b)$, $(?b\,pwc:isNearTo\,?c) \rightarrow (?a\,pwc:isNearTo\,?c)$

Example:

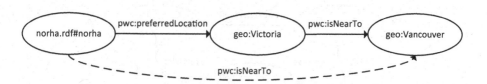

Fig. 12. Inferring implicit context facts with Rule 10

SMARTERCONTEXT uses Rule 10 to infer location-based context facts for the identification of relevant products, services, and retailers. This rule states that if an entity a is related to a location entity b by a $gc:locationRelationship$, and entity b is near to another location entity c, a valid conclusion is that entity a is near to c. By applying this rule to the example, given that Norha has Victoria as her preferred location, $pwc:preferredLocation$ is a subproperty of $gc:locationRelationship$, and according to the geo vocabulary Victoria is near to Vancouver, it is possible to infer that Norha is near to Vancouver. As a result, Norha may be interested in products, services, and deals not only available in Victoria, but also in Vancouver.

Rule 11 (shopping:FamilyShoppingList) $(?a\,pwc:relativeOf\,?b)$, $(?a\,shopping:toBuy\,?c) \rightarrow (?b\,shopping:toBuy\,?c)$

Example:

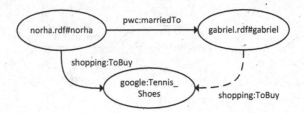

Fig. 13. Inferring implicit context facts with Rule 11

In our smarter commerce case study, Rule 11 is useful to infer products that could be included in the user's shopping list from the shopping lists of the user's relatives and vice versa. According to Norha's context sphere, tennis shoes and electric grills are product categories in her shopping list. Therefore, given that Norha is a relative of Gabriel, these two product categories could be suggested as Gabriel's shopping list products. Figure 11 depicts the application of the rule for tennis shoes.

Rule 12 (shopping:SocialBasedShoppingPreferences)
$(?a\ gc : social Relationship\ ?b), (?a\ pwc : likes\ ?c) \rightarrow (?b\ pwc : likes\ ?c)$

Example:

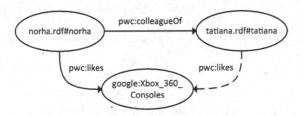

Fig. 14. Inferring implicit context facts with Rule 12

Rule 12 is comparable to Rule 11 but applies to more general social relationships (besides `pwc:relativeOf`) and to user interactions different than `shopping:toBuy` (i.e., `pwc:likes`, `pwc:dislikes`, and `pwc:isInterestedIn`). An example of the application of this rule involves the facts (`norha.rdf#norha pwc:likes google:XBox_360_Consoles`) and `norha.rdf#norha pwc:colleagueOf tatiana.rdf#tatiana`. Since Norha and Tatiana are colleagues and probably share interests and shopping preferences, it would be relevant to offer XBox 360 consoles or similar products to Tatiana.

Rule 13 (shopping:RelatedProductsPreferences)

$(?a\ shopping : relatedProductOrService\ ?b), (?c\ pwc : isInterestedIn\ ?a) \rightarrow (?c\ pwc : isInterestedIn\ ?b)$

Example:

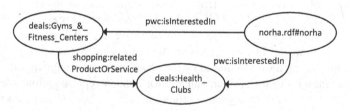

Fig. 15. Inferring implicit context facts with Rule 13

Relevant products, services and deals can be recommended by taking into account relevant products and services. Suitable ontologies for characterizing products, services and deals must support knowledge representation about related products (e.g., complementary products such as earrings and necklaces, or gyms and health clubs). In the example Norha is interested in deals related to gyms and fitness centers, therefore and taking into account that these deals are related to health clubs, she would be interested in deals related to the `deals:Health_Clubs` category.

9 Discussion and Related Work

Context modeling is an important component of the context information life cycle [22]. The smart internet and its applications such as the personal web require context models to represent the relevant aspects of entities that affect the interactions between users and systems, as well as the relationships between users and these entities. Ontologies are useful to describe concepts and the relationships among them. Therefore, ontology-based models are natural mechanisms to represent context information since context is a specific kind of knowledge [23]. The SMARTERCONTEXT ontology is a suitable mechanism for context representation and reasoning in the smart internet. It provides the mechanisms for the formal specification of the semantics of context data from a user-centric perspective [2]. Furthermore, an important modeling feature for realizing user-centric interactions and services in the smart Interent is knowledge sharing. The semantic web technologies supporting SMARTERCONTEXT not only allow the implementation of runtime context models, but also the interchange of context information among heterogeneous and distributed web entities.

Most context ontologies have been proposed for context representation and reasoning in pervasive and ubiquitous environments [2]. According to our systematic review of context modeling and management approaches, 49% of the surveyed approaches were proposed by the pervasive and ubiquitous computing research community. The remaining 51% are divided among several other communities: self-adaptive and self-organizing systems (12%), artificial intelligence and knowledge representation (11%), autonomic computing (8%), human computer interaction (5%), mobile computing and wireless networks (12%), and model-driven engineering (3%). To the best of our knowledge and according to relevant surveys on state-of-the-art context-aware computing, the SMARTERCONTEXT ontology is the first approach that has been proposed for user-centric context management in web applications [2,23,24].

Several ontologies are available for representing things in the semantic web. Examples of these ontologies are FOAF[10] (friend-of-a-friend), the ontology to connect people across the web [25]; GoodRelations,[11] the ontology for describing product and service offers on the web [26]; and GeoNames, the ontology that adds geospatial semantic information to the web.[12] In contrast to existing ontologies, SMARTERCONTEXT provides the common framework required by the smart internet to augment the semantics of existing ontologies to make them suitable for context representation. We envision SMARTERCONTEXT as the knowledge representation mechanism required to elevate the visibility of context information as demanded by smart web interactions and adaptive services. Nevertheless, without SMARTERCONTEXT, existing semantic web ontologies are useful to characterize and reason about web entities in concrete application domains with no awareness of user and system situations. For example, FOAF supports the representation of social relationships, GoodRelations the representation of online product and service offers, the Google Product taxonomy the representation of products, and GeoNames provides information about geographical places. The integration of these vocabularies into SMARTERCONTEXT instantaneously augments their semantics by converting their concepts into context entity types that can relate to each other to describe information about the user's situation. Therefore, these ontologies will represent not only web resources independent of the user, but relevant context about the user's situation. For example, FOAF would represent social context relationships that could be exploited to discover shopping preferences from the user's social network. GoodRelations and the Google Product taxonomy would describe not only products and services, but also the interactions between shoppers and online offers, thus enabling innovative approaches to leverage web interactions in business intelligence (BI) applications. Finally, the GeoNames ontology would represent not only places in the world, but geographical locations meaningful to improve the user's web experience.

10   Ongoing Research

Representing and managing context is not only critical for the realization of the smart internet and the personal web but also poses interesting research challenges. Our ongoing research concentrates on two of them: the management of trade-offs between expressiveness and performance, and the assurance of privacy and confidentiality of personal context data.

Performance is an important quality attribute to deliver user-centric smart interactions and services effectively. On the one hand, ontology-based knowledge representation approaches such as OWL expose performance limitations when reasoning on large data sets [8]. On the other hand, pure RDFS approaches lack semantic expressiveness

---

[10] http://www.foaf-project.org/

[11] http://www.heppnetz.de/projects/goodrelations

[12] http://www.geonames.org/ontology/documentation.html

for context reasoning [8,6,16]. An appropriate balance between expressiveness and performance is crucial to be able to reason about context situations with high amounts of context data. To balance this trade-off, we are investigating the application of computational biology algorithms and techniques to the mining of context facts [27,28]. Given the effective application of these techniques to the analysis of complex biological networks, we hypothesize that they can contribute to the analysis of complex RDF-based context models. These context mining techniques must be applied effectively not only to the analysis of individual context models, but also to the analysis of multiple context spheres (e.g., to correlate shopping preferences from personal context models of members of social networks). The development of suitable tools for the specification of context mining rules to be integrated into our context management engine at runtime complements this research.

To validate the SMARTERCONTEXT framework and the general applicability of the SMARTERCONTEXT ontology we are working on several case studies. Regarding the smarter commerce domain, we developed a deal recommendation system that exploits users' changing personal context information to deliver highly relevant offers. This application relies on recommendation algorithms based on collaborative filtering, and SMARTERCONTEXT. SMARTERCONTEXT provides the deal application with up-to-date information about user locations and product preferences gathered from their past and present web interactions. We conducted several experiments using real datasets to simulate personal context information gathered by SMARTERCONTEXT. For many deal categories the accuracy of the solution enhanced with SMARTERCONTEXT was between 3% and 8% better than the approaches we used as baselines. For some categories, and in terms of multiplicative relative performance, it outperformed related approaches by as much as 173.4%, and 37.5% on average [20].

Another relevant application to validate our research on context-awareness is the management of service level agreements (SLAs) in SOA governance [17]. The cornerstone of the SOA governance case study is the realization of *context-driven* SLAs, an extension of SLAs where context monitoring requirements are explicitly mapped to quality of service objectives to optimize the runtime control of contracted obligations. In our SOA case study, we extended the SMARTERCONTEXT ontology from the GC taxonomy to define the context types, and context relationships required to model, from SLA specifications, context monitoring requirements and context management strategies that change at runtime. Therefore, RDF graphs represent both context information and context management strategies (i.e., context gatherers and monitoring conditions).

A third case study we are conducting is the application of SMARTERCONTEXT to the monitoring of adaptation properties and goals for supporting runtime V&V of self-adaptive software [29]. In this research, the SMARTERCONTEXT ontology supports the representation of context monitoring requirements derived from adaptation properties and goals. For this, we mapped SMARTERCONTEXT types to the adaptation properties proposed in our evaluation framework for quality-driven self-adaptive systems [30]. Since adaptation goals can evolve over time, SMARTERCONTEXT supports dynamic changes in the monitoring infrastructure to preserve the relevance of monitoring strategies with the situation of the adaptive system.

11   Conclusions

Context awareness is a fundamental requirement to support the discovery, aggregation, and delivery of services according to user preferences and situations. Therefore, the effectiveness of smart interactions and services depends on the suitability of context representation and context reasoning techniques to understand the situation of users and systems. This paper explained the SMARTERCONTEXT ontology and its application to the smart internet using a personal web case study in smarter commerce. The SMARTERCONTEXT ontology exploits the semantic web to leverage context-awareness and thus optimize the user's experience in the smart internet. It provides a foundational framework to integrate existing semantic web vocabularies. This integration is crucial for raising the visibility of context information in user-centric, context-aware web applications. SMARTERCONTEXT augments the semantics of web resources represented by existing vocabularies. As a result, web resources with which the user interacts evolve from "things" in the web that are disconnected from the user into meaningful context entities that are now crucial for the understanding of personal preferences and situations. Most importantly, since SMARTERCONTEXT allows the understanding of the interactions between the user and web systems, web interactions evolve from simple data input mechanisms into the means to discover relevant context entities.

Finally, the formalization of a user model of the web centered on users and their goals constitutes one of the two main research challenges stated in the smart internet's research agenda [1]. Such a model must include the specification of user preferences and situations explicitly, and must provide runtime support for the manipulation of this context information. The SMARTERCONTEXT ontology provides the basis for context knowledge representation in the user-centered model of the web required by the smart internet.

Acknowledgments. This work was funded in part by the National Sciences and Engineering Research Council (NSERC) of Canada under the NSERC Strategic Research Network for Smart Applications on Virtual Infrastructures[13] (SAVI - NETGP 397724-10) and Collaborative Research and Development program (CRDPJ 320529-04 and CRDPJ 356154-07), IBM Corporation, University of Victoria (Canada), and Icesi University (Colombia).

References

1. Ng, J.W., Chignell, M., Cordy, J.R., Yesha, Y.: Overview of the Smart Internet. In: Chignell, M., Cordy, J., Ng, J., Yesha, Y. (eds.) The Smart Internet. LNCS, vol. 6400, pp. 49–56. Springer, Heidelberg (2010)
2. Villegas, N.M., Müller, H.A.: Managing Dynamic Context to Optimize Smart Interactions and Services. In: Chignell, M., Cordy, J., Ng, J., Yesha, Y. (eds.) The Smart Internet. LNCS, vol. 6400, pp. 289–318. Springer, Heidelberg (2010)
3. Coutaz, J., Crowley, J.L., Dobson, S.: Context is Key. Communications of the ACM (CACM) 48(3), 49–53 (2005)

---

[13] http://www.nsercpartnerships.ca/How-Comment/Networks-Reseaux/SAVI_AIIV-eng.asp

4. Bizer, C., Heath, T., Berners-Lee, T.: Linked Data — The Story So Far. International Journal on Semantic Web and Information Systems 5(3), 1–22 (2009)

5. Villegas, N.M., Müller, H.A., Muñoz, J.C., Lau, A., Ng, J., Brealey, C.: A Dynamic Context Management Infrastructure for Supporting User-driven Web Integration in the Personal Web. In: 2011 Conference of the Center for Advanced Studies on Collaborative Research (CASCON 2011), pp. 200–214. IBM Corp., Markham (2011)

6. Manola, F., Miller, E.: RDF Primer. Technical report, W3C (2004)

7. Munoz, J.C., Tamura, G., Villegas, N.M., Müller, H.A.: Surprise: User-controlled Granular Privacy and Security for Personal Data in SmarterContext. In: Proceedings 2012 Conference of the Center for Advanced Studies on Collaborative Research (CASCON 2012), pp. 131–145. IBM Corp., Riverton (2012)

8. Hitzler, P., Krötzsch, M., Rudolph, S.: Foundations of Semantic Web Technologies, 1st edn. Textbooks in Computing, vol. 33. Chapman & Hall/CRC (2009)

9. Berners-Lee, T., Hall, W., Hendler, J.A., O'Hara, K., Shadbolt, N., Weitzner, D.J.: A Framework for Web Science. Foundations and Trends in Web Science 1(1), 1–130 (2006)

10. The World Wide Web Consortium (W3C): RDF Vocabulary Description Language 1.0: RDF Schema (2004), `http://www.w3.org/TR/rdf-schema/`

11. The World Wide Web Consortium (W3C): OWL Web Ontology Language Reference (2004), `http://www.w3.org/TR/owl-ref/`

12. Berners-Lee, T., Fielding, R., Masinter, L.: Uniform Resource Identifier (URI): Generic Syntax (January 2005), `http://www.ietf.org/rfc/rfc3986.txt`

13. Fielding, R., Gettys, J., Mogul, J., Frystyk, H., Masinter, L., Leach, P., Berners-Lee, T.: Hypertext Transfer Protocol - HTTP/1.1 (1999), `http://www.w3.org/Protocols/rfc2616/rfc2616.html`

14. Knublauch, H., Fergerson, R.W., Noy, N.F., Musen, M.A.: The Protégé OWL Plugin: An Open Development Environment for Semantic Web Applications. In: McIlraith, S.A., Plexousakis, D., van Harmelen, F. (eds.) ISWC 2004. LNCS, vol. 3298, pp. 229–243. Springer, Heidelberg (2004)

15. The World Wide Web Consortium (W3C): XML Schema Part 2: Datatypes - W3C Recommendation. (May 2001), `http://www.w3.org/TR/xmlschema-2/`

16. The World Wide Web Consortium (W3C): OWL Web Ontology Language Overview (2004), `http://www.w3.org/TR/2004/REC-owl-features-20040210/#s3.1`

17. Villegas, N.M., Müller, H.A., Tamura, G.: Optimizing Run-Time SOA Governance through Context-Driven SLAs and Dynamic Monitoring. In: 2011 IEEE International Workshop on the Maintenance and Evolution of Service-Oriented and Cloud-Based Systems (MESOCA 2011), pp. 1–10. IEEE (2011)

18. Google Inc.: The Google Product Taxonomy (2012), `http://support.google.com/merchants/bin/answer.py?hl=en&answer=160081`

19. Groupon: The Groupon Deal Categories (2012), `https://sites.google.com/site/grouponapiv2/api-resources/deals`

20. Ebrahimi, S., Villegas, N.M., Müller, H.A., Thomo, A.: SmarterDeals: A Context-aware Deal Recommendation System based on the SmarterContext Engine. In: Proceedings 2012 Conference of the Center for Advanced Studies on Collaborative Research (CASCON 2012), pp. 116–130. IBM Corp., Riverton (2012)

21. Carroll, J.J., Dickinson, I., Dollin, C., Seaborne, A., Wilkinson, K., Reynolds, D.: Jena: Implementing the Semantic Web Recommendations. In: 13th International World Wide Web Conference (WWW 2004), pp. 74–83 (2004)

22. Hynes, G., Reynolds, V., Hauswirth, M.: A Context Lifecycle for Web-Based Context Management Services. In: Barnaghi, P., Moessner, K., Presser, M., Meissner, S. (eds.) EuroSSC 2009. LNCS, vol. 5741, pp. 51–65. Springer, Heidelberg (2009)

23. Bettini, C., Brdiczka, O., Henricksen, K., Indulska, J., Nicklas, D., Ranganathan, A., Riboni, D.: A Survey of Context Modelling and Reasoning Techniques. Pervasive and Mobile Computing 6, 161–180 (2009)

24. Hoareau, C.: Modeling and Processing Information for Context-Aware Computing: A Survey. New Generation Computing 27(3), 177–196 (2009)

25. Graves, M., Constabaris, A., Brickley, D.: FOAF: Connecting People on the Semantic Web. Cataloging & Classification Quarterly 43(3-4), 191–202 (2007)

26. Hepp, M.: GoodRelations: An Ontology for Describing Products and Services Offers on the Web. In: Gangemi, A., Euzenat, J. (eds.) EKAW 2008. LNCS (LNAI), vol. 5268, pp. 329–346. Springer, Heidelberg (2008)

27. Pavlopoulos, G., Secrier, M., Moschopoulos, C., Soldatos, T., Kossida, S., Aerts, J., Schneider, R., Bagos, P.: Using Graph Theory to Analyze Biological Networks. BioData Mining 4(1), 1–27 (2011)

28. Milo, R., Al, E., Biology, C.: Network Motifs: Simple Building Blocks of Complex Networks. Science, 824–827 (2002)

29. Tamura, G., Villegas, N.M., Müller, H.A., Sousa, J.P., Becker, B., Karsai, G., Mankovskii, S., Pezzè, M., Schäfer, W., Tahvildari, L., Wong, K.: Towards Practical Runtime Verification and Validation of Self-Adaptive Software Systems. In: de Lemos, R., Giese, H., Müller, H.A., Shaw, M. (eds.) Software Engineering for Self-Adaptive Systems. LNCS, vol. 7475, pp. 108–132. Springer, Heidelberg (2013)

30. Villegas, N.M., Müller, H.A., Tamura, G., Duchien, L., Casallas, R.: A Framework for Evaluating Quality-driven Self-Adaptive Software Systems. In: 6th International Symposium on Software Engineering for Adaptive and Self-Managing Systems (SEAMS 2011), pp. 80–89. ACM, New York (2011)

Simplifying the Task of Group Gift Giving

Shadi Ghajar-Khosravi, Louisa Holub, David Canella, William Sharpe,
and Mark Chignell

Interactive Media Lab, University of Toronto, Toronto, Canada
{ghajar,chignell}@mie.utoronto.ca,
{sharpewi,louisaholub,david.canella}@gmail.com

Abstract. Gift Giving is a complex and ubiquitous task that would benefit from
the simpler and more user-centred style of interaction offered by the Personal
Web vision. In this paper we begin by reviewing relevant literature on gift giving, and we identify key roles and requirements of gift giving. We examine current approaches to the support of group gift giving online and review some of
their deficiencies. We then discuss the role that recommender systems and social media can play in facilitating gift giving interactions. As a first step towards simpler and more effective group gift giving in the Personal Web, we review results of research studies that we have conducted showing opportunities
and challenges with respect to further development of gift giving online communities, and group gift giving services. We conclude with suggestions on future directions for online group gift giving noting the contribution that the Personal Web approach can make in this domain.

Keywords: Group Gift Giving, Social Media, Requirements Gathering,
Recommender Systems.

1   Introduction

This paper will focus on the impact that social media and the Personal Web are likely
to have on what people buy, looking at the particular case of products purchased as
gifts.

In the introduction paper in this book, the Personal Web is described as a unified
web platform in which web users can easily build the interactive functionality that
they require from an array of web services spread across different Web sites in the
current Web. Instead of initiating web requests to fulfill their tasks, users can delegate
task-related activity to Web services working on their behalf. Users can act as supervisory controllers [1] and set up reminders and guide task automation at a high level,
assisted by tools aware of their professional, social and personal context and history.

How can online gift giving be reconfigured to fulfill these goals? The essence of
the Personal Web approach is to simplify tasks for the user by integrating over sites
and services in an intelligent way [2]. However, before applying a Personal Web
perspective to online gift giving, we first consider the properties of online retail in
general, and online group gift giving in particular. We define group gift giving as the

M. Chignell et al. (Eds.): The Personal Web, LNCS 7855, pp. 185–220, 2013.
© Springer-Verlag Berlin Heidelberg 2013

purchase of something by a group of people, for a single recipient. Since coordination of group decision-making is inherently complex, online facilitation of group gift giving seems like a natural next step for group gift giving. But how does the group interaction fit in with each individual's personal view of the Web? Let's start by looking at the changing role of Web users.

In a world where users can construct their own personal view of the Web, and of the best places to buy the many versions of a product available online, the power of the user is increasing. Users often have access to a wealth of information about products, much of it from people like themselves:

"...after people have bought a product, they can turn themselves into broadcasters as they comment on the experience they have just had, rate the product they have just bought, apply their own "tags" to label it in ways that are meaningful to them, and comment about the product on the blog or news site that may have originally led them to the product. Their participation then assists those who come later and can read their comments" [3].

Through their mobile phones, in particular, people are continuously connected to vast collections of product catalogues and reviews, making it increasingly challenging for retailers to control what a person hears about products and to capture loyal customers and then extract price premiums based on that loyalty.

B2C (business to consumer) e-commerce is changing from a push model where products are pushed through retail channels, to a pull model where product offers are made in response to demand from consumers. While it could be argued that retailers always seek to meet customer demand, in practice present methods are inefficient, with often poor matches between supply and demand. The current system is wasteful because many products are pushed down through the retail distribution channel and then returned or sold off at a loss because of mismatches between supply and demand.

The ongoing online revolution in retail will have a big impact for society in general because of the major role that retail plays in most economies. Retail currently accounts for around 17% of the U.S. economy and the National Retail Federation states that it is responsible (directly or indirectly) for 24% of the jobs in the U.S. economy (according to numbers posted by the National Retail Federation [4]). In February 2012, the US Department of Commerce reported that $194.3 billion (out of a total of about $2.5 trillion in retail spending) was spent online in the US in 2011, with a 16% growth in sales over the previous year [5]. Hence, retail is becoming a highly competitive activity, which has led to a great deal of change, particularly in recent years, as retailers seek to gain an advantage over their competitors using new technologies such as social media.

The growth of social media has created a forum for gift discussion and a greater chance for traditional marketing messages to be outweighed by messages from friends and trusted others. The potential for such discussion and interchange can be seen in the growth of sites and applications such as Pinterest and Instagram. Increasingly, functions such as photo storage are being re-expressed in a social media context. Traditional activities are also being repositioned, as seen in the facilitative role of

Pinterest in areas such as wedding planning [6]. In the case of gift giving, the availability of social media discussions enables multiple individuals to coordinate the process of giving a gift to a particular recipient.

Startups, armed with disruptive technologies, have sought to capitalize on the growing interest in social commerce and social shopping, exploiting novel areas where nimble competitors may conceivably outmaneuver larger and more established retailers. The logic seems simple and has been persuasive, with millions of dollars having recently been invested in ventures for group gift giving (as of this writing). For example, eBay paid $20 million in September 2011 for The Social Project in order to create their own gift giving service (available at http://groupgifts.ebay.com).

In this paper we review past research on gift giving, and we discuss how online gift giving systems can be enhanced using a Personal Web approach, focusing on group gift giving in particular. In contrast to the extensive research conducted on gift giving in general, gift giving by groups of people has not been extensively studied. Therefore, two user studies on the requirements of online group gift giving have been conducted and their results will be reported in the final sections of this paper.

In writing this paper we sought to answer the following questions, which seemed particularly relevant to the goal of creating a Personal Web style of interaction for online gift giving.

- How does the nature of gift giving change when it is performed online?
- When would people like to participate in online group gift giving and what types of interaction can facilitate online group gift giving?
- How does the role of the user change when the gift giver is a group of people rather than an individual?
- How can shopping search engines and gift recommender systems make the gift selection process less effortful and more effective, while reducing gift selection anxiety and the likelihood of gift failure?
- What are the characteristics of givers that determine when and how group gift giving should be implemented?
- How should people interact with each other when choosing a group gift?

In the following sections, we will provide a brief background overview on the Personal Web framework, the nature of gift giving, and the recommender systems challenges and opportunities for a Personal Web oriented group gift giving service. In sections 3, we will present an overview on some of the currently existing online gift giving services. In section 4, we will report on recent research that we have conducted to explore requirements for online gift giving, and group gift giving systems. We summarize the research results in section 5 and we discuss implications for the Personal Web framework in section 6.

2   Background

2.1   The Personal Web Framework

IBM CAS Research Canada has developed a new framework for the web, entitled the Personal Web The Personal Web allows users to interact with the web as an integrated whole, instead of dealing with multiple independent domains [2].

The Personal Web has 5 main principles:

- Instead of servers as silos - an integrated web, no longer user pulling information from multiple sites. Content is created and pushed to users based on their current matters of concern.
- The Web as a Platform for Optimal Cognitive Support - the system provides cognitive support by reducing demands on working memory (by offloading storage tasks to the web), assisting with prospective memory (reminders to do something), and enabling user control and freedom (releasing the user from the need for programming expertise).
- Context Awareness of Users - relevant information is brought to the right person at the right time.
- Task Oriented Semantics - system is aware of the meaning of connections between users and items on the Web through knowledge of users, what they want to do (tasks), and the associated resources and information.
- Social Oriented Semantics – the System is aware of the meaning of connections between individuals through knowledge of the social structure between individuals (friends, friends of friends, etc).

The Personal Web is an integration of many ideas that are being worked on, but it is the focus on user-centeredness and cognitive support of the user, that distinguishes it from other initiatives. Thus it is envisioned that the Personal Web framework will provide a more user-centric web experience, one that is contextually aware of the user and the user's current task so that it can bring relevant sources of information to users when they need it without users having to remember to search for multiple sources of information, and at particular times.

2.2   The Nature of Gift Giving

Gift giving has been defined as an exchange of goods or services [7]. Although gift giving is regarded as voluntary, there are often strong social and cultural pressures that influence what is given, to whom, and when.

Gift giving is a social activity that confirms and strengthens relationships [8]. Gifts express feelings and emotions of various kinds [9-10]. Gifts also represent stages and types of relationships. As a relationship evolves, gifts help define social boundaries and confirm the status of the relationship. In romantic relationships, for example, gifts such as flowers or chocolates might be given on a first date, with gifts such as jewellery, apparel or other more personal items being given later as the relationship becomes longstanding and intimate [11].

According to [12], gift giving can be described as a three-stage exchange process. In the "gestation" stage, the gift giver searches internally for information about the self, the recipient, and the gift, and then externally searches for appropriate vendors and products. Next, the "presentation" stage involves the gift exchange with respect to time, place, and means of transaction. In the "reformulation" stage, the gift is evaluated by the recipient, which has an impact on social bonds. For example, a relationship can be strengthened if a spouse receives a thoughtful and generous gift from her partner.

Gift Selection. As mentioned earlier, how the gift is evaluated by the recipient has an impact on social bonds. Gifts are laden with meaning, and thus selection of appropriate gifts is an important task and may be the stage of gift giving where the Personal Web approach is most relevant. Since potentially relevant gifts, reviews, and relevant advice are scattered across many websites, the integration of that information into a user-centred Personal Web is critical in providing an online gift giving service that carefully takes into account the needs and preferences of its users.

Type of Gift. The type of gift given is generally a reflection of the type of relationship between the gift giver and recipient [10], [12]. A study by Parsons, Ballantine, and Kennedy [11] found that gifts from those who are close to the recipient should have greater symbolic meaning. An example of a symbolically meaningful gift is hand-made artwork from a child. The symbolism of this type of gift is associated with love and commitment, coming of age, and recognition [9].

Previous studies have found that age and gender of the recipient play a role in what type of gift is given. A study by [13] found that age and gender of the recipient had a significant influence on what type of Christmas gift they were given. For example, 91% of the decorations and ornaments, and 87% of the jewelry, were given to females, while 88% of the tools, and 76% of the sports equipment were given to males. Not surprisingly, a gift is more highly valued by the recipient if it uniquely suits the recipient or demonstrates a particular understanding of the recipient's desires [10].

However, recommendation of gifts based on characteristics of recipients is still in its infancy. Often recommendations are based on simple stereotypes. For instance, Gifts.com (www.gifts.com), as of this writing, recommended gifts based on the following stereotypes for men: "Guy's guy", "Geek", "Devoted dad", "Outdoor adventurer", "Metro man", "Activity", "Intellectual" and "Sports fan". When the site was reviewed by the authors in June 2012, collections of gift suggestions were attached to these eight types, and no criteria were given for determining how to assign different men to each of these types.

Ideally, a user-centered Personal Web, following the Social Oriented Semantics principle, should provide gift ideas that take into account the recipient's characteristics (e.g. age, gender, or personality) and the relationship between the recipient and giver(s). We assume that the Personal Web technologies discussed elsewhere in this book should facilitate the kinds of personalizing transactions envisioned here.

Gift Giving Anxiety. Gift giving is risky because gifts can fail to please recipients. Failed gifts are costly, not just in terms of the price of the product, and the wasted effort required to select, purchase, and send/give the gift [14], but also in terms of the potential damage that bad gifts can do to relationships. Thus, the very real prospect of gift failure will sometimes lead to anxiety about what gifts to give.

While gifting has been facilitated by improved communication technologies, such as smart phones that allow individuals to quickly and easily discuss gift ideas, problems undoubtedly remain. Online gift giving systems, when combined with a user-centred Personal Web approach, have the potential to reduce gifting anxiety and the likelihood of gifting failure by reducing the risk and effort associated with selecting and acquiring the products to be used as gifts.

2.3   Recommender Systems Opportunities and Challenges

The most difficult part of the gift giving task is generally the selection of the gift and reaching consensus in the case of group gift giving. Instead of requiring the user(s) to search or browse through many gifts, Personal Web interaction should simplify the task of gift giving for individuals and groups by making helpful suggestions that are in keeping with the preferences and relationship between gift givers and recipient, and that are consistent with the communicative requirements of the occasion. Thus, recommender systems should be a useful technology in implementing a Personal Web approach to online gift giving in general, and group gift giving in particular by incorporating the "task-oriented semantics" and "social-oriented semantics" of The Personal Web framework. Recommender systems have the potential to create recommendations for group members based on:

- Group members' past preferences and the preferences of users similar to them
- Group members' initial criteria with respect to the gift to be purchased (e.g. occasion, price, type, brand, etc.) and the preferences of users similar to them
- Gift recipient's past preferences (if available on the system), or wishlists
- Gift recipient's attributes (e.g., age, gender, personality, etc.)
- Group members opinions as expressed through voting and other decision making processes
- Group members' ideas shared with the group in an online shared space

Recommender Systems (RS) are systems that provide suggestions or recommendations for items to be of use or interest to a user [15]. These recommendations are normally based on what is known about users and their preferences (e.g., demographics, friends, groups, interests, ratings, activities history, etc.) According to Resnick and Varian, RSs augment the social process by which we rely on recommendations from other people.

RSs and social media are both highly relevant to a Personal Web view of gift giving. Social media introduces new types of data that can be used by RS algorithms (e.g., tags, comments, votes, explicit social relationships). RSs, in turn, improve social media user experience by providing users with the most relevant items that suit their preferences [16].

There are a variety of types of recommender system available to support Personal Web interaction. A content-based RS recommends items similar to the ones that the same user liked in the past. In other words, the RS *links* the active user to a list of items based on *items similarity* metrics. Items that are more similar will have stronger *connections*. The similarity of items is determined based on the descriptions or attributes of items or user's feedback history.

In contrast, a collaborative filtering RS recommends items that other users with similar tastes liked in the past. It provides a kind of automation of the process of "word of mouth" by *linking* the active user to items based on *users similarity* metrics.

Users that are more similar have stronger *connections*. Examples of users' similarity measures include similar user attributes, similar rating history, users' social networks, similar pages visited, co-location, etc.

The growing popularity of social networks has led to a rising interest in social recommender systems. The idea behind the design of such systems is that users rely more on the recommendations of their friends rather than anonymous individuals; i.e., familiarity is preferred over anonymous similarity [17].

Personal Web interaction may sometimes benefit from recommender system technologies but even when recommender systems are not explicitly used, Recommender issues can provide useful insights for Personal Web interactions. Personal Web interactions, like Recommender systems, tend to require that more work be done in the background on the user's behalf. Thus, Personal Web interaction is likely to share some of the challenges that recommender systems face, particularly with respect to the degree of transparency provided to the user concerning the reasoning that is being carried out in the background as well as when and how explanations should be provided [18].

In the context of group gift giving, recommendations may be made to individuals (with their selections and votes then being aggregated in some way to form a group decision), or recommendations may be made to the entire group. However, research on group recommender systems is at an early stage. It is not clear when recommendations should be made to individuals (prior to group discussion) and when they should be made to the group. Other challenges include: explaining group recommendations, aggregation strategies, and user interface design. Explanation does not have to be complicated to be useful. For instance, "Star Wars" might be recommended as a movie and the explanation could be that it stars Harrison Ford, who appeared in other movies that the person had rated previously.

It seems likely that recommendations for group gift giving will be particularly challenging, because the suitability of a gift depends jointly on who the gift givers are and who the gift recipient is. Gift recommenders have to recommend gifts for a recipient who is not involved in the decision making process but whose preferences are at least as important as those of decision makers. As a result, for group RSs there is the challenge of developing an aggregation strategy that not only takes into account the past preferences of gift givers and the social dynamics among them [19-20], but also takes account of the preferences of the gift recipient.

3   Current Online Gift Giving Systems

In this section we briefly discuss current (as of this writing) systems and services for providing support for gift giving online, focusing in particular on group gift giving services. The following are just a sampling of the many sites that were set up for group gift giving in the 2011-2012 time period: Giftiki, eBay Group Gifts, edivvy, SocialGift, Wraply, FrumUs, Wrapp, FromEveryone, Shareagift, theBIGgift, LetsGiftIt, Socialwise, and FriendFund.

Online retailers and entrepreneurs have responded to a perceived need for online group gifting by offering a variety of tools, Facebook apps, and web sites. Online group gifting sites have promoted the following common features to consumers:

- Inviting friends and managing budget: Online group gifting services help to automate the process of sending invitations to donors, collecting money, tracking the fundraising status of the gift, sending reminder emails to group members, and making the payment, which minimizes the burden imposed on the organizer of the group gift.

- Flexible privacy settings: Features such as anonymity of contributions and voluntary contribution amounts ease the awkwardness and peer pressure imposed on potential donors.
- Discussion forums: Web sites provide a forum for contributors to discuss and vote for gift ideas. Not only does this discussion provide information and opinions from peers, but it may also reduce gift anxiety by helping people choose gifts that are approved by people in their social network.
- Product Catalogues: Many online group gifting web sites also offer a product catalog to simplify the process of gift selection and purchase. This feature is helpful for gift givers who do not start off with a clear idea about what they would like to buy as a gift.

Group gifting also provides the following potential benefits for retailers:

- Increase in sales of higher-priced products (people can afford to spend more on a gift when they team up).
- Social channels like Twitter and Facebook help pull people in and create social media discussions about products that can lead to a kind of viral advertising effect.

According to Friendfund founder and CEO Harry McCarney: "We make products more affordable by allowing a group payment method and in the course of creating a pool, an invitation is sent out in social networks and anything that happens, it's mentioned in a Twitter or Facebook stream so merchants can get a huge visibility boom." [21].

However, group gift giving has been slow to take off in spite of the commercial interest, and this slow start may be attributable to a number of practical concerns that relate to group gift giving:

- Problems arise if not enough money is raised for the purchase of the gift by the contribution deadline. A decision needs to be made whether or not to extend the contribution deadline, and all parties involved might need to deal with PayPal or credit card refunds and cancellation fees, or else resort to alternative solutions such as convert the donated money into a gift voucher for the recipient.
- There can be complications when a gift is over-funded. A decision then has to be made about what to do with the excess funds.
- Aside from money issues it may be hard for a group of people to agree on what type of gift is suitable for a particular recipient and occasion, and they may not agree on how much should be paid for the gift.
- Relatively little is known about current attitudes towards group gift giving and for what types of occasion different groups of people would want to give gifts as a group.

3.1   An Example Group Gift Website: eBay Group Gifts

A website reviewed and analyzed for the purpose of this work was eBay Group Gifts website, a group gifting service offered by eBay after its acquisition of The Gifts Project in September 2011. We will provide a brief presentation of this service in the following paragraphs.

eBay Group Gifts has a particularly straight-forward user experience when it comes to starting a group gift, inviting contributors, and handling who-pays-how-much. On the Group Gifts homepage, for example, the three main steps are clearly illustrated and the user can enter the occasion and recipient directly on the page (see Fig. 1).

Fig. 1. Getting started with eBay Group Gifts

Fig. 2. Find a gift for the recipient using eBay Group Gifts

The next step, Find a Gift, leads the user to the eBay product search engine. Although a simple and clean interface (Fig. 2), it lacks any customized recommendations for the selected recipient.

The third step is to invite friends to chip in. The screenshot in Fig. 3 shows how eBay Group Gifts enables the user to import contacts, specify contribution suggestion settings, and enter PayPal account information all in a single easy-to-use form.

The eBay process for group gift giving is one of many that have been implemented. In the following subsections we give further examples of the different interactions that have been designed to handle the various steps in online group gift giving. We illustrate the interactions with screenshots that were representative of content for the corresponding sites as of the first half of 2012.

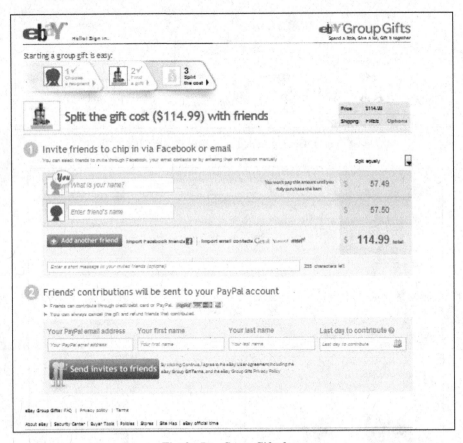

Fig. 3. eBay Group Gifts form

3.2   Selecting the Gift Recipient

The first step in any gift giving activity is the process of selecting the gift recipient and the reason, or occasion, for making the gift. Giftiki, a group gift giving service, simplifies the process of selecting the gift recipient using Facebook information. When the user logs in to the Facebook app, it automatically displays upcoming friends' birthdays. The user can click directly on the friend's photo, or select a different Facebook friend for the group gift (Fig. 4).

Fig. 4. Selecting a gift recipient on Giftiki

From the Personal Web perspective the interaction shown in Fig. 4 has a number of desirable features. First, by showing the friends' birthdays in the context of a gift giving interaction it takes the load off the user's memory system and it also avoids the need to check a different Website (e.g., Facebook) for the birthday information. In addition pictures are provided, which likely improves gift giving motivation, and the birthdays are ordered in time, so that the person can determine urgency and also set priorities (e.g., if several people are having birthdays in the next month (who are the most important people to send gifts to?). By providing the right information at the right time in this way, the process of gift giving is made smoother and more reliable.

3.3   Creating Invitations

Another important step in a group gift giving activity is creating and sending invitations to gift contributors. The eDivvy.com site supports this process with an attractive user interface (Fig. 5) that is simple to use and that has good affordances (i.e., it is obvious to the user what can be done and how it should be done).

Similar to Evite.com, eDivvy.com offers a selection of colourful, themed invitation templates to choose from. The designs are also categorized by occasion or event type. From a personal web perspective, the use of design templates in this way is reducing user effort and the choice of templates reinforces the communicative and ritualistic norms of gift giving.

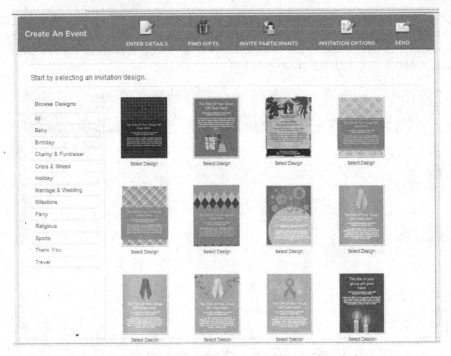

Fig. 5. eDivvy.com's interface for selecting invitation design

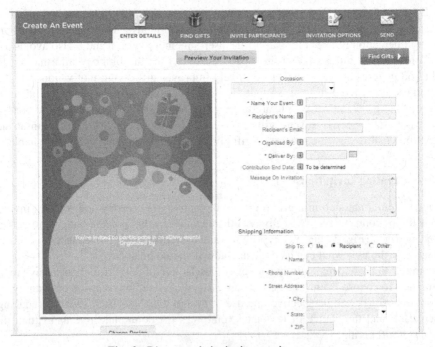

Fig. 6. eDivvy.com's invitation preview screen

eDivvy.com also has a visually appealing form for setting up the gift pool (Fig. 6). The invitation on the left-hand side of the screen is updated dynamically as the user enters information in the adjacent fields. One feature of this screen is that it puts all the information about the gift on one screen, reducing the number of steps required in the interaction.

Another feature in this interaction is the "Delivery By" field. Consistent with the Personal Web approach, loads on prospective memory (i.e., memory for future events) should be avoided. Once the delivery date has been set, the user shouldn't have to worry about whether or not the gift will be delivered at the right time. However, this desirable Personal Web interaction now needs to be backed up with a back-end process that ensures that a gift is chosen in time so that it can be shipped by the delivery by date, and that the shipping process is correspondingly reliable. For some occasions (e.g., birthdays) it is best that gifts arrive on a specific date, which requires more of the shipping process than simply delivering as quickly as possible given the level of service that the user is willing to pay for.

3.4   Choosing a Gift: Comments and Voting

Further task automation for group gifting can be seen in a service called FrumUs that provides a message board and voting tool directly on the gift tracking web page (Fig. 7). Contributors can use this gift tracking page to post suggestions for gifts and cast votes. The process of creating the poll is a simple one-step task of filling in the blanks and clicking on "Create Poll". This screen also shows how a number of steps (listed below) can be integrated onto one screen thereby simplifying the task for the user.

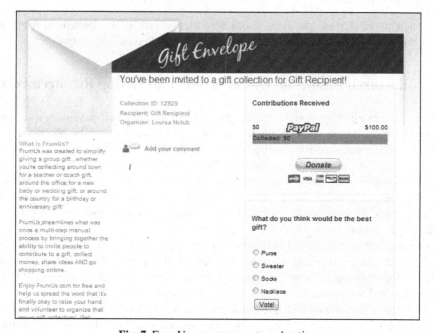

Fig. 7. FrumUs user comments and voting

- See who has already contributed
- Make your own contribution
- Vote on what type of gift to give
- Add a comment (i.e., communicating in context without the need to open up email or some other communication tool)

3.5   Paying for the Gift

One of the most challenging aspects of online group gift giving is how to coordinate payments by a group of people. Issues include:

- How much each person should pay (should it be divided equally, according to need, etc.)?
- Who should pay for the product/gift (e.g., a facilitator acting on behalf of the groups, or each person in the group paying their share individually)?
- If people pay individually should the individual payments be made directly to the merchant (currently problematic as most merchants don't know how to handle multiple transactions for a single product) or to a third party (e.g., a gift giving service) which then pays the merchant?
- If the product is paid for by a facilitator on behalf of the group then how should the facilitator be reimbursed by the group? Payment options could include PayPal, bank transfers, cheques and cash. A webpage can also be used where the facilitator can record payments and where the group members can easily see who is not paying their fair share.

Although we raise these payment issues here for the sake of completeness, it is not clear that they can be simplified or facilitated through a Personal Web approach.

4   Research Results on Online Group Gift Giving Requirements

There is an extensive research on gift giving from sociological, psychological, and anthropological perspectives. While this literature is potentially useful in the design of gift giving and gift recommendation systems, it does not directly address the issues and challenges relating to the design of online group giving systems. There has been little research into the requirements of online group gift giving, and into how and when it should be used, and by whom. It is our thesis that the emerging sector of group gift giving, while promising, will not succeed until human factors requirements and design challenges are met.

Our research group carried out two studies to explore requirements for online gift giving, and group gift giving systems. The results of the two studies are reported in this section of the paper. The findings are discussed in terms of their implications for the design and development of online group gift giving services.

The first study interviewed five participants about their attitudes towards gift recommendation systems and group giving. The second study was based on an online survey filled-in by 249 respondents. The survey examined the impact of age, gender, and personality on factors such as amount spent on gifts and level of online purchasing, and attitudes towards group gift giving.

4.1 Study One

A user study was run over the course of one week on five Canadian participants. The purpose of this pilot study was to explore how people buy group gifts offline through physical retailers, how people buy or would buy group gifts online, and also what would be the initial expectations of online users of an online gift recommender system. Each session lasted about one hour. The interview consisted of three major sections:

- Past offline group gifting experiences
- Past online group gifting experiences
- Envisioning an online gift recommender system.

Both sections of the interview focused on a particular past offline/online group gifting experience. If the participant did not have a relevant past experience, they were asked to answer questions imagining their best friend's birthday was just around the corner and that they would like to buy a gift with a group of mutual friends.

Group Gift Giving Start-up. Participants were asked about the details of a past group gifting process including where they started from, who was invited to the group, and whether or not they asked the gift recipient for his/her preferences. 4 out of the 5 participants liked their gifts to be a surprise (Table 1) and none of the participants thought it was a good idea to let a gift giving group get expanded by inviting

Table 1. Summary of Comments on how participants would start an online group gift giving process (i.e., what would be their first action)

Participant#	Start time	Group members	Friends of friends	Group gift giving starting point	Asking gift recipient?
1	1 mth before	3 common friends	Not accepted	Looking for Photography equipment	No – wanted to surprise
2	3-4 wks before	4 common friends	Not accepted	Initial ideas of the group + agreeing on budget	No – wanted to surprise
3	2wks before	3 common friends	Not accepted	Deciding on which stores to go to	No – wanted to surprise
4	Couple of mths before	5 common friends	Not accepted	Agreeing on budget + checking websites	No – wanted to surprise
5	1 mth before	4 common friends	Not accepted	What the recipient had mentioned before + checking favorite online websites	Yes, but she was shy to say anything or wanted to get surprised.

friends of friends to the group. All of the interviewees preferred to buy the group gift with their own close friends. Four out of the five participants mentioned that research for online gifts (as opposed to offline gifts) needed to start earlier to allow for order processing and shipping time. All of the participants regarded the prospect of an online group gifting service positively.

Gift Ideas Comparison Factors. When the interviewees were asked about how they would compare gift ideas or decide on what to buy, "price" and "the gift recipient's taste" were the two most cited factors playing a role in their decision making process. In the specific context of online group gift buying, "user reviews" and "shipping options" (e.g. cost, duration, and availability) were also among the factors that were cited by at least four of the five participants as being important in choosing what to buy as a gift.

Envisioning a Group Gift Giving System. Participants were also asked about what features should be added to an individual gift giving system in order for it to work for a group rather than an individual (i.e. what was their view as to how a group gift giving system would work). Most of the responses to this question were concerned with how the group could share their ideas and preferences in such an online environment and with how a voting system could help the group reach a final decision. A summary of the responses made is shown in Table 2.

Interaction preferences with Recommender Systems. The participants were questioned about their attitudes towards gift recommender systems. In their responses, all of the five people interviewed emphasized the need for simplicity and clarity in interacting with the recommender system. Also, all five participants preferred to enter information in multiple steps rather than in one step. They did not trust an automated system to take all their information at once and give them an answer right away. Instead they wanted more of an interactive dialogue, where the system would provide interim feedback and provide an opportunity for them to give further input and guidance to the recommendation process. Respondents wanted the opportunity to browse a wider range of products before getting more specific about their preferences.

4.2   Study Two

A survey was then developed to explore attitudes towards giving, and group giving, further. The questionnaire development, data collection process, and an overview of the analysis method are discussed below.

Method. The questionnaire, shown in Appendix A, consisted of 15 questions, split into seven different parts. The seven parts of the questionnaire were: (1) Demographics, (2) Frequency of online social networking and online purchases, (3) a Five-Item Personality Inventory, based on the Big-Five Model of Personality (BFI) [22]; (4) Gift expenditure history; (5) Gift selection preferences and behaviour; (6) Preferences for online group gift features; and (7) Online group gift scenarios. The last two questions (#14 and #15) collected contact information for the draw prize and future surveys.

Table 2. Summary of particicpants' expectations of an online group recommender system

Participant #	Features of Group Recommender Systems
Participant1	- Each group member should be able to **save the results** of their individual search - Each group member should be able to **share the results** of their individual search (or their gift ideas) with the group. - Each group member should be able to indicate which one of the shared items they **like**. - The need for a **shared space** or page similar to a shopping cart that everyone could add gift ideas to - Each group member should be able to add a **limited number** (2-3) of items to the cart - A **voting** feature to finalize the decision
Participant2	- System should ask **everyone** for their preferred gift **category** - Recommendation results should be based on **everyone's preferences** - **Voting, commenting,** and **liking** features - Everyone should be able to see what other group members **like** and why
Participant3	- Each group member should be able to see how other group members are **searching** for gift ideas (i.e., their search criteria) - Each group member should be able to see the **results picked** by others - Decision on the final gift should be made **among people** and not through the system - Group members should be able to see the **preferences** of one another
Participant4	- Group members should be able to view **each other's preferences** - **Summarize preferences** - **Top 3** choices of **each** group member could be displayed to the group - **Commenting** feature beside each product - **Voting** feature
Participant5	- Displaying items that have been recommended to each of the group members so that group members will be able to see what others are looking for. - **Voting** feature - **Commenting** and **liking** - Photos of the gift recipient with the clothing on them

In Part 3, the five personality categories measured were Extroversion, Emotional Stability (i.e., anxious vs. calm), Open to New Experiences, Agreeableness, and Conscientiousness (i.e., disorganized vs. reliable). In order to reduce acquiescence bias (the tendency to agree with statements as presented), the five personality questions were a mix of both positive and negative personality traits selected from a ten item short form of the BFI [23].

Questions were worded to avoid biases, and were detailed and explicit to minimize potential assumptions made by respondents. For example, questions in Part 6 ("Preferences for online group gift features") were based on a specific scenario about a group of friends chipping in to buy a bicycle for a friend's birthday. The rationale is that preferences might be different depending on the occasion and type of relationships involved in the group gift.

The survey was carried out by Vocalage Inc. (and branded with its GiveButtons service), using materials and methods developed by the authors.

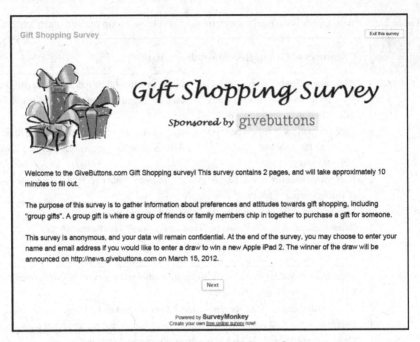

Fig. 8. The Online Survey Welcome Screen

Results. The online survey was completed by 249 participants (84 males, 164 females, and one person with undeclared gender). 212 participants were from Canada, 29 from the United States, five from the United Kingdom, and one each from Australia, Malaysia, and the Dominican Republic. United States and United Kingdom respondents were recruited through Facebook advertising, while the other respondents were recruited through snowball sampling beginning either with friends and family of two of the researchers, or else with a mother's group that one of the researchers belonged to. The incentive for participating in the survey was the chance to win one of two iPad2's that were offered in a random draw to those who completed the survey (the iPads were 32GB 3G models).

Age. The average age of the respondents was 32, but as expected there was a strong age effect on the use of social networking sites such as Facebook. The average age of people visiting those sites daily was 29, whereas for those who were not daily users of social networking the average age was over 40.

An analysis of variance showed that there was a significant association between age and frequency of online social networking use ($F(4, 241)=16.03$, $p<0.001$). People who were younger in age used Facebook or other social networking websites more frequently than people who are older (Fig. 9).

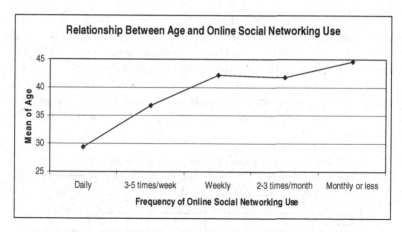

Fig. 9. Relationship Between Age and Online Social Networking Usage

The majority of participants reported spending $1000 or less per year on gifts, although most reported spending more than $500.

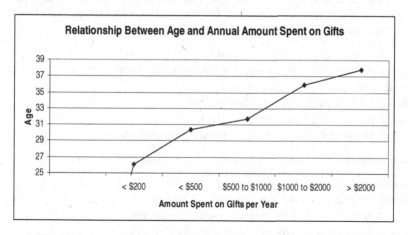

Fig. 10. Relationship Between Age and Annual Amount Spent on Gifts

Age was a strong predictor of the amount of money spent on gifts, with Analysis of Variance showing a statistically significant effect ($F(4,241)=6.457$, $p<0.001$). As age increased gift spending went up, from a mean age of 26 for those spending less than $200 per year to a mean age around 40 for those spending more than $2000 a year (as shown in Fig. 10).

Personality. Exploratory cluster analysis was carried out on the self-reported personality ratings in order to identify different combinations of personality types that could be tested as possible differentiators in gift giving preferences. K-means analysis was used, as implemented in the IBM SPSS statistical package.

After a number of preliminary analyses, a final cluster analysis was run with three of the personality factors - extroversion, anxiety, and conscientiousness – as the variables. The other two personality factors – warm and sympathetic, and openness - were removed because they did not differentiate clusters in the earlier iterations of the cluster analysis. The final analysis found six clusters, which were then tightened up by removing outliers. The survey participants were distributed fairly evenly between the clusters, with the smallest cluster containing 32 participants and the largest cluster containing 54 participants.

Table 3. Mean Personality Ratings for each of the Clusters

	Cluster					
	1	**2**	**3**	**4**	**5**	**6**
Extrovert	5	5	6	3	5	2
Anxious	5	2	5	5	2	3
Organized	6	6	3	3	3	6

Based on the results shown in Table 4 (note that values for Organized have been recoded so that higher values represent organization, in order to facilitate interpretation), the six clusters can be characterized as follows:

- Cluster 1: extroverted, anxious, organized (conscientious)
- Cluster 2: extroverted, not anxious, organized (conscientious)
- Cluster 3: extroverted, anxious, disorganized
- Cluster 4: introverted, anxious, disorganized
- Cluster 5: extroverted, not anxious, disorganized
- Cluster 6: introverted, not anxious, organized (conscientious)

The following relationships were investigated regarding characteristics of gift buyers:

- Frequency of online social networking use x Personality Clusters
- Amount of online purchases x Personality Clusters
- Amount of money spent on gifts x Personality Clusters
- Method for generating gift ideas x Personality Clusters
- Preferences for contribution confidentiality x Personality Clusters
- Preferred communication method for exchanging gift ideas x Personality Clusters

The only statistically significant relationship involving personality was *Preference for using an online message board to exchange gift ideas x Personality cluster (p<.05 as assessed using Chi-squared analysis)*. Personality Cluster #6 (Introverted, Not Anxious, Organized) was the outlier among all Clusters, with only 22.2% of the group reporting that they would like to use an online message board to exchange gift ideas with others. In contrast, over half (between 54.5% and 59.4%, depending on the cluster) of respondents in the other clusters reported that they would be interested in using an online message board.

There was also a potential relationship between *Amount of money spent on gifts x Personality Clusters (p<.10)* as shown in Fig 11.

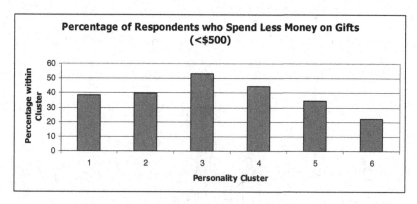

Fig. 11. Possible Effect of Personality Cluster on Tendency to Spend Less on Gifts

Respondents within Personality Cluster #3 (Extroverted, Anxious, Disorganized) had a tendency to spend less money on gifts, with 53.2% of respondents within the group reporting that they spend $500 or less on gifts per year. Only 28.2% of Cluster#3 participants reported spending $1000 or more on gifts per year. In contrast, only 22.2% of respondents within Personality Cluster #6 (Introverted, Not Anxious, Organized) reported spending less than $500 on gifts in a typical year. Cluster#6 participants reported spending the most money on gifts per year compared to all other groups, with 44% of the group reporting that they spend over $1000 on gifts each year.

Interest in Group Gift Giving. Respondents were then classified into two groups, those who had a general interest in group gift giving (group givers), and those who generally had less interest in group giving (non-group givers). In order to make this classification, average interest in group giving was computed across all the gift giving occasions surveyed in the final question (occasions such as weddings, baby showers, mother's/father's day, child's birthday, etc.), i.e., question 13 as listed in the Appendix of this paper.

The histogram of average group giving interest, calculated from the survey responses, is shown in Fig 12. The average value of group giving interest is 3.34, or just above the neutral point of the scale for interest in group gift giving (note that a value of 3 on the response scale represents neither agreeing nor disagreeing with the statement that a particular occasion would be good for group gift giving). We chose a cutoff of 3.8 to distinguish people who had a greater interest in group gift giving. This cutoff was half a standard deviation above the mean of the sample. While this cutoff is just under the somewhat agree value of four on the scale, it represents the average across a number of gift giving occasions, some of which were seen as being generally unsuitable for group gift giving. Thus, the people that we classified as having greater interest in group gift giving tended to be interested in group giving for those occasions where it was generally regarded as being suitable. People with an average interest score of 3.8 or more were classified as group givers and the rest were classified as non-group givers.

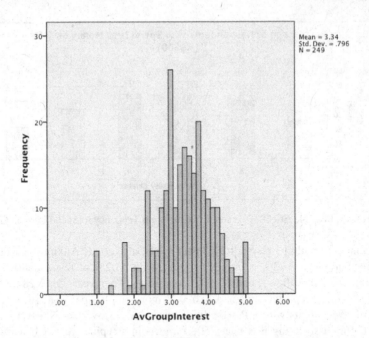

Fig. 12. Average Group Giving Interest Histogram

Gender. A higher proportion of women (31%) were group givers than men (18%) with this difference being statistically significant based on chi-squared analysis ($p<.05$). In contrast, there was no significant difference in age or personality type between the group givers and the non-group givers.

Other gender effects could be seen in how people preferred to communicate when discussing group gifts. Males had a significantly stronger preference for using the phone and instant messaging to pass and share gift ideas, while females had a significantly stronger preference for using emails.

Group Gift Giving Occasions. The occasions that generated the most interest in group gifts were:

- Co-worker or colleague's retirement or farewell gift (average interest rating = 3.95)
- Thank-you gift for a teacher, coach or volunteer (average interest rating = 3.84)
- Baby shower/baby gift (average interest rating = 3.67)
- Wedding gift (average interest rating = 3.59)
- The occasions with the least amount of interest in group gifts were:
  - Child's birthday (friend or relative's child) (average interest rating = 2.84)
  - Christmas gift for a close friend or relative (average interest rating = 2.87).
  - A close friend or relative's birthday (average interest rating = 2.96).
  - Mother's or Father's Day gift (average interest rating = 3.14).

It is interesting to note that the occasions judged less suitable for group gift giving seem to be more intimate, involving close friends and families (what sociologists refer to as "strong ties"). Perhaps it should not be surprising that group gift giving is more suitable for relationships involving weak ties. Most groups of people, especially those who are meeting online and who are not members of the same family, will not be composed exclusively of people who have strong ties with each other. Thus, it is generally unlikely that a group of people will have strong ties with the same person. Furthermore, to the extent that gifts to close ties are special and communicate more intimacy, it may be inappropriate to give them with a collection of other people. However, there may be special cases where a group may give a gift to someone that they all have a close tie with (e.g., a graduation gift to a family member, or an anniversary gift, such as a cruise, to grandparents).

While women were overall more interested in group gifts, statistically significant (p<.05, as assessed by chi-squared analysis) gender differences in preferences for group gifts were only observed for three of the gift giving occasions that were examined in the survey. Those occasions were baby showers, weddings, and gifts for a co-worker's retirement or farewell occasion (with women having a greater interest in group gifts for all three of the occasions).

Gift Ideas Start-Up. One of the questions in the survey asked how the respondent normally started looking for gift ideas. The top responses to this question were getting ideas from friends and family (79%), asking the recipient what he or she wanted (63%), and walking into retail stores (56%). In contrast, people were less likely to use online resources, with 41% browsing online stores for gift ideas, 21% using a search engine to get gift suggestions, and only 4% using online gift recommendation systems (see Fig. 13). It remains to be seen whether or not online methods for searching and recommending gift ideas can be improved to the point where the current reticence to get gift ideas from online sources is overcome.

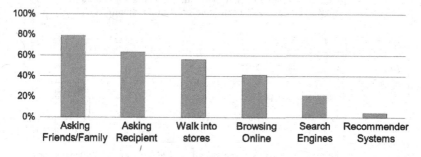

Fig. 13. Methods of looking for gift ideas

Gift Ideas Search Factors. People were also asked which factors were most important to them when looking for gift ideas. The three dominant factors were the gift recipient's tastes and preferences (78%), the usefulness of the gift (72%), and price (68%). Style was an important factor for only 16% of the respondents, and other factors such as brand, promotion, and shipping features were important to only 10% or fewer of the sample. Since shipping is known to be important in online purchase decisions, these results suggest that there is a dissociation between selecting gift ideas and actually making purchase decisions.

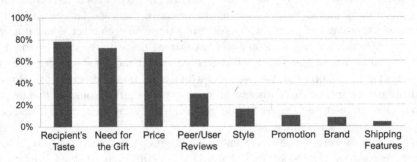

Fig. 14. Relevance of Factors when looking for gift ideas

We also examined a possible interaction between the factors that people looked for in selecting gifts, and which occasions they thought would be suitable for group gift-giving. While style and price were associated with one occasion each, it was promotions that seemed to interact most with group giving (being significantly related to three of the gift giving occasions that we studied). People who considered "Promotions" as an important factor in gift selection tended to be significantly (as assessed by chi-squared analysis) more interested in group gift giving for the following occasions: a work colleague's retirement or farewell occasion (p<.05), a Christmas gift for a close friend or family member (p=0.01), and a close friend's birthday (p<.06).

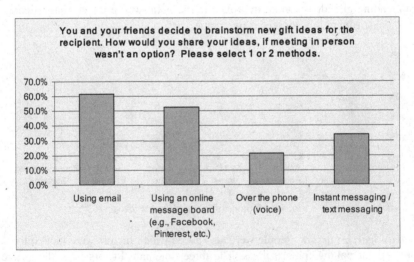

Fig. 15. Group discussion methods

Group Gift Giving Discussions. One of the major tasks in group gift giving is coordinating decision making (and possibly payments, depending on how they are made) within the group. This requires discussion and for most groups it is impractical to hold these discussions in a face-to-face setting. Respondents in our survey expressed their degree of willingness to use each of four different methods of communication during group gift giving discussions (email, online message board, phone, text messaging). As shown in Fig 15, only one fifth of the sample would use the phone for this discussion and only a third would use instant messaging. The most popular methods in our survey were an online message board (just over half of the sample) and email (almost two thirds of the sample)

Other gender effects could be seen in how people preferred to communicate when discussing group gifts. While overall there was a greater interest in using email to communicate gift ideas than to use the phone or instant messaging, there were significant gender differences relating to phone and instant messaging (p<.01 in both cases, as assessed by Chi-Squared analysis). Males had a significantly stronger preference (versus females) for using the phone to communicate gift ideas with other people. 31% of male respondents selected "Phone" as one of their two preferred communication methods, compared to only 14.6% of female respondents. Males also have a significantly stronger preference for using instant messaging to exchange gift ideas with other people. 40.8% of male respondents selected "Instant Messaging" as one of their two preferred communication methods, compared with only 21.5% of female respondents. Females in our sample tended to have a stronger preference for email (p<.10). 69.4% of female respondents selected "Email" as one of their two preferred communication methods, compared to 56.3% of male respondents.

Fundraising. Organizers of group gifts are faced with many tradeoffs. One of these is concerned with fundraising. Should the money be collected first, and the gift choice then be made based on the amount of money available? Or should the gift be chosen first with the amount of money to be collected being determined by the cost of the gift? In the first method the focus is on the money, in the second method it is on the gift. In our review of group gift Web sites, we found that the vast majority of the sites made an assumption that group gifts are based on raising enough funds to pay for a pre-selected gift with a fixed price tag. Our respondents were asked to choose between the two methods across three different types of gift giving occasion. The resulting preferences are shown in Fig 16. The donation approach was judged more favorably for the retirement and thank you gifts, but was unpopular for the birthday gift to a close friend or relative. This suggests that online group gift giving services need to work differently, depending on the occasion.

Underfunding. When a gift cannot be purchased by a group because of insufficient funds, that group is faced with a dilemma. Should they give up and return the money or should they try again either with a different gift or with a gift certificate. In this study, almost half of the participants felt that the available money should be spent on a gift certificate and most of the rest favoured buying a different (less expensive) gift that would match the available budget (Fig. 17).

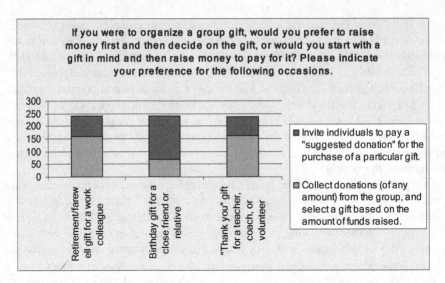

Fig. 16. Preferred Funding Raising Methods for Different Gift Giving Occasions

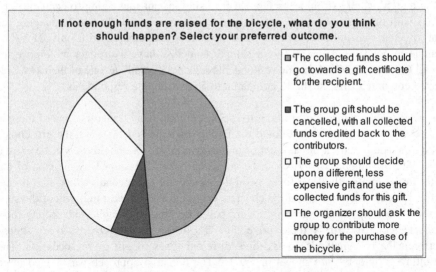

Fig. 17. Preferred Courses of Action When a Gift is Underfunded

Males and females had different opinions on what to do in case of insufficient funding for a group gift ($p<.001$ as assessed by Chi-Squared analysis). A much larger proportion of female respondents preferred to cancel the group gift if insufficient funds were raised (58.7% of female respondents, compared to 31.4% of male respondents), as shown in Fig 18 below. On the other hand, a larger proportion (22.9%) of males preferred to attempt to raise additional funds to buy the gift, compared to only 6.5% of female respondents. Males were also more interested in putting raised funds towards a gift certificate for the recipient.

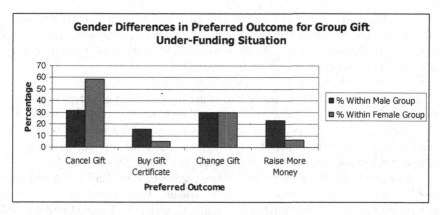

Fig. 18. Gender Differences in Preferred Outcome for Group Gift Under-Funding Situation

4.3   Summary

The results of the two studies are instructive for the design of an online group gift giving service within a Personal Web framework. Such an online group gift giving service:

- brings useful gift ideas to the group members taking into account: a) the characteristics (e.g., age, gender, or personality) of the recipient and each group member, b) the preferences of the recipient and group members (e.g. product ratings), c) the connections among group members through knowledge of social structure between group members, and d) the gift occasion.
- provides cognitive support by providing a shared online space where user could share, discuss, and vote on gift ideas
- enables user control by allowing users to invite as many friends as possible, share gift ideas from any retail website, set various fundraising approaches, search gift ideas based on variety of search factors, or modify/revise their search criteria at any time.

5   Discussion

Our interpretation of the overall pattern of results concerning giving behaviour is that gift selection is a two stage process where a first stage of generating and comparing gift ideas is then followed by a stage of choosing where and how to buy the gift idea that was selected in the first stage. This suggests that gift giving sites that attempt to generate sales while people are examining gift ideas will have trouble getting conversions except from the most impulsive people, or when there are compelling incentives that can over-ride the normal decision making processes.

Gender was found to be important not only for determining how likely a person was to be interested in group gift giving, but also in determining how a group gift giving system should work. The survey results demonstrate that there are a number of challenges for online group gift giving systems. Perhaps most importantly, people differ in how much interest they have in group gift giving, and men, in particular, currently have little interest in it. There is also little interest overall in group gift giving when the recipients are close friends and family.

Opportunities for online gift giving sites were indicated in responses to a question that asked what method people would like to use to brainstorm gift ideas with others. Only 20% chose to use the phone, with 36% willing to use text chat. In contrast, 62% would use email and 53% would use online message board functionality such as that provided by Facebook or Pinterest. This suggests that brainstorming gift ideas in a group is an important function that people would like online sites to provide.

Perhaps the strongest message from the two studies reported here is that group gift giving systems need to be targeted, first at particular types of occasion (involving weak tie recipients) that are suitable for group gift giving, and second at the people (and women in particular) who are inherently most interested in group giving. In early ventures into online group giving it seems that support of gift idea discussions is a very good place to start, and this may explain the success of sites like Etsy and Pinterest, which perhaps not surprisingly, are particularly appealing to women.

6   Implications for the Personal Web

The psychology and sociology of gift giving and receiving have always been interesting and complex areas of research. When combined with online shopping and collaborative gift giving scenarios, gift selection and purchase takes on yet another dimension of complexity. In order to create an effective online gift giving process that supports collaborative buying, Personal Web interactions are needed that respect the motivation and psychology of gift giving.

We conclude by considering the questions posed earlier in the paper in the context of the Personal Web.

How does the nature of gift giving change when it is performed online?

Retail is becoming a multi-channel experience that is being increasingly influenced by social media. How will gift giving (with its attendant challenges of gift anxiety and the possible consequences of gift failure) change in response to these changes in the retail experience? It seems clear that certain types of gift giving will become more social experiences. Even when gifts are not given by groups, they will be visible to groups of people and commented on by them. For some, this may create a desire for more unique gifts and a search for "one of a kind" gifts that have not already appeared on someone's blog or Facebook page. For others, increased information about the gifts that people have given may allow them to choose more fashionable and trendy gifts that will be less likely to fail (i.e., be unattractive to the recipient). As recommendation technologies improve and add features like social recommendation, we expect that online gift giving services will reduce the effort, risk, and anxiety associated with gift giving.

From a Personal Web perspective, we expect that the tasks and workflow of gift selection will continue to change. In the past, gift selection online was presumed to most likely occur when searching within an online catalogue. The rise of search engines and search engine marketing in the first decade of the twenty-first century created a new way of guiding customers to particular catalogues or products based on the needs or interests implied in their search queries. Advertising and brand awareness helped drive customers to retailer websites. With the rise of Web 2.0, the blogosphere, and affiliate marketing (predominantly advertising on blogs), the potential touchpoints between products/brands and customers have increased enormously. Affiliates can embed advertisements in content in many different ways, but when done right the product offer is compelling because it is a natural extension of, or response to, the content being read on the blog.

Shopping search engines and price comparison services have been another way for people to find information specifically about products. By late 2012 Google's early entry into this space (Froogle) had evolved into Google Shopping with paid search operating much the way that adwords worked when searching the general Google search engine. As of late 2012, the experience of looking for products on Google Shopping and two other the other search and comparison platforms (Pricegrabber and Shopzilla) were very similar. Users could input a product type (such as nail polish organizers, tennis rackets, or headsets) and get back a list of product options with pricing and vendors. Each of the services provided a compare prices buttons and with one or two clicks users could go to a vendor site and purchase the product.

1. Buy your friend a gift

Pick out the perfect gift, add your message and it's ready to ship - no address needed.

2. Your friend is notified instantly

Friends enter their own shipping info and can swap for a different size, flavor or style before the gift ships.

3. The gift arrives!

Your beautifully packaged gift gets delivered right to your friend's door.

Fig. 19. The Facebook Gift Function (Advertised as coming soon: Screenshot taken November 8, 2012)

As of this writing, the potential for using social media discussions to facilitate gift giving remained largely unrealized, although trends in that direction were starting to emerge. For instance, sites like Pinterest facilitated product browsing and discussion, and Facebook showed clear intent to plunge into the gifting space (Fig. 19).

From the Personal Web perspective, what is currently missing from online gift giving services is multi-site user-centered integration. Sites like Amazon, e-Bay, and Etsy provide interesting features and offer many attractive products that may be suitable as gifts, but they are largely silos designed for browsing and search. Current solutions typically assume an effortful and focused search or browsing approach to gift selection. As noted earlier, gift recommendation systems, where they exist, tend to be primitive. Gift selection is not a restful process and people cannot start sketching out ideas and have them filled in over time, as they interact with different suggestions, and provide their feedback about what seems interesting or relevant. The focus tends to be on the retailer rather than the gift, and on the purchase process rather than the selection process.

When would people like to participate in online group gift giving and what types of interaction can facilitate online group gift giving?

Our research results suggest that online group gift giving will be most attractive for groups of people connected by weak ties to the gift recipient and for formal (e.g., retirement of a colleague) rather than intimate (e.g., birthday of a close family member) occasions. However, there may be special cases where a group may give a gift to someone that they all have a close tie with (e.g., a graduation gift to a family member, or an anniversary gift, such as a cruise, to grandparents).

Discussion through social media appears to be a promising way to facilitate online group gift giving, but it is clear that discussion tools will have to be designed and promoted carefully. At present, the default discussion method appear to be email, and whatever new methods are developed for gift discussion, they will need to provide at least as much functionality as email and be as easy to use. One aspect of email is that the sender can tailor who the email is sent to and one challenge will be how to create systems that allow people to tailor who sees different parts of gifting discussions in social media.

From a personal web perspective, gift giving should be less effortful and laborious. One strategy for reducing effort is to build gift giving into existing workflow. For instance, automatically generating gift events for people within groups or families who have upcoming birthdays, weddings, etc. Simplifying workflow to create effective personal web interaction should be useful for individual, as well as group, gifts. Real workflows may be fragmented, and in group gifting discussions there may be shifting coalitions of people involved. Different subgroups should be able to have different gifting discussions, and discussions amongst groups of people should be able to occur across different websites and forums. For instance, a gifting discussion might begin with the creation of a gift event page on some service and then transition to Etsy for inspiring ideas, followed by further research on Pinterest, then discussions on Facebook followed by synchronous meetings on skype or Google Hangouts. In the Personal Web approach Gift selection and discussion workflow should be facilitated so that it becomes like a template that guides the activities of a group of people over time. This kind of guidance should be carried out in such a way that the focus of the people is on the gift ideas and associated discussions, not on the mechanics of constructing search strategies, choosing sites to look at, scheduling meetings, and so on.

How does the role of the user change when the gift giver is a group of people rather than an individual?

In principle, group gifting reduces the load on the individual giver. However, if gift selection and discussion becomes too complex, or too divisive, the process may be more difficult or more annoying than simply doing the job oneself. There is also the issue of how a gift is facilitated. While software could in principle play the role of facilitator, much as software manages auctions in a service like eBay, in practice there is a strong human element to gift giving which may predispose people to expect assistance from a human facilitator. Depending on how the role of the facilitator is implemented, other users in a gift giving group may fall along a continuum of interactive involvement from simply paying the required price for their share of the group gift to being actively involved in selecting the gift to be given. However, providing that social media discussion around gift selection doesn't become too onerous and drawn out, the role of the user can be simplified in group gift giving. Gift anxiety should also be reduced as participation in the group reduces the level of personal risk associated with the potential for gift failure.

How can shopping search engines and gift recommender systems make the gift selection process less effortful and more effective, while reducing gift selection anxiety and the likelihood of gift failure?

The central theme of the Personal Web is that the coordination of Web services should be user centric rather than server centric. By synthesizing information available about products on various websites, and by also synthesizing social media discussion around those products, the Personal Web view of gift giving is consistent with well integrated shopping search engines and gift recommender systems. The principles of the Personal Web should assist in the design of online gift giving systems. Interactions should occur on a single site or page (perhaps constructed by a Personal Web browser or toolbar as a composite view of data that might exist on many different websites). The tasks of the user should be simplified to the extent possible without diminishing the communicative and social goals of gift giving. Most importantly gift giving workflow should be automated as much as possible. This might include automated set up of friends and family birthdays as gift events, and flexible ways of alternating between individual and group giving strategies depending on the occasion, and on the person's relationship with the recipient.

What are the characteristics of givers that determine when and how group gift giving should be implemented?

While women are currently more interested in group gift giving than men, this may change if men find an opportunity to have rewarding social interactions during group gifting discussions, or if group gifting can reduce gift anxiety and reduce the effort that men would otherwise have to make in selecting and presenting gifts. Aside from gender of the giver and the strength of social ties with the recipient, other personal characteristics of the giver and recipient may also be relevant to the decision of when to make group, rather than individual, gifts. It seems likely that interest in group gift giving will depend a great deal on how online group gift giving services are implemented and what kinds of interaction are available when using them. More research is needed to determine what personal characteristics drive the decision of when to use group gift giving. It seems likely that the relationship between personal characteristics and propensity or interest in giving group gifts may well depend on the types of group gift giving interactions that are available.

How should people interact with each other when choosing a group gift?

While our research results indicated a preference for email interaction when choosing a group gift (particularly amongst women) we do not believe that this is the best solution in future online group gift giving systems. Email is unwieldy when dealing with groups of people where some members of the group may be more willing to get involved in discussions than others. When people express a preference for email those preferences may be due to the degree of control that email provides, in contrast to the alternative of broadcasting to everyone on a discussion page. We believe that one of the key challenges for successful implementation of online group gift giving on a large scale will be the development of gift selection discussions that combine the ease and transparency of communication on discussion boards with email's ability to send out specific messages to different subsets of people.

In summary, online gift giving represents a large opportunity for companies wishing to re-invent online retail through greater social media discussion. However, there are significant challenges to realizing the vision of large scale online group gifting. Group gift giving is likely to work best for particular types of people and occasion. Given that current methods for online group gift giving are relatively primitive and have not been sufficiently informed by research on the requirements and needs of gift givers, it is suggested that new methods of gift selection discussion be explored, informed by a Personal Web approach to interaction.

References

1. Sheridan, T.B.: Supervisory Control. In: Handbook of Human Factors and Ergonomics, 3rd edn., pp. 1025–1052 (2006)
2. Chignell, M., Cordy, J.R., Ng, J.W., Yesha, Y.: First symposium on the Personal Web. In: Proceedings of the 2010 Conference of the Center for Advanced Studies on Collaborative Research, pp. 327–329. IBM Corp. (2010)
3. Rainie, L., Wellman, B.: Networked: The New Social Operating System. MIT Press (2012)
4. National Retail Federation. Retail's Impact by Numbers. Downloaded from, http://www.retailmeansjobs.com/data-home (June 20, 2012)
5. Vertical Web Media, Internet Retailer Top 500 Guide (2012), Downloaded from, http://www.internetretailer.com/top500/ (June 20, 2012)

6. Barker, O.: Pinterest changes the way brides plan their weddings. USA Today (April 12, 2012) Downloaded from,
   http://www.usatoday.com/life/lifestyle/story/
   2012-04-11/pinterest-wedding-planning/54188942/1 (May 9, 2012)
7. Belk, R.W.: Special Session Summary: The Meaning of Gifts and Greetings. In: Corfman, K.P., Lynch, J. (eds.) Advances in Consumer Research, vol. 23(13), Association for Consumer Research, Provo (1996)
8. Hollenbeck, C., Peters, C., Zinkhan, G.: Gift Giving: A Community Paradigm. Psychology and Marketing 23(7), 573–595 (2006)
9. Otnes, C., Ruth, J.A., Milbourne, C.C.: The Pleasure and Pain of Being Close: Men's Mixed Feelings about Participation in Valentine's Day Gift Exchanges. In: Parsons, A.G. (ed.) Brand Choice in Gift-Giving: Recipient Influence (2002); Journal of Product and Brand Management 11(4), 237–249 (2002)
10. Belk, R.W., Coon, G.S.: Gift Giving as Agapic Love: An Alternative to the Exchange Paradigm Based on Dating Experiences. Journal of Consumer Research 20, 393–417 (1993)
11. Parsons, A.G., Ballantine, P., Kennedy, A.: Gift Exchange: Benefits Sought by the Recipient. International Journal of Sociology and Social Policy 31(7), 411–423 (2011)
12. Sherry, J.F.: Gift Giving in Anthropological Perspective. Journal of Consumer Research 10, 157–168 (1983)
13. Caplow, T., Chadwick, B.A., Bahr, H.M.: Middletown Families: Fifty Years of Change and Continuity. University of Minnesota Press, Minneapolis (1982)
14. Areni, C.S., Kiecker, P., Palan, K.M.: Is it better to give than to receive? Ex-ploring gender differences in the meaning of memorable gifts. Psychology and Marketing 15, 81–109 (1998)
15. Resnick, P., Varian, H.R.: Recommender Systems. Communications of the ACM 40(3), 56–58 (1997)
16. Guy, I., Carmel, D.: Social Recommender Systems. In: Proceedings of the 20th International Conference Companion on World Wide Web (WWW 2011), pp. 283–284. ACM, New York (2011)
17. Guy, I., Zwerdling, N., Carmel, D., Ronen, I., Uziel, E., Yogev, S., Ofek-Koifman, S.: Personalized Recommendation of Social Software Items Based on Social Relations. In: Proceedings of the Third ACM Conference on Recom-Mender Systems (RecSys 2009), pp. 53–60. ACM, New York (2009)
18. Herlocker, J.L., Konstan, J.A., Riedl, J.: Explaining Collaborative Filtering Recommendations. In: Proceedings of the 2000 ACM Conference on Computer Supported Cooperative Work (CSCW 2000), pp. 241–250. ACM, New York (2000)
19. Gartrell, M., Xing, X., Lv, Q., Beach, A., Han, R., Mishra, S., Seada, K.: En-hancing Group Recommendation by Incorporating Social Relationship Interactions. In: Proceedings of the 16th ACM International Conference on Supporting Group Work (GROUP 2010), pp. 97–106. ACM, Sanibel Island (2010)
20. Shang, S., Hui, P., Kulkarni, S.R., Cuff, P.W.: Wisdom of the Crowd: Incorporating Social Influence in Recommendation Models. In: Proceedings of IEEE 17th International Conference on Parallel and Distributed Systems (ICPADS 2011), pp. 835–840. IEEE, Tainan (2011)
21. Kim, R.: Is Group Gift Buying Poised for Take-Off? GigaOm (May 17, 2011) Downloaded from,
    http://gigaom.com/2011/05/17/is-group-gift-buying-poised-for-take-off/ (June 20, 2011)

22. McCrae, R.R., Costa, P.T.: A Five-Factor Theory of Personality. In: Pervin, L.A., John, O.P. (eds.) Handbook of Personality: Theory and Research 2, pp. 139–153. Guilford Press, New York (1999)
23. Gosling, S.D., Rentfrow, P.J., Swann, W.B.: A Very Brief Measure of the Big-Five Personality Domains. Journal of Research in Personality 37, 504–528 (2003)

Appendix A: Online Survey Questions Used in Study Two

Note that in addition to the questions shown below, respondents were also asked to supply their age and gender).

1. Approximately how often do you visit social networking websites? (e.g. Facebook, Google+, etc.)

- o   Daily
- o   3-5 times a week
- o   Once a week
- o   2-3 times a month
- o   Once a or month or less

2. Approximately how many online purchases (business or personal) have you made over the past year?

- o   0
- o   1 – 3
- o   4 – 6
- o   7 – 9
- o   10 or more

3. Please tell us about your personality by rating the following characteristics. (each of the options below was rated on a 7-point Likert scale of Strongly Disagree to Strongly Agree)

- o   I see myself as extroverted
- o   I see myself as anxious
- o   I see myself as "open to new experiences"
- o   I see myself as sympathetic and warm
- o   I see myself as disorganized

4. Approximately how much money do you personally spend on gifts (including gifts you buy with other people) in a typical year?

- o   Less than $200
- o   Up to $500
- o   Between $500 and $1000
- o   Between $1000 and $2000
- o   More than $2000

5. When buying a gift for someone, how do you normally start looking for gift ideas? Please select the top 3 methods you use.

- o   Using a search engine (e.g. Google) to get suggestions
- o   Getting ideas from friends or family
- o   Looking at the recipient's Facebook profile

- o   Using an online gift recommendation system (e.g. Amazon.com Gift Organizer, Gifts.com, etc.)
- o   Browsing online stores
- o   Walking into retail stores
- o   Asking the recipient what he or she wants
- o   Other (please specify)

6. Which factors are most important to you when looking for gift ideas? Please select the top 3.

- o   Promotions
- o   Gift recipient's taste/preferences
- o   Brand
- o   Style
- o   Friends and family feedback or user reviews (if online)
- o   Price
- o   The need for, or usefulness of, the gift
- o   Shipping features (if available)
- o   Other (please specify)

7. Which factors are most important to you when looking for gift ideas? Please select the top 3.

- o   Promotions
- o   Gift recipient's taste/preferences
- o   Brand
- o   Style
- o   Friends and family feedback or user reviews (if online)
- o   Price
- o   The need for, or usefulness of, the gift
- o   Shipping features (if available)
- o   Other (please specify)

8. If not enough funds are raised for the chosen gift, what do you think should happen? Select your preferred outcome.

- o   The collected funds should go towards a gift certificate for the recipient.
- o   The organizer should ask the group to contribute more money for the purchase of the bicycle.
- o   The group should decide upon a different, less expensive gift and use the collected funds for this gift.
- o   The group gift should be cancelled, with all collected funds credited back to the contributors.

9. You and your friends decide to brainstorm new gift ideas for the recipient. How would you share your ideas, if meeting in person wasn't an option? Please select 1 or 2 methods.

- o   Using email
- o   Using an online message board (e.g., Facebook, Pinterest, etc.)
- o   Over the phone (voice)
- o   Instant messaging / text messaging

10. If you were to organize a group gift, would you prefer to raise money first and then decide on the gift, or would you start with a gift in mind and then raise money to pay for it? Please indicate your preference for the following occasions.

o   Retirement/farewell gift for a work colleague
o   Birthday gift for a close friend or relative
o   "Thank you" gift for a teacher, coach, or volunteer

13. For which people and occasions would you be most interested in participating in an online group gift? With real-life relationships in mind, please rate your level of interest for each occasion (interest was rated on a five-point Likert scale ranging from not at all interested to very interested).

o   Mother's or Father's Day gift (chipping in with siblings)
o   A close friend or relative's birthday
o   Child's birthday (friend or relative's child)
o   Baby shower / baby gift
o   Christmas gift for a close friend or relative
o   "Thank you" gift for a teacher, coach, or volunteer
o   Co-worker or colleague's retirement or farewell gift
o   Wedding gift

Author Index

Canella, David   185
Chechik, Marsha   11
Chignell, Mark   185
Consens, Mariano P.   87

Ghajar-Khosravi, Shadi   185

Holub, Louisa   185

Jacobsen, Hans-Arno   49

Lau, Alex   65
Liaskos, Sotirios   11
Lo, Jimmy   113

Martin, Patrick   113
Matheson, Marie   113
Müller, Hausi A.   151

Nejati, Shiva   11
Ng, Joanna   1, 65, 113

Sabetzadeh, Mehrdad   11
Salay, Rick   11
Samavi, Reza   87
Sharpe, William   185
Simmonds, Jocelyn   11
Stroulia, Eleni   131

Tan, Daisy   113
Thomson, Brian   113
Topaloglou, Thodoros   87

Upadhyaya, Bipin   65

Villegas, Norha M.   151

Xiao, Hua   65

Ye, Chunyang   49
Yoon, Young   49

Zou, Ying   65